KV-259-601

Palgrave Studies in the History of the Media

Series Editors: **Dr Bill Bell** (Centre for the History of the Book, University of Edinburgh), **Dr Chandrika Kaul** (Department of Modern History, University of St Andrews), **Professor Kenneth Osgood** (Department of History, Florida Atlantic University), **Dr Alexander S. Wilkinson** (Centre for the History of the Media, University College Dublin)

Palgrave Studies in the History of the Media publishes original, high-quality research into the cultures of communication from the Middle Ages to the present day. The series explores the variety of subjects and disciplinary approaches that characterize this vibrant field of enquiry. The series will help shape current interpretations not only of the media, in all its forms, but also of the powerful relationship between the media and politics, society, and the economy.

Advisory Board: Professor Carlos Barrera (University of Navarra, Spain), Professor Peter Burke (Emmanuel College, Cambridge), Professor Denis Cryle (Central Queensland University, Australia), Professor David Culbert (Louisiana State University, Baton Rouge), Professor Nicholas Cull (Center on Public Diplomacy, University of Southern California), Professor Tom O'Malley (Centre for Media History, University of Wales, Aberystwth), Professor Chester Pach (Ohio University)

Titles include:

Michael Krysko
AMERICAN RADIO IN CHINA
International Encounters with Technology and Communications, 1919–41

Christoph Hendrik Müller
WEST GERMANS AGAINST THE WEST
Anti-Americanism in Media and Public Opinion in the Federal Republic of Germany 1949–68

Joel Wiener
THE AMERICANIZATION OF THE BRITISH PRESS, 1830s–1914

Forthcoming titles:

James Mussell & Suzanne Paylor
NINETEENTH-CENTURY IN THE DIGITAL AGE
Politics, Pedagogy and Practice

Jane Chapman
EMPIRE, WOMEN AND MEDIA
Citizenship and Consumption in Press and Radio, 1863–1947

Martin Conboy & John Steel
THE LANGUAGE OF NEWSPAPERS IN NINETEENTH-CENTURY ENGLAND
Commercializing the Popular

Palgrave Studies in the History of the Media
Series Standing Order ISBN 978–0–230–23153–5 hardcover
Series Standing Order ISBN 978–0–230–23154–2 paperback
(*outside North America only*)

You can receive future titles in this series as they are published by placing a standing order. Please contact your bookseller or, in case of difficulty, write to us at the address below with your name and address, the title of the series and one of the ISBNs quoted above.

Customer Services Department, Macmillan Distribution Ltd, Houndmills, Basingstoke, Hampshire RG21 6XS, England

---

Also by Joel H. Wiener

THE WAR OF THE UNSTAMPED: The Movement to Repeal the British Newspaper Tax, 1830–1836

A DESCRIPTIVE FINDING LIST OF UNSTAMPED BRITISH PERIODICALS, 1830–1836

GREAT BRITAIN: Foreign Policy and the Span of Empire, 1689–1971 (A Documentary History)

GREAT BRITAIN: The Lion at Home (A Documentary History of Domestic Policy, 1689–1973)

RADICALISM AND FREETHOUGHT IN NINETEENTH-CENTURY BRITAIN: The Life of Richard Carlile

INNOVATORS AND PREACHERS: The Role of the Editor in Victorian England

PAPERS FOR THE MILLIONS: The New Journalism in Britain, 1850s to 1914

WILLIAM LOVETT

ANGLO-AMERICAN MEDIA INTERACTIONS, 1850–2000 (*with Mark Hampton*)

3065613

The Americanization of the British Press, 1830s–1914

Speed in the Age of Transatlantic Journalism

Joel H. Wiener
Emeritus Professor of History, the City University of New York, USA

UNIVERSITIES AT MEDWAY LIBRARY

palgrave
macmillan

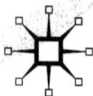

© Joel H. Wiener 2011

All rights reserved. No reproduction, copy or transmission of this publication may be made without written permission.

No portion of this publication may be reproduced, copied or transmitted save with written permission or in accordance with the provisions of the Copyright, Designs and Patents Act 1988, or under the terms of any licence permitting limited copying issued by the Copyright Licensing Agency, Saffron House, 6–10 Kirby Street, London EC1N 8TS.

Any person who does any unauthorized act in relation to this publication may be liable to criminal prosecution and civil claims for damages.

The author has asserted his right to be identified as the author of this work in accordance with the Copyright, Designs and Patents Act 1988.

First published 2011 by
PALGRAVE MACMILLAN

Palgrave Macmillan in the UK is an imprint of Macmillan Publishers Limited, registered in England, company number 785998, of Houndmills, Basingstoke, Hampshire RG21 6XS.

Palgrave Macmillan in the US is a division of St Martin's Press LLC, 175 Fifth Avenue, New York, NY 10010.

Palgrave Macmillan is the global academic imprint of the above companies and has companies and representatives throughout the world.

Palgrave® and Macmillan® are registered trademarks in the United States, the United Kingdom, Europe and other countries

ISBN 978-0-230-58186-9   hardback

This book is printed on paper suitable for recycling and made from fully managed and sustained forest sources. Logging, pulping and manufacturing processes are expected to conform to the environmental regulations of the country of origin.

A catalogue record for this book is available from the British Library.

Library of Congress Cataloging-in-Publication Data
Wiener, Joel H.
   The Americanization of the British press, 1830s–1914 : speed in the
   age of transatlantic journalism / Joel H. Wiener.
      p. cm.
   Includes bibliographical references and index.
   ISBN 978-0-230-58186-9 (alk. paper)
   1. Press–Great Britain–History–19th century. 2. Press–Great
   Britain–History–20th century. 3. Journalism–Great Britain–
   History–19th century. 4. Journalism–Great Britain–History–20th
   century. 5. Press–United States–Influence–History–19th century.
   6. Press–United States–Influence–History–20th century. I. Title.
   PN5117.W46 2011
   072.09–dc23
                                                          2011021394

10   9   8   7   6   5   4   3   2   1
20   19   18   17   16   15   14   13   12   11

Printed and bound in Great Britain by
CPI Antony Rowe, Chippenham and Eastbourne

For Erika, Andrew, Adam, Lexi, Emma and Rebecca
The next generation of newspaper readers

Contents

Acknowledgements

Over the course of years I have acquired innumerable debts while writing this book. Many librarians have courteously assisted me, particularly at the following institutions: British Library, Colindale Newspaper Library, New York Public Library, Columbia University Library and the House of Lords Library. I am grateful to the British Library for kindly giving permission to reproduce the cover illustration to this book.

Through the years many friends and colleagues on both sides of the Atlantic have helped me with information, suggestions for additional reading and comments on earlier versions of this book or portions of it. They include the following: Dennis Griffiths, Dilwyn Porter, Laurel Brake, the late Robert A. Colby, Eric Landesman, Aled Jones, Robert Glen, Michael Harris, Ray Boston, Sally Mitchell, Christopher Kent, Richard Fulton, the late David Linton, Peter Mellini, John Byrne, James Startt, Matthew McIntyre, Jonathan Rose, Patrick Leary and the late Joseph Baylen. I am extremely grateful to Craig Parish for his generous help with technical matters related to this book, to Chandrika Kaul for getting me involved in this excellent series and providing helpful comments on the manuscript, and to Ruth Ireland of Palgrave Macmillan for her expert editorial advice and assistance. Mark Hampton has been an inspiration as well as a continuous fount of knowledge. Most of all I owe a profound debt of gratitude to my wife Suzanne, who is always at my side. I thank her for her unstinting encouragement, her intellectual curiosity and for sharing with me an unfailing enthusiasm for the world of print.

List of Illustrations

*"NEVER FORGET THAT MEN HAVE TAMED AND CAUGHT
THE LIGHTNING; CLAD IT IN A LIVERY KNOWN AS NEWS"*

(John Davidson, 1903)

Introduction

Imagine a middle-class family sitting down to breakfast in July 1829, in the well-to-do Bayswater section of London. *The Times* is face upwards on the table, its dense, unbroken text conveying dramatic news about political events in Paris. The newspaper recounts a drift towards autocracy in the government of Charles X, as well as the emergence of a popular opposition. None of this news appears on the front page, however, the latter being given over instead to small advertisements ("personals") that concern mostly house lettings and job opportunities. News reports, from Paris and other European capitals, which are lifted primarily from Continental newspapers, appear on the two inside pages of the four-page paper next to several of the leading articles. The remainder of the inside matter (the fourth page also consists of advertisements) includes summaries of legal cases, accounts of public meetings, letters from correspondents and financial intelligence. Occasionally a prurient bit of news sneaks its way into the *Times*, such as an account of a murder or rape. And during the months when parliament is in session a portion of the paper's space is given over to lengthy summaries or verbatim texts of important speeches. But there are no pictures, headlines, crossheads or by-lines. At seven pence a copy (about 13 American cents), the *Times* provides a compact and reassuring, if somewhat unimaginative, read for the family seated at the London breakfast table.[1]

Four thousand miles away, on Bowling Green in lower Manhattan, a New York City family of comparable means sits down to read a newspaper on the same morning. Most likely, this family will be perusing Colonel James Webb's *Morning Courier and New-York Enquirer*, which sells for six cents and circulates predominantly among the city's business and professional classes. The family will not learn anything about the dramatic political events in Paris for another five or six weeks, when the sailing ships that carry London and Continental newspapers reach Sandy Hook, Long Island, where they will be met by schooners hired by Colonel Webb or his formidable competitor, Gerard Hallock, owner of the New York *Journal of Commerce*, for the purpose of bringing the news to American readers.[2] Until then the New York inhabitants will have to make do with "stale" international news, some of it lifted without attribution from the *Times* and other London newspapers. To be sure, the *Morning Courier's* Washington news reports are reasonably up to date and, as it happens, presented in a lively style by the paper's Washington correspondent, James Gordon Bennett, an ambitious young journalist recently arrived from Scotland who also sends reports from Saratoga Springs and Albany, New York.[3] If anything, the *Morning Courier* is more businesslike and concise in tone than the *Times*. It provides minimal news coverage (including a section entitled "Miscellanies" in the right hand column of the front page), fewer editorials and a layout that is equally dense. Like the *Times*, it is a compendium of commercial and political news interspersed with advertisements. It has no visual or typographical breaks of any consequence in its text. It contains little in the way of local news and prints most of its news reports on the inside pages. "Staid, prosy, and expensive" is a descriptive phrase used by a contemporary journalist that can apply equally well to the leading London or New York newspaper in 1829.[4]

If we turn the clock forward almost a century to the summer of 1914, the framework will have shifted enormously. During the intervening 85 years millions of new readers have come to the fore in both cities, and they are as likely to be found on public trams and underground trains ferrying people to and from work, as in smart drawing rooms or seated around comfortable breakfast tables. These readers would be able to choose from a more entertaining selection of newspapers. If they live in London there is a reasonable possibility that they will be reading Alfred Harmsworth's halfpenny *Daily Mail*, founded in 1896; if in New York, perhaps the *New York Evening Journal*, a penny newspaper owned by William Randolph Hearst that boasts the largest circulation in the United States. Consumers of the Hearst paper are likely to be entertained by banner headlines on the front page that summarize in journalistic shorthand the details of the latest gruesome crime to afflict the city. For example, on the first day of July the newspaper directs its attention almost exclusively to the titillating saga of a prominent Long Island woman shot to death in her doctor's office. Suggestive headlines jump out from the front page: "ASSASSIN SHOOTS PATIENT: MEANT TO KILL DOCTOR: SCANDAL IS BEHIND SLAYING OF WOMAN

IN PHYSICIAN'S OFFICE." Photographs of the scene of the crime are prominently displayed, together with detailed accounts of the police investigation.[5]

Most of the remainder of the paper is taken up with bold display advertising and an assortment of news about New York, much of it dealing with crime. International news coverage is minimal, and the *Evening Journal* includes only a few condensed wire service reports from places like Mexico City, where a revolution is under way, and Sarajevo, in distant Bosnia, where the heir to the Austrian throne has just been assassinated. Of greater interest to the paper's readers are its familiar features: Dorothy Dix's renowned "advice to the lovelorn" column; the two popular comic strips, "Krazy Kat" and "Polly and her Pals"; baseball news provided by Sam Crane and a new breed of effervescent sports reporters. Serialized versions of two recently released movies, "The Pearl of the Punjab" and "The Perils of Pauline," are another popular feature of the paper. The *Evening Journal* is easy to read and diverse in its coverage. It reflects, crudely to be sure, the drama of ordinary life in a way that none of the newspapers of 1829 could even remotely aspire to.

The London *Daily Mail* is more restrained than the Hearst paper. For one thing it still prints nearly all of its news on inside pages, a practice it will stubbornly adhere to until the outbreak of war with Germany in 1939. But its single column decked headlines catch the eye, it has photographs, and portions of its eight pages are given over to sports, serialized fiction and subjects like cooking and fashion that are deemed to be of special interest to women readers.[6] A large amount of space is also devoted to crime and news from the divorce courts. The *Daily Mail* describes itself robustly on one of its ears as "The Busy Man's Daily Journal." While it would not come close to meeting this specification if published in this form either in London or New York 75 or so years later, it is vastly more spirited and energetic than the staid *Times* of 1829.

The transformation of Anglo-American journalism between the 1830s and 1914 was an event of revolutionary importance. It ushered in a great age of print, lasting nearly two centuries and now, perhaps, facing the prospect of extinction. It was an era in which popular newspapers on both sides of the Atlantic came to dominate the reading habits and daily consciousness of ordinary people. This New Journalism (to use the name by which it is best known in Britain), or Yellow Journalism (as it was referred to in the United States), or Tabloid Journalism (a twentieth century generic label on both sides of the Atlantic) emphasized human-interest, visual matter, typographical boldness and rapid, speedy news coverage.[7] It replaced a press nurtured in a traditional format, political and pedagogical in orientation and read by relatively small numbers of people, with one catering to every conceivable taste. By responding to, and transforming, the reading habits of millions of people, it made newspapers an integral facet of popular communications.

This revolution in journalism forms the core of this book, which considers the ways in which British and American press experiences in the nineteenth century interacted and exerted influence on each other. While popular journalism in Britain pioneered the retailing of gossip and the use of pictures, most of the key transformations in journalism occurred a little earlier and had a greater impact in America. Beginning in the 1830s, with the rise of a penny press, American newspapers began to exhibit some of the characteristics of modern mass circulation journalism. Newly developed technology was harnessed to the press, while urban reporting, with its use of the personal interview, by-lines and speed in its search after human-interest stories, took hold there first. Best known, in this regard, was the journalism of Joseph Pulitzer and Hearst near the close of the century with its focus on crime and scandal, large headlines and enthusiasm for investigative reporting.

But it is important to emphasize that the press revolution took place on both sides of the Atlantic. By 1914, popular newspapers were being read by millions of people throughout the transatlantic world; published in daily, evening and Sunday editions; and filled with pictorial advertising, gossip, sports, features intended to attract women and children, and fast-breaking news stories transmitted by wire services at unprecedented rates of speed. These papers looked and felt different than their predecessors. They were cheap, visual and (by the standards of the time) sensational in tone. Their staffs were both professionally trained to some extent and unwieldy in size. The technology that produced them was constantly developing new applications. And their goal was to provide entertainment as well as news and, above all, to make a profit for their owners.

These newspapers were the joint products of a common culture and indefinably transatlantic in sensibility. The many parallels to be found in American and British journalism during the nineteenth century are not fortuitous. Both nations were steadily reconfigured by comparable economic and political developments, including the evolution of representative forms of government and the restructuring of traditional social and ethical relationships. By their ephemeral nature newspapers are best able to depict and embody such transformative events. They are a token of the speed of modern life, which enables human activity to be expressed in all of its variety. When newspapers are crabbed and restrictive, as they were for much of the century, political and social patterns can legitimately be interpreted as resistant to change. When popular elements of journalism come steadily to the fore, as they did in both the United States and Britain, a movement towards cultural democracy, with its attendant stresses and tensions, is clearly under way. Unfortunately, even some of the very best work on the British and American press in recent years has failed to recognize that these changes in journalism were a product of a common framework of democratization and of joint cultural formation.

Much work on the popular press has tended to view it from the perspective of its commercial imperative, and in some instances to emphasize the neutering of political consciousness that this has brought about. It has frequently been maintained that the ordinary reader is a victim of the forces of advertising, or of social control, and that the replacement of the values of liberal journalism and of the public sphere by a passive "mass culture" reflects a wrong turning in press history. There is much to savor in such analyses, portions of which have been influenced by the writings of Jurgen Habermas, Theodor Adorno and others. But to focus on the production of newspapers at the expense of their consumption, especially when dealing with the rise of the modern press, is, I believe, to oversimplify a crucial strain in the history of journalism.[8] It is essential that historians take into account the ways in which the dissemination of cheap print enormously enlarged opportunities for personal choice. To whatever degree commercial factors distorted the popularization of journalism, and however much one approves or disapproves of the end product, the creation of a mass circulation press fulfilled the expectations (and more) of a new readership. That, it seems to me, is the key explanation for its enormous success throughout the nineteenth and twentieth centuries, a success that is now being challenged by an extraordinary technological revolution that is proffering its own claims to cultural democracy.[9]

It is not my intention to set forth a theoretical model of press development in this book, though, admittedly, some of the best work in media history on both sides of the Atlantic is currently being done in the area of theory. Mark Hampton, Laurel Brake, Martin Conboy, James Curran and Andrew King are names that come immediately to mind, and I am grateful to them and others for providing insights into the structure of press dynamics.[10] My purpose, however, is somewhat different. It is to demonstrate in concrete ways that changes in journalism are long-range, and do not rest exclusively on the innovations of a few key individuals, or (in the context of transatlantic history) the contributions of a single nation.[11] Journalism is richly layered and, in the best sense of the word, a collaborative activity. During the nineteenth century, sub-editors and engravers were as critical to its success as overseas reporters and compositors. So, too, though many of the details remain elusive, were rewrite men, "penny-a-liners" and beat reporters. The great household names of the century – James Gordon Bennett, Hearst, Stead, Pulitzer, Alfred Harmsworth – were of central importance to the transformation of journalism (their influence is more than reflected in the pages of this volume), but numerous "lesser breeds" also participated in the maturation of Anglo-American journalism. As a way of emphasizing the evolutionary nature of changes in the press I have focused on themes like the collection and distribution of news; the reconfiguration of newspaper content; developing relationships among proprietors, editors, and reporters; and the impact of an innovative technology that came increasingly to be defined by speed. It is hoped that such a perspective on the changes that transformed transatlantic journalism, and on the process of "Americanization" that accompanied it, will facilitate discussions of how ideas and cultural standards are communicated, about the nature of professionalism, and about whether or not traditional literary quality can (or even should) be maintained during periods of great change.

Several caveats are in order. First, there are gaps and distortions in this book, a few by intent, others because of inadequate sources of information. Published writings about the press in America and Britain are, in a curious way, both voluminous and relatively scarce. In recent years there has been an explosion of interest in the history of journalism among scholars on both sides of the Atlantic. Organizations such as the Research Society for Victorian Periodicals (RSVP) and the American Journalism Historians Association (AJHA) sponsor annual conferences and have stimulated much new work in the field. Journals like *American Journalism*, the *Victorian Periodicals Review* and *Media History* reflect the intensity of interest in the subject. The ongoing digitization of newspapers and magazines has also generated a host of profitable studies in a multiplicity of areas. Nonetheless, important spaces remain unfilled. Relatively little work has been done, for example, on the daily content of the nineteenth-century popular press, including crime, sports, and sex, the trinity of themes that define modern tabloid journalism. Nor has pictorial journalism received its full due, or gossip journalism, or to select another example at random, sub-editing, the relatively mundane task that provided much of the cement of print journalism. And while numerous biographies of journalists are available, a number of them very good, gaps remain to be filled: to name a few, Stead, Archibald Forbes, Melville Stone, Winifred Black.

By choice I have given a disproportionate emphasis to the journalism of London and New York. The breakfast tables, railway and tram stations, and reading rooms of these two great metropolises loom large in this book, at the expense of cities that also produced an impressive array of daily and weekly newspapers, including Manchester, San Francisco, Birmingham, Chicago, Leeds, St. Louis, Glasgow and Boston. I believe there is a justification for this emphasis. In the case of Britain it is based upon the fact that despite the increasing importance of the provincial press, a London-centered "national press" existed from the outset of the nineteenth century and has continued to dominate much of the journalism of that country. Furthermore, key elements of mass circulation journalism derived from the experience of the London press. Between 1830 and 1914 an overwhelming number of aspiring journalists regarded work in London as the pinnacle of their ambition. They migrated to "Fleet Street" when and if they were able to do so, and sought to write for newspapers located there. London, dominant in so many ways, was, clearly, a forcing ground for journalistic creativity.

The United States presents a trickier situation. Metropolitan journalism was less concentrated there, and a regional press prevailed in many aspects of the nation's life.[12] The enormous size of the country had a great deal to do with this, as did the segmented pace of economic change, which I have tried to take into account. Still, the bulk of the analysis in this book focuses on the newspapers of New York because, like London, this hugely significant urban center was the epicenter of change throughout much of the nineteenth century. It attracted ambitious, talented journalists from every walk of life, provided a burgeoning market for the sale and distribution of news, and by its symbolic commitment to speed and size appeared to invite the process of journalistic change to germinate within its boundaries.

There is a final general point to be made. I believe that scholarly insight is enriched by comparative analysis, and that when applied to journalism such an approach deepens contextual understanding, for example, making it easier to measure the accuracy of words like "sensationalism" or "speed." It is, of course, possible to focus on countries other than Britain and the United States, as Simon Potter, Chandrika Kaul and others have demonstrated so effectively. But the two countries I have selected exerted measurable influences on each other and have the added advantage of being inextricably linked by language and culture.[13] I also have a confession to make: similarities and differences between British and American newspapers are, at bottom, personally fascinating to me. I have been an unabashed (and unapologetic) consumer of the quality and tabloid press of both countries for many years (including the recently departed *News of the World*) and am lured by the seductiveness of Anglo-American interactions. Many questions arise, some of which I have tried to answer in this book. Why do lead stories appear on different sides of the front pages of broadsheets in each country: Britain's to the left, America's to the right? To what degree are the reporting styles of the two countries different? Why has "tit and bum" journalism become a defining feature of British tabloid newspapers like the *Sun*, while less able to take root in America other than in the so-called supermarket tabloids?[14] Why did newspaper technology in Britain lag behind for several decades? Why were and are American journalists more likely to undertake serious investigative reporting than their British counterparts? As with journalism itself, such questions (and the answers they provoke) have the potential to be endlessly fascinating, especially at a time when print journalism seems to be confronting a grave challenge from Internet technology, one that may presage its ultimate destruction.

Notes

1 For example, see the *Times*, 15 September 1829. Late-breaking news, highlighted by words such as "Express from Paris," was placed just before the leading articles, which were on the second page.

2 See James L. Crouthamel, *James Watson Webb: A Biography* (Middletown, Ct.: Wesleyan University Press, 1969).

3 By modern standards even news from the nation's capital was stale. An elaborate "pony express" system installed by Webb in 1830 took about 30 hours to bring news from Washington to New York. In 1831 Webb introduced a steamboat from Baltimore and cut the time to 15 hours. Crouthamel, *Webb*, 29–30.

4 See especially *Morning Courier and New-York Enquirer*, 1 August 1829 and 1 October 1829. The phrase is taken from Frank O'Brien, *The Story of "The Sun": New York: 1833–1928* (New York: D. Appleton and Company, 1928), 82.

5 See especially *New York Evening Journal*, 1 July 1914 and 6 July 1914. Harmsworth was ennobled as Viscount Northcliffe in 1905, though I use his family name throughout this text for purposes of clarity.

6 Page seven of the *Daily Mail* featured "Women's Realm," edited by a succession of female journalists.

7 The phrase New Journalism, first used in Britain in the 1880s, has not frequently been employed in American press history. But in the 1960s a group

of American writer-journalists, including Norman Mailer, George Plimpton and Tom Wolfe, developed a distinctive "non-fictional" style and came to be referred to as New Journalists. See Tom Wolfe, *The New Journalism: With an Anthology Edited by Tom Wolfe and E. W. Johnson* (New York: Harper & Row, 1973) and Robert S. Boynton, *The New New Journalism: Conversations with America's Best Nonfiction Writers on Their Craft* (New York: Vintage Books, 2005).

8 Commercial influence on the press features prominently in Alan J. Lee, *The Origins of the Popular Press, 1855–1914* (London: Croom Helm, 1976); Gerald J. Baldasty, *The Commercialization of News in the Nineteenth Century* (Madison: The University of Wisconsin Press, 1992); Jean K. Chalaby, *The Invention of Journalism* (Macmillan, 1998). For social control, see the relevant essays in George Boyce, James Curran and Pauline Wingate (eds), *Newspaper History: From the 17th Century to the Present Day* (London: Constable, 1978), and in James Curran, Anthony Smith and Pauline Wingate (eds), *Impacts and Influences: Essays on Media Power in the Twentieth Century* (London: Methuen, 1987). An exceptionally fine study that focuses on readers rather than economic supply is Thomas C. Leonard, *News for All: America's Coming-Of-Age With the Press* (New York: Oxford University Press, 1995).

9 Two impressive studies dealing with cultural democratization are Michael Schudson, *Discovering the News: A Social History of American Newspapers* (New York: Basic Books, 1978) and John Carey, *The Intellectuals and the Masses: Pride and Prejudice Among the Literary Intelligentsia, 1880–1930* (London: Faber and Faber, 1992).

10 Samples of recent theoretical work are Mark Hampton, *Visions of the Press in Britain, 1850–1950* (Urbana: University of Illinois Press, 2004); Laurel Brake, *Print in Transition, 1850–1910: Studies in Media and Book History* (Houndmills: Palgrave, 2001); Martin Conboy, *Journalism, a Critical History* (London: Sage, 2004); Andrew King, *The London Journal, 1845–83: Production and Gender* (Aldershot: Ashgate, 2004).

11 Raymond Williams, *The Long Revolution* (London: Chatto and Windus, 1961) continues to be an immensely influential study. It has given a stimulus to a "democratic" perspective on literacy and journalism and strengthened theoretical work in more general cultural areas. See Stuart Hall and others (eds), *Culture, Media, Language: Working Papers in Cultural Studies, 1972–1979* (London: Hutchinson, 1980).

12 A brilliant study of regionalism in British journalism is Aled Gruffydd Jones, *Press, Politics and Society: A History of Journalism in Wales* (Cardiff: University of Wales Press, 1993).

13 See Simon J. Potter, *News and the British World: The Emergence of an Imperial Press System* (Oxford: Clarendon Press, 2003); Chandrika Kaul, *Reporting the Raj: The British Press and India, c. 1880–1922* (Manchester: Manchester University Press, 2003). For Britain and the United States, see the collection of essays in Joel H. Wiener and Mark Hampton (eds), *Anglo-American Media Interactions, 1850–2000* (Houndmills: Palgrave Macmillan, 2007).

14 Even the supermarket tabloids are different. Papers like the *Star* and the *National Enquirer*, published in the United States, feature preposterous stories of gossip and scandal but rarely anything sexually explicit.

1
The Fear of Americanization

The phrase "Americanization of the British Press" appears to have been used for the first time in a leader in the *Pall Mall Gazette* in 1882 and then, in a more substantive way in 1887, in the concluding pages of Henry Fox Bourne's magisterial two-volume history of English newspapers. Bourne, a dispassionate observer who was himself a journalist, was seeking to describe a critical moment in the history of Anglo-American journalism, when traditional forms of print were ceding ground, seemingly in a rush, to popular modes of expression. The changes to which he was alluding, given an impetus earlier in the decade by William T. Stead in Britain and Joseph Pulitzer in the United States, did not create sudden new structures of journalism. They were instead the product of a process that had been evolving for half a century, much of which appeared to be driven by American models.

Even in 1829, in the days of Colonel Webb's *Morning Courier*, the United States was thought by many to epitomize a kind of cultural primitiveness. By the end of the century, "Americanization" had become a cultural buzzword, framed almost invariably in negative terms, even when employed, as by Bourne, with seeming impartiality. It connoted a vision of advancing democratization with consequent attendant vices, foremost among them being a threat to hierarchical stability. The adjective "transatlantic," which began to be widely used in the 1880s, likewise communicated a specter of egalitarianism and vulgarity.[1]

New Journalism and Yellow Journalism were widely employed phrases that entered the public consciousness in the final decades of the century. They referred to the seeming speed with which the press in Britain and America was being transformed into a sensationalist organ of communication. Matthew Arnold, a fierce critic of cultural democracy, gave support to these forebodings in an article entitled "Up to Easter," that

10

was published in May 1887. In it he derided the New Journalism as "feather-brained" since, in his words, it threw out "assertions at a venture because it wishes them true; does not correct either them or itself, if they are false; and to get at the state of things as they truly are seems to feel no concern whatever."[2] Arnold linked this journalism to an ill-educated populace whose presence threatened to undermine the stability of modern culture. In his view, such a populace was devoid of the idea of perfection, which he envisaged as a counterweight to the constricting pressures of democracy with its narrow social vision. In the late nineteenth century American journalism appeared to many observers to be in the vanguard of this shabby process as it spread inevitably and rapidly across the Atlantic. According to Arnold, "If one were searching for the best means to efface and kill in a whole nation the discipline of respect, the feeling for what is elevated, one could not do better than take the American newspapers. The absence of truth and soberness in them, the poverty in serious interest, the personality and sensation-mongering are beyond belief."[3] He maintained that this contagion was entering Britain in the first instance via the *Pall Mall Gazette*, whose youthful editor, Stead, was derided as the leading advocate and practitioner of this New Journalism.

Theodore Child, a lesser known art critic and journalist, provides an even more extreme example of British fears of an American mass culture. He presented his views in "The American Newspaper Press," an essay published in the influential *Fortnightly Review* in 1885. He openly contemned American-style egalitarianism because of the alleged threat it posed to cultivated life in Britain. Child, who served as a Paris correspondent of the New York *Sun* for many years, commented that "even the blubber-lipped negro is the political equal of the man whose boots he blacks and whose votes he can nullify or confirm." Newspaper writing in America, he maintained, was a "coarse art" that emanated from a "fidgetty and purposeless civilization." It eschewed "simple decency" in favor of "sensationalism and vulgarity."[4] George Flack, the "scissor editor" in Henry James's incisive novel *The Reverberator*, published in 1888, made a similar point, if by indirection. Flack boasted: "I always rush. I live in a rush. That's the way to get through."[5] American journalism was supposedly constructed on a foundation of speed and noise, a corrosive union that was incapable of doing other than paying court to hordes of semiliterate readers. The implications of this for Britain with its history of institutional stability and adherence to conventional standards were dangerously self-evident.

Arnold's anathemas, the hysterical ministrations of Child, and a plethora of negative allusions to "Americanization" and "transatlantic journalism" in the British periodical press testify to a pervasive concern about the impact of mass journalism during the final years of the century. Feelings fraught with cultural anxiety were being expressed sometimes with an anger that was barely suppressed. At the same time many readers continued to enjoy a traditional level of comfort with their newspapers, including the *Times*, which produced a steady miscellany of well-crafted leaders, unbroken typography and authoritative news content that relied heavily on British and Continental sources. For such readers newspapers like the *Times* represented "the civilisation and intelligence of England," in the blunt words of the journalist and literary biographer, John Forster, who claimed to be speaking for "the real English people." Avatars of popular journalism such as Stead and Thomas P. O'Connor, his American-inspired companion-in-arms, might initiate change for its own sake, or (it was suggested) as a means of lining their pockets with profits. But that was insufficient justification for literate newspaper readers to surrender to the excesses of a mass circulation press, with its informality of style and coarse emphasis on "human interest" and speed. If traditionally reliable standards were to be preserved, journalists needed to continue to do what they had been doing for more than two centuries: give space to "the periodical expression of the thought of the time, (and) the opportune record of the questions and answers of contemporary life."[6] In the words of W. J. Stillman, the correspondent of the *Times* in Rome, the alternative was to allow the press to become an exclusive agency for "collecting, condensing, and assimilating the trivialities of ... human existence."[7] Stead and O'Connor, not to speak of other New Journalists such as the Irish-born Frank Harris of the *Evening News* (who was regarded by some contemporaries as much worse), might try to bore holes in the foundations of journalistic respectability. But if the traditionalist script held firm, they were doomed to defeat.

Unfortunately for advocates of the Old Journalism (as it came to be referred to), the traditionalist script was not so easily maintained. And the continuing debate regarding standards in journalism (and literature generally) proved to be more complex than anticipated. Larger issues were at stake than the size of type used to head a news story, the number of column inches reserved for parliamentary oratory, or even the sensationalist treatment of street crimes. Led by Arnold, James, Thomas Escott, who edited the *Fortnightly Review*, and a bevy of writers and journalists, defenders of a traditionalist press fought hard to proclaim the virtues of the current system and repel the unsettling features of a populist press. Thus American journalism in particular generated passionate convictions on both sides. It served both as vigorous antagonist and heroic protagonist in a full-bore debate about equality and the lessons it held for the future. "In the four quarters of the globe who reads an American book" (or, for that matter, an American newspaper?), sneered the Irish wit Sydney Smith.[8] During the final decades of the century, against a backdrop of political and social transformation that involved psychological as well as material anxieties, it became clear that an increasing number of people on both sides of the Atlantic did, a situation that only served to intensify the conflict.

It is important to focus on the transatlantic aspects of this debate because during the nineteenth century the histories of Britain and the United States were closely intertwined. Both nations were evolving slowly into democratic entities and experiencing moments of significant industrial and political change. Their populations were increasing to an unprecedented degree and in each a literate working class was taking form. During the century state schools were established, the right to vote extended to adult males, and the standard of living of poor people of both sexes substantially improved. Better opportunities for consumer choice were becoming available, with the publication and distribution of newspapers providing a central facet of this market revolution. Although considerable disparities in comfort and wealth existed within each nation, conditions of life and work were substantially better by 1914 than they had been at the outset of the nineteenth century.

Yet these generalizations overlook important differences between Britain and the United States, where the advancement of a democratic culture was taking place at a more rapid rate. To be sure, America was not, and never has been, the social and political utopia that some radical reformers in Britain imagined it to be. Inequality continued to be a defining aspect of its history until well into the twentieth century.[9] There were hundreds of thousands of very poor white people living in the United States; millions of impoverished black slaves (up to the mid-1860s); huge numbers of recently arrived immigrants who lacked adequate food and shelter; and not unlike the situation in Britain, widespread feelings of deprivation and anger. The English artisan William Lovett's plaintive expression of belief in the Edenic qualities of American society, where "the will of the American people, expressed through their legislatures, has raised them from such poor and heterogeneous origin to become a nation 'better educated than any other under the sun....'," rested on an inadequate picture of reality.[10]

Yet testaments to the existence of an American cultural democracy, expressed by numerous visitors from abroad and conjured up figuratively by millions of others who never came close to crossing the Atlantic, were not entirely amiss. For by comparison with Britain, a substantial basis for democracy did exist in the United States. Well before the twentieth century, the forms and much of the substance of popular participation had been established. Equal rights were broadly enforced, literacy was widespread, and elected officials from humble backgrounds were not infrequently chosen to serve. Social mobility was accepted in ways that were not nearly as prevalent in Britain. So too (and particularly relevant for its cultural implications) was the reading of newspapers. The "paper fever burns" in the United States, one observer excitedly reported, though not, surely, to the extent claimed by Francis Grund, an English visitor in the 1830s, who maintained that there was "hardly a village or a settlement of a dozen houses in any part of the country, without a printing establishment and a paper."[11] Without giving too much sanction to verbal license of this kind, Andrew Carnegie, the Scottish-born industrialist, was probably not far off the mark when he described America as an "editor's Paradise," where "every man is a politician; and a nation of politicians is the journalist's favorite field."[12] Relevant in this context is Laurence Levine's observation that nineteenth-century America was culturally democratic because all of its classes shared to a degree in its public life.[13]

During these final years of the century, as harsh claims and counterclaims were being made by partisans squaring up to do battle, key questions began to be posed: Was popular journalism devoid of intellectual substance? Was it a minor subset of culture, or on the contrary a more fundamental expression of modern life? Were its protagonists in too much of a hurry to take time to establish their credentials? Was America, as some British reformers contended, a beacon of journalistic experimentation that, notwithstanding its defects, represented a visionary hopefulness? More negatively, did mass circulation journalism (in particular its American version) portend the worst of future possibilities, a transatlantic world of diminished standards and unrestrained commercialism, where intellectual solidity was unlikely to find a resting place? Was it, as Henry James suggested in a moment of notable bleakness, a situation from which "the faculty of attention has utterly vanished," with journalism being nothing more than "the criticism of the moment at the moment."

The fundamental charge made against a popular press was its perceived ephemeral nature. Critics carped at the inability of popular newspapers to grapple with the concrete and to focus overwhelmingly on the passing moment. The writer and historian Alexander Kinglake observed that "the literary difference between (my) own earlier days and those into which (I) lived was that everyone now hurried to print what nobody thought it worthwhile to say then." He concluded that the unfettered pursuit of news, especially at the level of semiliterate reader response, inevitably produced a fleeting sensationalism.[14] James Bryce, whose penetrating study, *The American Commonwealth* (1888), was a landmark in transatlantic cultural analysis, agreed at least in part. Bryce maintained that newspapers were ingested rapidly because "the habit of mind produced by a diet largely composed of (them) is adverse to solid thinking and dulling to the sense of beauty."[15] A leading English critic, Evelyn March Phillips, endorsed Bryce's point, though in sharper terms. She affirmed that the "craze for novelty and excitement threatens to minimize the effect of much that is admirable"; in her view, modern journalism (as signified by the odious American practice of interviewing people and assigning instant celebrity status to them) is drawn to "any mediocrity who o'ertops his fellows by an inch."[16] According to Phillips and others of her contemporaries who attacked a mass press, readers would become disengaged unless their newspapers produced a compelling news story each morning. As an observer noted caustically, such a process would lead inevitably to "restlessness and superficiality." Or, in the words of another commentator: "We print to-day what everybody will burn tomorrow."[17] George Gissing's novel *Born in Exile,* published in 1892, sheds acrid light on this situation. "We must write for our public," stated Jarvis Runcord, the editor and co-proprietor of the book's "Weekly Post." His friend John Earwaker wrote serious essays for a radical newspaper and strongly demurred at Runcord's statement. But Godwin Peak, another associate, quickly put him to rights: "They are too strong for you, Earwaker. They have the spirit of the age to back them up."[18]

The "spirit of the age" did not encompass at least one important group of journalists who were not to be found in the popular press of either country. These were the so-called "higher journalists," men of letters who contributed to the leading political and literary magazines on a regular basis. Recruited primarily from Oxford and Cambridge, and in the case of America from Harvard and Yale, such men (women being mostly excluded from the company) were avatars of respectable professions such as religion and the law. John Gross, who has written extensively about them, concludes that they "served the interests of the most powerful section of the community, and ... reflected the prosperity of their readers."[19] Writers such as Leslie Stephen, James Knowles and Walter Bagehot were regarded as essayists who had something interesting to say to their readers. In the words of the journalist James Grant, their aim was to "enlighten the minds, and to elevate the character of mankind in general."[20] Such activity was assumed to be at work not only in the pages of a quarterly like the *Westminster Review* or in the intellectually combative *Saturday Review*, a weekly journal dating from 1855 that featured a more "popular" style of writing, but in the leaders of influential newspapers such as the *Daily News* and, to be sure, the *Times*.[21] This "higher journalism" was conceived of as durable in a way in which the daily press, increasingly subject to popular input, rapidly transforming trends and, above all, a contagious Americanizing process, could never be.

Inevitably, whenever "higher journalists" were brought into the discussion the United States came up particularly short, a point that was central to many of the harsh attacks leveled against American journalism. For many critics believed that an aristocracy of letters (accepted without demur in Britain) could never be successfully nurtured in a democracy, despite the circulation of eminent American literary journals like the *North American Review*, the *Atlantic Monthly* and *Lippincott's Magazine*. Bryce ruefully noted that ordinary Americans "look around to one another, carrying to its extreme the principle that in the multitude of counsellors there is wisdom."[22] Alexis de Tocqueville, who provided one of the best analyses of social trends in nineteenth-century America, was even more scathing in this regard. Tocqueville bewailed the absence of an overarching literary group whose manners and influence would be able to soften the rough edges of an immature civilization. John Forster reached similar conclusions after paying an extended visit to the United States in 1842. Unlike Tocqueville, Forster correctly discerned the existence of a "small and select community" of intellectuals in America. But he concluded that even these writers lacked gravitas sufficient "to guide (American democracy), to elevate, to redeem it, to conduct it to a noble and enduring destiny"; as a result, American newspapers were "degrading (and) disgusting."[23] His close friend Charles Dickens expressed a comparable point of view in the *Life and Adventures of Martin Chuzzlewit*, when he had Colonel Diver, the editor of the fictitious "New York Rowdy Journal," observe wittily that there was an aristocracy of "intelligence and virtue in New York. And of their necessary consequence in this republic. Dollars, Sir."[24]

In fact, a "higher journalism" did exist in the United States but it was mostly confined to the eastern seaboard and rooted in a magazine culture far removed from the daily newspaper press that drew the attention of most visitors. It was believed that this situation promoted cultural and sectional fragmentation. "The country is parcelled out among small cliques, who settle things their own way in their own particular districts," commented a writer in *Blackwood's*.[25] Some visitors uncovered the odd nugget of gold buried within the interstices of American popular journalism, even in a paper as widely excoriated as James Gordon Bennett's *New York Herald*, which was the prototype for Dickens's "New York Rowdy Journal." But even they concluded that in the absence of a moderating, cohesive center to impart good taste, the fortuitous inter-play of market forces would ensure the survival of bad journalism at the expense of a better product.

The absence of an elite group with the ability to foster traditional cultural standards, especially in the press, meant in the view of many that the acquisition of money was the overriding goal, and as Christopher Mulvey has amply demonstrated in his studies of Victorian travelers, this became a key social fact linked to America.[26] Beginning with Frances Trollope and Dickens, and progressing full speed to Arnold Bennett, George W. Steevens and a host of writers and journalists at the end of the century, the refrain was a consistent one. Americans represented "smart dealing" and a "universal pursuit of money." They worshipped profit as a "hobby, passion, vice, monomania." Business, or so it was unquestioningly concluded, was "everything," without "any end or boundary to it."[27]

Thomas Escott intoned that because of this pervasive commercial ethos, journalism was being transformed from a "liberal profession to a branch of business." "Facility and accuracy in précis-writing," asserted Escott, "can be soon acquired by a sharp lad, and can always be turned to paying account in the newspaper office for the production of literary 'pemmican'."[28] Writing from a self-described moral per-spective, A. E. Fletcher, a former editor of the *Daily Chronicle*, stated that journalism needed to be "rescued from the control of mere profit-mongers, and kept alive as an informing, inspiring, and guiding-force, helping men and nations onward in the direction of the realisation of ideals that alone made life worth living."[29] Possibly the most wound-ing comment was reserved for another one of Gissing's characters: Jasper Milvain, the ambitious pressman on the make in *New Grub Street*. Milvain was determined to rationalize his arduous climb up the ladder of literary success and told his interlocutors: "Most people would imagine I had been wasting my time these last few years, just sauntering about, reading nothing but periodicals, making acquain-tance with loafers of every description. The truth is, I have been collecting ideas, and ideas that are convertible into coin of the realm, my boy; I have the special faculty of an extempore writer. Never in my life shall I do anything of solid literary value; I shall always despise the people I write for. But my path will be that of success."[30] It accomplished little to point out, as many observers did, that newspapers had always relied upon an income for survival and that, even during the comparatively staid 1820s, the revenue from advertising had provided a secure economic foundation for both John Walter, who owned the *Times* and Colonel Webb, the proprietor of the *Morning Courier*. Clearly, what counted most in the view of the critics was the ability to sustain self-evident cultural benchmarks, as a bulwark against the sweeping forces of a transatlantic journalism that seemed to be not only rooted in commercialism but entirely reflective of it.

The conclusions reached by opponents of both New Journalism and Yellow Journalism were therefore unfailingly negative: that standards would inevitably crumble as a mass circulation press, carved into shape in America, extended its tentacles into Britain. Assertions became common that the language of journalism was becoming corrupted ("slipshod slang," Andrew Lang called it), that newspapers were prostituting themselves by pursuing false leads and errant news stories, that people's mental faculties were being endangered by exposure to snippets of information and that time-tested beliefs were being replaced by a public dialogue rooted in invective and sensationalism.[31] The essence of traditional print was becoming "sorely vulgarised and vitiated" by American newspapers, attested a writer in the *British Quarterly Review*, who complained of the abysmal level of education in that country.[32] American journalism, "personal in the extreme," was even linked to the supposedly violent proclivities of frontier life. Thus an image of unrestrained rowdyism – complemented by the occasional reported physical shootout between newspapermen – provided further evidence that cultural standards were under dire threat.

In an influential article in the *Nineteenth Century* in 1887, shortly after Arnold's initial attack on the New Journalism, Arnot Reid, an English journalist, conceded that American newspapers sometimes displayed "vitality, enterprise, and independence of precedent," together with a surfeit of hard news (which he reminded his readers was mostly copied without attribution from English sources). But he predictably maintained that American journalists were solely aiming to satisfy the visceral needs of their readers. According to Reid, the modern daily newspaper, British as well as American, was characterized by "bright, racy, trivial, contemptible stuff, which should interest no one of intellectual capacity, and which does interest ninety-nine people out of a hundred." Henry Lucy, Reid's colleague, concurred. He claimed that American papers "with frenzied haste and fervid imagination (the latter not infrequently supplying the facts) work up the details of personal and private matters its London contemporaries would not even barely record."[33]

Edward Delille, an American-born journalist who had lived in Paris for many years, also came down hard on the "sidewalk journalism" of New York, especially Pulitzer's newly-minted *World*, which he described as "more tawdry, more coarse, more vulgar" than any other newspaper. While accepting that a cheap press was a "social necessity" in America because its restless populace preferred pictures to text (a point not fully borne out by the facts), Delille obsessed about the transatlantic consequences of this situation: "Its example is not only bad, but contagious," he asserted. "It is rather a portent than a subject for just boast."[34] Richard Whiteing, a British writer of popular fiction who had a stylistic affinity for certain aspects of the New Journalism, emphasized the context of this historic shift. Traditionally, Whiteing observed, the press served up "solid masses of nutriment." Now it did little more than proffer abridgements and "induce people to think this way or that, without formally inviting them to think in any way at all."[35] The pedagogical functions of journalism, he maintained, were being tossed out in the rush to transform it.

Quite clearly, those who disparaged popular journalism in the pages of newspapers and influential magazines in Britain (and to some extent in America) dominated the cultural debate. They fired a steady fusillade of ammunition at progenitors of a New Journalism, conjuring a prospect of imminent deterioration. Perhaps, they conceded, British journalism would never quite sink to the level of the American gutter press. As Charles Whibley, writing in *Blackwood's*, crudely expressed it, the "mixed population" of the United States (a euphemism for its huge numbers of immigrants) created a special circumstance because readers of that nation's press, "if they must read, can best understand words of one syllable and sentences of no more than five words."[36] But the situation in Britain was thought likely to become almost as dire. Already by the 1880s, it was maintained that the "mainstream" penny *Daily Telegraph*, founded in 1855, had begun to amend its content for the worse to take into account the demands of semiliterate readers. At the same time, erudite editors like John Morley of the *Pall Mall Gazette* were beginning to cede ground to dangerous pressmen such as Stead and O'Connor, not to speak of lesser breeds such as Horace Voules, a sub-editor on the halfpenny

Echo, who was characterized by a fellow journalist as "the most universal utility man known to the press in his day" because he could "equally ... write printer's copy and ... set it up himself."[37]

Yet if the doomsayers mostly drowned out the voices of those sympathetic to popular journalism, they did not have the field entirely to themselves. There was a genuine debate about the nature of mass journalism and its future possibilities. Defenders of a cheap press fought back hard, led by many of the New Journalists. A small number of the latter issued ringing calls for change. O'Connor stated vigorously that journalism should try to "tell the story of each day in the briefest, the most picturesque, the most graphic situation," while in New York Pulitzer offered the view that newspapers must be "not only bright but large, not only large but truly Democratic"[38] Stead produced an even more exhilarating formula. An article that he wrote for the *Contemporary Review* in 1886, entitled "Government by Journalism," became a manifesto of the New Journalism. In it he described the function of the press to be "at once the eye and the ear and the tongue of the people. It is the visible speech if not the voice of the democracy. It is the phonograph of the world."[39]

Others joined the fray, including several British writers who had been to America on lucrative lecture tours and returned not entirely disheartened by what they had observed.[40] Their reactions were mostly ambivalent, similar, perhaps, to those of foreign visitors to the United States today, who are attracted and repulsed in equal measure by what they experience. The speed and coarseness of American life provoked disparagement in these nineteenth-century visitors (what Daniel Snowman has wittily referred to as the "Disneyland principle").[41] Yet the seeming brashness, vigor and experimental quality of American life engendered a modicum of respect. Few expressed unqualified admiration for America, perhaps because this represented too much of a plunge into the unknown, or as one historian has deftly expressed it: "It was much harder to go from a country that did not spit to one that did than vice versa."[42] Nonetheless, a perception of unremitting energy and lack of deference (equated by critical observers with an unnerving disrespect for privacy) could be at least faintly attractive, as is evident in the accounts of Dickens, Thackeray, Frances and Anthony Trollope, Harriet Martineau, Frederick Marryat and others. Arnold Bennett spoke for an entire century of bewildered literary tourists when during his first visit he characterized New York as an "enfevered phantasmagoria" and "an enormous and overwhelming incoherence."[43] On both sides of the Atlantic many agreed that both America as a whole and its journalism embodied a series of contradictions.

To some America seemed reminiscent of an adolescent in the process of weaning itself away from a reluctant parent. It had, thankfully, retained some traditional values but, as is often the case, the leap into maturity felt bumpy and uncomfortable. A moment of cultural weaning (if that is what it was) appeared to take place around the third quarter of the century, just as many Britons were beginning to come to the United States to have a look at it. Both nations were affected by this cultural interaction, characterized as it was by tentativeness and uncertainty. But whereas Britain appeared to some outsiders to be hemmed in mentally by the weight of convention, America seemed at relative liberty to do what it chose to do.

Dickens, who visited the United States twice, embodied these contradictory perceptions. During his initial visit in 1842, he was appalled by American journalism, which he described as a "monster of depravity" that imposed an informal blanket of "rampant ignorance and base dishonesty" upon its readers. He maintained that the extent of this "transatlantic blackguardism" could not be believed. Still, he was partly consoled by the "warmth of heart and ardent enthusiasm" of the ordinary people he met.[44] Amidst a pervasive stream of mediocrity, American newspaper readers demonstrated, in the opinion of Dickens, a capacity for personal growth that, he felt, lacked a counterpart in Britain. This fitful optimism shone even more brightly during his second visit to the United States in 1867–8, when he found "the general aspect of America and Americans decidedly much improved," not because of institutional changes but due to the development of a national character and the existence of a crude level of egalitarianism.[45]

From the outset Anthony Trollope was more open to the qualities of American culture than Dickens, though he was, perhaps, compensating for an earlier family slight. His mother Frances had set a pattern for nineteenth-century America-bashing with her diatribe in *Domestic Manners of the Americans*, published in 1832. She had condemned the "universal reading" of newspapers in the United States, believing like many others that journalism (defined as bad) and literature (defined as good) were incompatible. "When newspapers are the principle vehicles of the wit and wisdom of a people," Frances observed, "the higher grace of composition can hardly be looked upon."[46] Anthony, who lived in America for nine months during the 1860s, was likewise repelled by the poor quality of some of the newspapers he read. They were "ill-written, ill-printed, ill-arranged," and, in many instances, "glanced at, and thrown away."[47] This stinging jab at the vacuities of modern consumerism was nonetheless counteracted by a grudging admiration for the benefits of productivity. American newspapers, he pointed out, published considerably more hard news than those printed in Britain. And while their intrusiveness and preening egalitarianism appalled him, he appreciated the opportunities they provided to those people (millions of them) who were capable of reading print with a degree of seriousness. The possibility of achieving a state of cultural nirvana from American newspaper print was, admittedly, non-existent; yet, with the assistance of a cheap press millions of Americans were able at least to anticipate a measure of success, "in commerce, in mechanics, (and) in the comforts and luxuries of life."[48]

T. Wemyss Reid of the *Leeds Mercury*, a skillful practitioner of the Old Journalism, endorsed some of Trollope's views, praising American journalism for "its brightness, (and) its close grip of actualities," while at the same time Paul Blouët, a French writer who contributed to numerous British and American periodicals under the pen name "Max O'Rell," applauded the narrative qualities of American newspapers. According to Blouët, these produced "a huge collection of short stories" that encapsulated the lives of millions of common people. As such, they were nearer to the pulse of everyday existence than papers that focused on the distant world of high politics or parliamentary legerdemain.[49] While denigrating elements of American journalism, another critic praised its "easy personal style, that trick of bright colloquial language, that wealth of intimate and picturesque detail, and that determination to arrest, amuse, or startle."[50]

The most cogent and effective defense of the American press was that it exemplified populism in action, what David Croly, the editor of the New York *Daily Graphic*, described as "the common sense of common men."[51] Such a press was no better or worse than the cultural level of readers who sought it out, even if in practice it was little more than an "adult kindergarten," in the words of a not entirely unfriendly observer.[52] "The press represents the nation," a writer stated, and on this basis the seeming contradiction resolved itself according to how one assessed the quality and potential of the populace.[53] At the very least, Americans might be said to demonstrate a receptivity to change, though perhaps something a little bolder existed, of the kind enunciated in the writings of Harriet Martineau, an influential journalist and a leading advocate of the theories of political economy. Martineau bewailed the relatively depressing quality of American newspapers while foreseeing (and predicting) considerable improvement in them. As early as the 1830s, she wrote that "the influence of the will of the awakening (American) people is ... seen in the improved vigor or in the tone of the newspaper against outrage."[54]

The more positive assertions of Martineau, Croly and others lead to some general conclusions about nineteenth-century popular journalism, which feature in three important contemporary analyses: Bryce's *American Commonwealth*; Joseph Hatton's *To-Day In America: Studies for the Old World and the New*, published in 1881; and Blouët's *A Frenchman in America*, which appeared in 1891. Bryce and Hatton agreed that American culture encompassed speed, materialism and, at its best, only a thin layer of intellectualism. But they were impressed by the marked degree of fluidity in America, combined with a practical kind of equality that "with all its virtues and its defects, was a part of everyday life." These qualities informed journalism in important ways. As Hatton observed: "Love of fun, written, spoken, acted, is a powerful factor in American life, and the entire press of the Republic administer to it."[55] Bryce described the American press as a weathercock that functioned as an "index and mirror of public opinion" and believed this was central to the smooth working of journalism in a democratic society. Although he disapproved of much of the content of the press, he praised American newspapers for their receptivity to new ideas. His conclusions are insightful: "American democracy has certainly produced no age of Pericles. Neither has it dwarfed literature and led a wretched people ... into a barren plain of featureless mediocrity."[56] Blouët's analysis was similar. He contended that the press in America embodied the "whole character of the nation," and that both people and journalism were characterized by traits such as "spirit of enterprise, liveliness, childishness, inquisitiveness, (a) deep interest in everything that is human, fun and humor, indiscretion, love of gossip, (and) brightness."[57]

This century-long debate about popular journalism and the extent to which the American press presented a threat to the cultural stability of British life was waged with intensity because the stakes were seen to be high. It embodied opposing views about the nature of cultural dominance within the transatlantic world and, as well, the changing pattern of reciprocal cultural influences. Throughout most of the century Anglo-American literary culture was predominantly sustained and transmitted by means of book culture, which was much more firmly grounded in Britain than in the United States. For decades Americans eagerly awaited the latest published writings of Scott, Dickens, Tennyson, Stevenson, Wilkie Collins, Hardy, Conan Doyle and others. The absence of copyright protection before 1891 made it relatively easy for British literary works to circulate cheaply in America. Fictional and critical texts imported from Britain were assumed to embody a set of canonical truths. They exuded a "confident authority" and served as a cultural surrogate for the opinion-shaping hierarchy that was assumed to be missing in America.

By the third quarter of the century, this pattern began to change, as American writers such as Hawthorne, Twain, Longfellow, William Dean Howells and (interestingly) the western author, Bret Harte, attracted a following in Britain. There were intimations of the beginnings of a shift of power in the cultural sphere. But it was the American newspaper, non-literary by consensus and bearing in its train the banner of democratization, that most directly threatened the cultural dominance of Britain. In Britain an institutional conservatism continued to inhibit the pace of cultural change as well as the public response to it. America, on the other hand, was reshaping itself more rapidly. Its popular newspaper press increasingly permeated transatlantic literary life in the final decades of the nineteenth century and was at the core of an Americanizing process that was to affect Britain profoundly.

Notes

1 The word "transatlantic" dates from the 1760s but was used in a variety of contexts throughout the nineteenth century.
2 Arnold, "Up to Easter," *Nineteenth Century*, XXI (1887), 638.
3 Matthew Arnold, "Civilization in the United States," in *Civilization in the United States: First and Last Impressions of America* (Boston: Cupples and Hurd, 1880), 177–8.
4 Theodore Child, "The American Newspaper Press," *Fortnightly Review*, new series, XXXVIII (1885), 831, 834.
5 Henry James, *The Reverberator* (New York: Grove Press, 1979; first published in 1888), 6.
6 John Forster, "The Answer of the American Press," *Foreign Quarterly Review*, XXXI (1842), 255, 264.
7 W. J. Stillman, "Journalism and Literature," *Atlantic Monthly*, LXVIII (1891), 689.
8 Quoted in Amanda Claybaugh, "Toward a New Transatlanticism: Dickens in the United States," *Victorian Studies*, XLVIII (2006), 440.
9 See Daniel Walker Howe, *What Hath God Wrought: The Transformation of America, 1815–1848* (New York: Oxford University Press, 2007) and Sean Wilentz, *Chants Democratic: New York City & the Rise of the American Working Class, 1788–1850* (New York: Oxford University Press, 1984).
10 Like most other English workingmen Lovett never got to see the country of his dreams. The quote is taken from an Address Issued by the London Working Men's Association, as cited in G. D. Lillibridge, *Beacon of Democracy: The Impact of American Democracy upon Great Britain, 1830–1870* (Philadelphia: University of Pennsylvania Press, 1955), 31. Gordon S. Wood, *The Radicalism of the American Revolution* (New York: Alfred A. Knopf, 1992), gives support to Lovett's dreams by describing early nineteenth-century America as "the most liberal, the most democratic ... people in the world." (p. 7).

11 The reference to "paper fever" is in Edward Delille, "The American Newspaper Press," *Nineteenth Century*, XXXII (1892), 14. For Grund's statement see Francis J. Grund, *The Americans in Their Moral, Social, and Political Relations* (London: Longman, Rees, Orme, Brown, Green, & Longman, 1837), I, 198. Francis Trollope provided anecdotal evidence to support Grund: "I have seen a brewer's drayman perched on the shaft of his dray and reading one newspaper, while another was tucked under his arm." (*Domestic Manners of the Americans* (London: George Routledge and Sons, 1927; first published in 1832), 76.

12 Andrew Carnegie, *Triumphant Democracy, or Fifty Years' March of the Republic* (New York: Charles Scribner's Sons, 1886), 344.

13 See Laurence W. Levine, *Highbrow/Lowbrow: The Emergence of Cultural Hierarchy in America* (Cambridge, Massachusetts: Harvard University Press, 1988).

14 I have put T. H. S. Escott's paraphrase of Kinglake's remarks into quotes. Escott, *Masters of English Journalism: A Study of Personal Forces* (London: T. Fisher Unwin, 1911), 347.

15 James Bryce, *The American Commonwealth* (London: Macmillan, 1888), III, 566.

16 Evelyn March Phillips, "The New Journalism," *New Review*, XIII (1895), 183, 188.

17 Stillman, "Journalism and Literature," 690; Sydney Brooks, "The American Yellow Press," *Fortnightly Review*, new series, XC (1911), 1137. The actress Fanny Kemble's first impressions of New York testify to this sense of speed and transience. The city reminded her of "an irregular collection of temporary buildings, erected for some casual purpose, full of life, animation, and variety, but not meant to endure for any length of time; a fair, in short." Quoted in Christopher Mulvey, *Anglo-American Landscapes: A Study of Nineteenth-Century Anglo-American Travel Literature* (Cambridge: Cambridge University Press, 1983), 165.

18 George Gissing, *Born in Exile* (London: The Hogarth Press, 1985; first published in 1892), 111, 185.

19 John Gross, *The Rise and Fall of the Man of Letters: Aspects of English Literary Life since 1800* (London: Weidenfeld and Nicolson, 1969), 68–9. On this subject see also N. G. Annan, "The Intellectual Aristocracy," in J. H. Plumb (ed.), *Studies in Social History: A Tribute to G.M. Trevelyan* (London: Longmans, Green and Company, 1955), 241–87.

20 James Grant, *The Newspaper Press: Its Origin-Progress-and Present Condition* (London: Tinsley Brothers, 1871), II, 456.

21 See Joanne Shattock, *Politics and Reviewers: The "Edinburgh" and the "Quarterly" in the Early Victorian Age* (London: Leicester University Press, 1989); Merle M. Bevington, *The Saturday Review, 1855–1868: Representative Educated Opinion in Victorian England* (New York: Columbia University Press, 1941). As a student at Christ's College, Cambridge, in the 1850s, Walter Besant, later to endorse aspects of popular journalism, stated the point sharply: "The only journalism that was accounted worthy of a gentleman and a scholar was the writing of leaders for the *Times*." Besant, *Autobiography* (New York: Dodd, Mead and Company, 1902), 92.

22 Bryce, *American Commonwealth*, III, 104.

23 Forster, "Answer of the American Press," 265, 281; John Forster, "The Newspaper Literature of America," *Foreign Quarterly Review*, XXX (1842), 197.

24 Charles Dickens, *The Life and Adventures of Martin Chuzzlewit* (Harmonds-worth, Middlesex: Penguin Books, 1968; first published in 1843–4), 321.

25 Charles Bristed, "The Periodical Literature of America," *Blackwood's Magazine,* LXIII (1848), 111.

26 Mulvey, *Anglo-American Landscapes* (1983); Mulvey, *Transatlantic Manners: Social Patterns in Nineteenth-Century Anglo-American Travel Literature* (Cambridge: Cambridge University Press, 1990), especially chapter 2. See also Allan Nevins (ed.), *America Through British Eyes* (New York: Oxford University Press, 1948).

27 Charles Dickens, *American Notes for General Circulation* (Leipzig: Bernhard Tauchnitz, 1842), 302–3; Trollope, *Domestic Manners,* 259; Arnold Bennett, *Those United States* (Leipzig: Bernhard Tauchnitz, 1912), 133; G. W. Steevens, *The Land of the Dollar* (Edinburgh: William Blackwood and Sons, 1897), 264.

28 T. H. S. Escott, "Old and New in the Daily Press," *Quarterly Review,* CCXXVII (1917), 366, 368.

29 Quoted in *Review of Reviews,* XXI (1900), 368.

30 George Gissing, *New Grub Street* (Boston: Houghton Mifflin Company, 1962; first published in 1891), 62. In *Island,* a novel by Aldous Huxley, the journalist Will Farnaby describes his work as "making money by turning out the cheapest, flashiest kind of literary forgery." (New York: Bantam Books, 1963; first published in 1962), 100.

31 The Lang reference to "slipshod slang" is in Marysa Demoor, "Andrew Lang's *Causeries,*" *Victorian Periodicals Review,* XXI (1988), 22.

32 "The American Press," *British Quarterly Review,* LIII (1871), 18.

33 Arnot Reid, "The English and the American Press," *Nineteenth Century,* XXII (1887), 230; Henry W. Lucy, "American Newspapers," *Sell's* (1904), 107. For a sampling of antipathetic views of the American press, see E. M. Palmegiano, "'BABY-BEER-BULLETS!!!': British Perceptions of American Journalism in the Nineteenth Century," *American Journalism: A Journal of Media History,* XXIV (2007), 47–8, 51–2.

34 Delille, "American Newspaper Press," 18–19, 28.

35 Richard Whiteing, "Old and New Journals," *T. P.'s Magazine,* I (1910), 16. Sir Edward Russell, the editor of the *Liverpool Daily Post,* bewailed the existence of a newspaper that believed it was "enough for people to get news of the world in snippets." Quoted in *Caxton Magazine,* I (1901), 91.

36 Charles Whibley, "The Yellow Press," *Blackwood's Magazine,* CLXXXI (1907), 536.

37 Escott, *Masters of English Journalism,* 268.

38 O'Connor's statement is in Hamilton Fyfe, *Sixty Years of Fleet Street* (London: W. H. Allen, 1949), 48–9. Pulitzer is quoted in Piers Brendon, *The Life and Death of the Press Barons* (London: Secker & Warburg, 1982), 93–4.

39 W. T. Stead, "Government by Journalism," *Contemporary Review,* XLIX (1886), 656.

40 More than 300 British visitors to the United States published accounts of their travels between 1824 and 1870. For information about the profitable lecture tours undertaken by many of these visitors, see Philip Collins, "'Agglomerating Dollars with Prodigious Reality': British Pioneers on the American Lecture Circuit," in James R. Kinkaid and Albert J. Kuhn (eds), *Victorian Literature and Society: Essays Presented to Richard D. Altick* (Columbus, Ohio: Ohio State University Press, 1983), 3–29.

41 Snowman's "Disneyland principle" is described as the "combined message of things American, the handy neologisms, the hamburgers, the jeans, the jazz and the rest." *Kissing Cousins: An Interpretation of British and American Culture, 1945–1975* (London: Temple Smith, 1977), 267.

42 Mulvey, *Anglo-American Landscapes*, 19.

43 *These United States*, 198. Broadway reminded Bennett of a "very remarkable deep glade" surmounted by "enormously moving images of things in electricity." (p. 33). On his first visit to New York in 1895 Winston Churchill characterized American journalism as "vulgarity divested of truth," while conceding that vulgarity was occasionally a "sign of strength." Martin Gilbert, *Churchill: A Life* (New York: Henry Holt, 1991), 57.

44 Dickens, *American Notes*, 301, 305.

45 Quoted in Harold Spender, *A Briton in America* (London: William Heinemann, 1921), 311–12.

46 Trollope, *Domestic Manners of the Americans*, 268.

47 Anthony Trollope, *North America* (eds), Donald Smalley and Bradford Allen Booth (New York: Alfred A. Knopf, 1951), 503. Trollope wrote: "When we express a dislike to the shoeboy reading his newspaper, I fear we do so because we fear that the shoeboy is coming near our own heels." 424.

48 *Ibid*, 538.

49 Stuart J. Reid (ed.), *Memoirs of Sir Wemyss Reid, 1842–1885* (London: Cassell and Company, 1905), 313; Paul Blouët ("Max O'Rell"), "Lively Journalism," *North American Review*, CL (1890), 366.

50 Phillips, "New Journalism," 182.

51 Quoted in Charles F. Wingate (ed.), *Views and Interviews on Journalism* (New York: F. B. Patterson, 1875), 338.

52 Lydia Kingsmill Commander, "The Significance of Yellow Journalism," *Arena*, XXXIV (1905), 155.

53 James E. Rogers, *The American Newspaper* (Chicago: The University of Chicago Press, 1909), xi.

54 Harriet Martineau, *Society in America* (London: Saunders and Otley, 1837), I, 152.

55 Joseph Hatton, *To-Day in America: Studies for the Old World and the New* (London: Chapman and Hall, 1881), I, 47.

56 Bryce, *American Commonwealth*, III, pp. 35, 38, 544.

57 Paul Blouët ("Max O'Rell"), *A Frenchman in America: Recollections of Men and Things* (New York: Cassell, 1891), 110.

2
The Beginnings of Sensationalism

Middle-class families in London and New York in 1830, with their comforting editions of the *Times* and the *Morning Courier* at hand, had little reason to contemplate the enormous changes that lay ahead. London had emerged from centuries of political and commercial activity in a dominant position, though provincial metropolises, including Manchester and Birmingham, were beginning to rival it as a result of considerable industrial changes under way in Britain. It continued, however, to be the largest city in the world, with a population of almost two million people. Its eight daily newspapers (four of them evening papers with small circulations), led by the *Times* and the *Morning Chronicle*, were the only ones of this type published in Britain; elsewhere, newspapers appeared weekly or, occasionally, two or three times a week. London was at the center of the nation's publishing trade, which featured book distribution, as well as influential weekly magazines like the radical *Examiner* and the literary *Athenaeum*. Virtually all news, domestic and international, was filtered through its communications pipeline. It was the chief entrepôt of print, although the majority of its publications were relatively high-priced and beyond the reach of ordinary people.

By contrast, New York was the foremost commercial city in the United States and a center of manufactures with a concentration of small factories and workshops.[1] As was the case with cities like Philadelphia and Boston, it was flexing its economic muscles in the early nineteenth century. Its rapidly growing population of nearly a quarter of a million people was still largely wedged into an area south of Canal Street, in lower Manhattan, and the publication and sale of its newspapers was concentrated in that neighborhood, especially in the avenues and streets adjacent to City Hall. Although the *Morning Courier* attracted the largest number of readers and advertisements, ten other newspapers were published daily in addition to several foreign language papers. The total number of daily newspaper readers was almost certainly less than that guessed at by foreign visitors (it probably did not exceed 30,000), but on a per capita basis it considerably surpassed that of London. At the same time, hundreds of newspapers in other parts of the United States were either in circulation or about to be published.[2]

On the surface, the world of print was relatively quiescent in both countries. News accounts in the morning dailies were securely defined, as were the expressed views of the papers' editors. On an everyday basis there was little that was likely to startle readers, unless news of an unexpected political upheaval abroad qualified. The bustling activities of ordinary people in both great cities went largely unreported in the press. A Bayswater resident, for example, would have at hand substantial reports of parliamentary activities at Westminster or news from Paris, St. Petersburg or, perhaps, Vienna. A speech by the Duke of Wellington, who was prime minister, or one by Henry Brougham, a leading spokesman for the pro-reform wing of the opposition Whigs, would almost certainly garner attention. Yet news emanating from Washington received little coverage, as did events in other parts of the United States. And although the *Times* and other London newspapers published miscellaneous theatrical and literary news from America, including reviews of some of the latest books, their readers were unlikely to have any substantive awareness of (or interest in) what was happening there. They possessed an inward-looking self-assurance that was not to be significantly challenged (at least as reflected in the daily press) for another half century.

The reading habits of New Yorkers were substantially different. For much of the century Americans gazed reverently across the Atlantic towards what they conceived to be a superior culture. They soaked up Continental news and avidly read British books and magazines. They paid handsome admission fees to attend lectures given by "literary lions" on tour from London and elsewhere. Those who could afford to travel went to Britain with considerable expectations and, for the most part, were not disappointed by what they saw. Many of them wrote appreciative comments after their visits, unencumbered by the negativism of their British counterparts. And dubiously, in the opinion of some observers, their publishing firms reprinted numerous British literary works, often in abridged versions and without paying any compensation to the authors. In the absence of an International Copyright Law, it was not required that they do so, though adequate remuneration was occasionally negotiated privately as a "trade courtesy."[3] These contrasting cultural experiences are crucial to an understanding of developments in transatlantic journalism. For they make clear that in the first half of the nineteenth century initiative and leadership in this area emanated decisively from Britain.

Before considering changes in the press that began as early as the 1830s, it is necessary to take into account the role of popular culture in the development of mass circulation journalism. For example, the transition from an oral culture to one dominated by print, which forms a critical backdrop to the emergence of cheap journalism in the nineteenth century, took place at differing rates of speed. By 1830 a shift to printed texts was virtually complete for middle-class families in both countries, who were mostly literate. Their books, periodicals and newspapers were of a reasonable standard of quality and they looked to a predictable world of print for the cultural reassurance they needed.

On the other hand, customary expressions of popular culture continued to flourish among the masses of people who were beginning to populate urban centers in Britain and the United States. This was especially true in the former country, where pockets of working-class illiteracy (in places ranging as high as 50–60 per cent of the adult population) remained a serious problem until later in the century. Hundreds of thousands of chapbooks, many of them poorly executed, were published in Britain in the early nineteenth century, as were almanacs that predicted climatic and agricultural prospects. Ballads recounting the exploits of highwaymen and folk heroes were sung or read aloud in small groups. A trade in the "Last Dying Speeches" of condemned criminals, often supplemented by broadsides and crude woodcuts that celebrated the deeds of criminals, continued to be brisk. Songbooks and children's tales were also published. And in the United States, where popular print culture relied to a significant extent on materials imported from Britain, "captivity stories" and adventure serials popularized the heroic travails of frontier settlers captured by savage Indians and forced to undergo the torments of contact with an infidel population.[4]

Cheap serialized fiction was likewise a prominent feature of the popular culture of both countries. The linkage between journalism and fiction has often been an intimate one, and this is especially true at the popular level. "Penny dreadfuls" and "shilling shockers" circulated widely in Britain in the 1820s and 1830s, and many were reprinted in the United States where they were sometimes referred to as "steam literature."[5] Such tales narrated romantic and perilous situations in relatively crude terms and were invariably resolved in acceptably moral ways. The literary style of the "penny bloods" and American adventure serials left a sharp impact on readers by elevating their emotions. Hack writers working in small printing shops produced the bulk of this sensational fiction. Some of these writers made a successful transition to popular journalism, though most, who were for the most part anonymous and poorly paid, did not.[6] But this "blood and guts" popular fiction, with its ties to stage melodrama and literary realism, offered a continuing link to the mass circulation press of subsequent decades, probably more than any other aspect of popular culture.

These elements of a common literary experience are central to the transatlantic revolution in journalism. For journalism fed upon, and in turn transformed, segments of demotic culture into a daily quotient of readable print. Fictional narrative structures were transmuted into techniques of reporting news, while a centuries-old fascination with personal improprieties was converted into a hunger for modern scandal and crime. Likewise, "human interest" news became a substitute for tales of derring-do and survival that had held semiliterate audiences in thrall for centuries.[7] The notion of a long revolution in journalism is therefore critical because the transition to cheap journalism, even during moments of political upheaval, took place at a time when forms of traditional culture continued to have a significant influence on the lives of ordinary people. Oral communication gave way to print; in an obverse fashion, print separated itself out from more ephemeral kinds of literature. The process was intricate and slow moving. But in both Britain and the United States, it was complemented by a significant transformation of the structure of journalism. In the words of Richard Brown, a "popular market of entertaining information" emerged on both sides of the Atlantic during the middle decades of the nineteenth century, as elite groups gradually lost their role as cultural gatekeepers for their less literate neighbors.[8]

Another point that bears emphasis concerns the relationship between popular politics and journalism, especially in a comparative context. Notwithstanding the increasing recognition of transatlantic studies as a productive academic discourse, events in early nineteenth-century America and Britain, which framed a decisive shift towards political and cultural democracy, continue to be viewed almost entirely within their national contexts. By mid-century, the process of democratization in the United States had moved well ahead of that in Britain, as is clear from the extension of voting rights within individual states and the emergence of relatively fluid class relations. And the years from 1825 to 1840 gave additional resonance to the concept of popular sovereignty.

The presidency of Andrew Jackson, beginning in 1829, strengthened a democratic sensibility (though scholars are right to reject the simplistic phrase "Jacksonian Democracy"). It gave force to a communications revolution, which while falling short of what was anticipated by many observers, had widespread popular reverberations. One key aspect of this democratizing process was the emergence of a penny press in the 1830s.[9]

Events in Britain took a different form, though one that bore some parallels with America. The political and social institutions of the country were not decisively reshaped during these years. But efforts to reconfigure the mold of traditional politics in Britain were successfully undertaken. By the late 1820s industrialization was well under way, in particular the growth of a cotton industry, which led to a concentration of population in northern cities and towns. The economic and social strains accompanying early industrialization were often severe. In the years following the Napoleonic wars a disaffected working class began to challenge the dominant political groups, and among those workers most decisively affected by these upheavals were skilled and semi-skilled artisans who regarded their prospects as insecure while, at the same time, aspiring to improved opportunities in work and education. Ties to popular journalism were notably strong among these artisans, and it was at this level that the roots of a culture of mass journalism began to be firmly imprinted.

One powerful form taken by working-class discontent in Britain was the struggle for a political penny press, focused in the 1820s around the efforts of journalists such as William Cobbett and Richard Carlile to win greater freedom for dissident views, and in the following decade, around the dramatic events that have come to be referred to as the War of the Unstamped. This latter movement involved a sustained agitation against the "taxes on knowledge," which consisted of imposts on newspapers, advertisements and paper that in total comprised an unacknowledged censorship of the "poor man's press." The War of the Unstamped brought the first organized network of vendors into the streets on either side of the Atlantic, and as with the establishment of a penny press in America during the same decade, it involved elements of "sensational" journalism.[10]

The concept of press sensationalism is, to be certain, a relative one.[11] It is capable of being applied to almost any form of media expression that adopts a strategy of giving its readers what it thinks they want. Definitions of sensationalism vary enormously over time, as does the technical ability to create and sustain them. The possibilities for sensational journalism were much greater in 1914 than they were in 1830.

By then photographs could be reproduced, news transmitted with enormous speed across telegraph and telephone wires, and newspapers were able to stay in intimate daily conversation with their expanding readerships by a variety of means. The contrast is obvious if one considers the differences between the *Morning Courier* and the *New York Evening Journal*. The former newspaper eschewed almost any topic that veered towards the "sensational" and conducted itself in such a way as to fulfill the modest anticipations of its readers. The *Evening Journal*, on the other hand, reveled in the ingredients of what came to be characterized as Yellow Journalism: violent crime stories, scare headlines, pictures that literally jumped off the front page, by-lined journalists who personalized explosive news events. A few muted touches of sensationalism were to be found in Webb's *Morning Courier*, including an occasional "human interest" story and some lively dispatches from Washington and Saratoga Springs written by James Gordon Bennett. But its departures from traditionally sedate forms of journalism were rare.

All of this is by preface to an analysis of the considerable innovations in popular journalism that began to take place in New York and several other American cities during the 1830s. Bennett and Benjamin Day, the two leading press pioneers during this decade, were based in New York. Day's chief contribution to modern journalism was to commence the New York *Sun* in 1833, the first successful penny daily newspaper in the world and one that was to maintain a preeminent position in the history of journalism until its demise in 1928. (Several short-lived Boston penny papers preceded the *Sun* by a few months, as did the abortive New York *Morning Post*, also begun in 1833, with which Horace Greeley was associated.) The *Sun*, tabloid-sized and featuring only three columns of text instead of the usual seven to eight columns, competed with broadsheets that sold for six cents such as the *Morning Courier* and the *Journal of Commerce*. Within four years the *Sun* had amassed an unprecedented daily circulation of 30,000 and was in a position to attract substantial advertising, a remarkable commercial feat considering that the average circulation of a morning newspaper in New York before 1833 was less than 3,000.[12] Even more striking, Day's *Sun* coaxed other cheap newspapers into existence, including Bennett's *New York Herald*, the best-known penny newspaper of the decade, which first appeared in 1835; the *New York Transcript* (1834–39), which specialized in crime news; the *Morning Star* and the *Daily Whig*, also published in New York; and successful penny newspapers in other cities such as the Boston *Daily Times*, the Philadelphia *Public Ledger* and the *Baltimore Sun*.[13]

What accounts for the rapid success of the *Sun* and these other penny newspapers? Why did a revolution in popular journalism take place in America in the 1830s? The answer has to do partly with a receptive commercial environment, which made it easier than in Britain to launch newspapers and transform them into profit-making enterprises. Likewise, the fluid nature of social and political relationships expanded readership possibilities and accelerated the trend towards separating newspapers from their customarily intimate ties to political parties. A ferment of pre-literate popular culture seems also to have been "in the air" in America (it has been described as a "carnivalesque ritual" by one historian), which made for a chaotic situation that was ripe for transformation.[14]

Day was a fertile innovator who took advantage of these opportunities. Initially he had worked as a printer on Samuel Bowles's *Springfield Republican*, an influential weekly paper published in western Massachusetts. After residing in New York for several years, the 22-year old reached the conclusion that the public was ready for a paper veering in the direction of "human interest" journalism. His techniques were bold for the time. He concentrated on classified advertising and popular news coverage, and pursued both vigorously. Feature stories in the *Sun* included a widely circulated series in August 1835 about life on the moon written by Richard Adams Locke, an Englishman with a fertile imagination who had immigrated to New York after a brief career in journalism in London and Bristol. Locke's "Great Moon Hoax" articles boldly described the topography and inhabitants ("bat-men") of the lunar environment in detail. They increased the circulation of the *Sun* considerably, even after the paper reluctantly confessed its deception to its readers.[15]

Of greater importance in the long term was Day's recognition of reader interest in local news. His work on the *Springfield Republican*, one of the few newspapers to cover local events in depth, propelled him in this direction. Prior to the 1830s, both the British and American press concentrated almost entirely on national and international news. They ignored local stories (with the exception of commercial news), believing these to be of scant interest to readers. Day intuited otherwise, and began the fundamental process of redefining and expanding the concept of news. With limited resources and a tiny staff, the *Sun* printed reports of local news in its pages, including accounts of fires, accidents and crimes. Some of these were lifted from rival newspapers because, as with books, copyright protection did not exist for newspapers at that time. This emphasis on local news reporting, increasingly emulated by other American papers, only became an integral part of British journalism much later in the century.

Day grasped the appeal of crime news in particular, although he offered squibs rather than detailed reports to his readers and overlaid his coverage of crime with a veneer of conventional morality. The links with Britain are especially close in this area. Crime stories have always been endemic to British popular culture. The *Newgate Calendar*, published during the eighteenth century and reprinted many times subsequently, included illustrated accounts of criminal trials that were intended to titillate readers. Speeches and "confessions" of murderers, accompanied by woodcuts, were likewise popular. In addition, police gazettes circulated in cheap editions, and Sunday newspapers and even daily papers such as the *Times* carried reports from Bow Street and other police courts as a part of their regular news coverage. In 1828, at the time of the gruesome Burke-Hare murders in Edinburgh, when the theft and sale of cadavers to medical schools for anatomical purposes was a common practice, crime coverage reached a temporary peak. Sensationalized accounts of bodysnatching were widely circulated, with even staid newspapers like the *Edinburgh Evening Courant* offering "scoops" descriptive of this phenomenon.[16] American popular culture reflected a similar fascination with crime, though, curiously, it derived from fewer indigenous sources and was more modulated. In seeming agreement with the advice tendered by a London street vendor that "there's nothing beats a stunning good murder after all," Day drew on the British interest in crime news to a considerable extent (and to a presumed American craving for it) when he launched the *Sun* in 1833.[17]

At the outset of the 1830s, crime reporting in America generally followed the anecdotal, "Bow Street" mode of writing then fashionable in London newspapers. This technique, which aimed at exaggerated comic effect, distanced the reader from "blood and gore," while providing a modestly sensational treatment of its subject. John Wight, a celebrated police reporter on the London *Morning Herald* in the 1820s, had given shape to such a style of reporting and its perceived objective, which was to provide entertainment for the "prosperous and orderly portion of society" and enlightenment for "what passes among the destitute and disorderly portion of it."[18] Early on the *Sun* departed from this approach when it hired as its crime reporter, George W. Wisner, who had previously worked for several newspapers in upstate New York. Wisner employed a style that eschewed ornate language. He printed the real names of alleged criminals and adhered closely to the "facts" of each case, which represented still another departure from customary practice.[19]

"Bow Street" crime reporting soon began to disappear from the American penny press. For example, the *New York Transcript*, a competitor to the *Sun*, initially hired William Attree, an Englishman, to report on police cases. Attree penned his accounts in the "Bow Street" fashion, as in this example from the *Transcript* (28 March 1835): "Pat Magill, a steam boiler maker, got his steam up so high over night that his boiler bursted in Broadway." However, the *Transcript* soon began to hire American-born police reporters who composed their accounts in a more melodramatic, hardboiled, style (similar to Wisner): "As she stood on the stand the excitement of the occasion caused the rich purple to mantle to her cheek in more than ordinary measure, giving to her face a glow of hauteur."[20] This linguistic shift, which lacked immediate stylistic antecedents in American popular culture, increasingly took root in the 1830s and paved the way for the subsequent crime coverage of Bennett's *Herald* and the even more spectacular version proffered by the *Evening Journal* and other newspapers later in the century. It has continued to characterize American crime reporting up to the present day.

If Benjamin Day was one of the pioneers of penny journalism, Bennett, his chief rival and sometime comrade in arms, was a more formidable talent. Contemporaries unmercifully vilified Bennett because of his patent disregard for traditional press standards. Yet he gave an immense stimulus to an emerging democracy of print, greater than that of any other journalist on either side of the Atlantic during the first half of the nineteenth century. Bennett was born in Scotland to a Catholic family and immigrated to the United States at the age of 24. He worked on American newspapers from the outset and sought inspiration from them rather than British models. Although he possessed keen commercial instincts he adhered to the democratic belief that newspapers must reflect the diverse interests of their readers. "I mean to make the Herald the great organ of social life, the prime element of civilization," Bennett asserted.[21] This egalitarian cultural vision did not equate to progressive views in politics. On the contrary, Bennett's opinions are best defined as rabidly conservative, since they included opposition to immigration, support for the institution of slavery, and periodic attacks on blacks and Irishmen, which were sometimes expressed in racial terms. At the same time, he rejected the longstanding ties between newspaper editors and political parties, which were customarily cemented by official patronage and subsidies. (Such connections remained powerful in Britain until much later in the century.) Instead he cultivated independent links between publisher and reader. "I have been a wayward, self-dependent, resolute, freethinking being from my earliest days," he mused in later years.[22] His notion of what should ideally appear in a newspaper was truly eclectic and, in effect, constituted a revolution in journalism. "The specialty of the daily newspaper," claimed Bennett, is to "give that part of the news of the day which interests the whole public."[23]

Before launching the *Herald* in 1835, Bennett worked as a reporter for several newspapers with a reputation for local news coverage, including the *Charleston Courier*. As with Day, these early experiences proved to be formative. The *Herald* became a champion of local and "ordinary" news, and within a short period of time easily surpassed the coverage of the *Sun* in both areas. Bennett's three years as a reporter for the *Morning Courier* (1828–31) also influenced him greatly. During that time he cultivated a distinct style of expression, injecting a personal voice into his dispatches from Washington and Saratoga Springs, and never losing sight of the intrinsic value of the events that inspired these reports. He emphasized the critical function of news and the need to adopt a neutral, if vigorously expressed, personal attitude towards it. The *Herald* became one of the first newspapers in the United States to assign reporters to cover stories in many of the leading American cities, one of the first to establish a congressional bureau in Washington, which it did in 1841, and the first to hire local stringers to report on news in major European cities, including London. Historians have sometimes referred to Bennett's years of innovation on the *Herald* as the "riotous era of news."[24]

It was Bennett's recognition of the ineffaceable role of news, as well as the need to fundamentally redefine it, that made him such a decisive influence in transatlantic journalism. To be sure, news had an important role in the British press at the time, but in deference to the prevailing model of journalism, which was primarily pedagogical, it was mostly relegated to second place in favor of leader writing. The *Times,* for example, posted correspondents in leading European capitals and prided itself on its ability to collect news from Continental and overseas sources and disseminate it to its readers as rapidly as possible. But there was little cohesiveness or structure in its dense columns, which relied preponderantly on the coverage of parliamentary and official events. They were appendages to the paper's two chief objectives, which were to sustain the political loyalty of its readers and to influence opinion. Occasionally it even presented important news in its leader columns, because in this way its editor (John T. Delane from 1841 to 1877) could convey in authoritative terms what he had learned from highly-placed sources.

Bennett's approach to news coverage was totally different, and this difference helps to clarify the reconfiguration of essential elements of transatlantic journalism. He actively searched for news, and with a reporter's instinct for a good story, attempted to publish it in a systematic, if tantalizing, way. The *Herald* was one of the first newspapers in the world (none existed at the time in Britain) to present accounts of fires, crimes, political news, even religious sermons, in the form of a sequential narrative, meaning that a portion of its news was sometimes held over to the following day so as to give it a structured quality. Wherever possible Bennett also aimed at accuracy. He was one of the first New York publishers to refuse to give credence to the *Sun's* "Great Moon Hoax," partly because the paper was a fierce competitor, though primarily because he knew the story to be false. In the 1830s the boundaries separating fact and fiction had not yet been professionally delimited, as is evident from the susceptibility given to moon stories and other "tall tales" circulating in the press. Bennett helped to create new professional boundaries, even if these continue to be somewhat problematic (and inconsistent) up to the present day.[25]

The very idea of a modern news story can be seen in the *Herald's* extensive coverage of the Robinson-Jewett murder case in 1836. More than any other event, this celebrated crime established for better or worse the reputation of the paper. In April of that year a prominent man about town was accused of murdering a fashionable prostitute with a hatchet. Bennett broke new ground in his coverage of this homicide, which was also sensationally featured in the other New York penny papers. He contended that the murder agitated the "public mind beyond any event that we ever heard or saw in any city," and published ongoing developments about the murder on a daily basis, whetting the appetites of his readers every morning by providing driblets of information and assuring them that more was to be made available the next day. Bennett published intimate details about the prostitute, Ellen Jewett, including several of her love letters. He printed an interview with the landlady of the boarding house where the crime took place, which he characterized suggestively as being of an "extraordinary nature."[26] He also published artists' sketches recreating the "scene of the crime," which are among the earliest attempts at pictorial crime journalism in Anglo-American history.

The Robinson/Jewett crime story ended successfully for Bennett (and for the accused murderer) when a jury acquitted Robinson, since the *Herald* had consistently championed his innocence.[27] Yet, in larger terms, the case helped to shape an emerging democratic perspective in journalism. To be sure, Bennett was condemned for the salaciousness that marked the paper's treatment of the murder, including accusations that he was "creating" news as well as reporting it. (Similar accusations were to be consistently leveled against Hearst in later years).[28] But the public craved this type of "human interest" news story and it soon made its way to Britain where it provoked harsh opposition, especially after a similar London homicide (referred to as the "Paddington Tragedy") was reported on, if more discreetly, in the British press during the year 1837.[29]

Bennett's *Herald* helped to create a modern popular press in other ways as well. For a number of years it featured daily "Money Market" articles that he wrote himself. These retailed information (not advice) about stock prices and financial transactions, and were of special interest to New York's mercantile community, which made up a solid portion of the paper's readership base. These articles became a paradigm for financial columnists in subsequent decades, such as Henry Labouchere, who in the 1870s wrote similar "City" reports for the *World* and *Truth*, two of London's widely circulated society weeklies, and Harry Marks, an American-influenced journalist who founded the *Financial News* in 1884. The investigative component of Bennett's articles is of interest. He did not systematically try to expose the alleged criminal machinations of New York's businessmen, principally because he lacked the resources to do so. But he requested that readers send him "facts, names, dates, (and) accounts" of malefactors, and while promising to maintain strict confidentiality he pursued such "insider" tips to the best of his ability, sharing information with his readers whenever he could.[30] In effect he employed the *Herald* as an engine of opposition to financial corruption, a technique pursued by journalists later in the century on both sides of the Atlantic.

British journalists have always had a more tenuous relationship to investigative journalism than their American counterparts, in part because of the existence of a more restrictive legal system in that country. Nonetheless, the penchant for gossip in the British press, some of it fused with investigatory tendencies (the fortnightly magazine *Private Eye* comes to mind) seems, curiously, to have served as an inspiration to Bennett in this area. Throughout the eighteenth century, London newspapers freely disseminated innuendos about aristocrats and churchmen. Much of this was scuttlebutt, though some of it secured a foothold in the mainstream press. In the 1830s scandal sheets such as Barnard Gregory's *Satirist* and Renton Nicholson's *Town* (the latter was "neither intended for the eyes of ladies, nor to be read in the refined circles of the drawing-room") began to flourish. They purveyed a potent mixture of ribald gossip and sexual suggestiveness, and occasionally engaged in the nefarious, if profitable, practice of extorting money from well-to-do individuals.[31] More respectable British newspapers sported a similar, if diluted, tradition of exposure, as in their frequent condemnations of the mistreatment of the indigent poor in parish workhouses. Both William Cobbett and the *Times* waxed indignant on this subject and shared information with their readers about the wasteful spending of public money and the horrifying conditions to be found in cotton factories. To a degree Bennett imitated this British practice. Yet he went considerably beyond it. He pursued investigations that bordered on actual detective work, vowing to "tell the Truth and care for nobody." His financial articles, and complementary denunciations of land speculators, customs agents, bankers, manipulators of stocks and other unsavory commercial and financial predators, became part of a chronicle of nefarious deeds that was published on a regular basis in the pages of the *Herald*.[32]

Bennett integrated additional elements of popular culture into his paper, including more extensive coverage of sports news than that provided elsewhere. As with crime reporting, the indigenous roots of British (as well as American) popular culture undoubtedly influenced his journalism in this area. Beginning with the Regency years of the early nineteenth century, when aristocratic "swells" began to ape working-class styles of life, a veritable mania for prizefighting and horse racing developed in Britain. Sporting prints and caricatures were popular, as were journalists like Robert S. Surtees, who successfully turned his hand to inditing comic novels about fox-hunting. Sunday papers such as the *Weekly Dispatch* and the *Sunday Times*, deemed beyond the pale by "respectable" readers, provided news of the ring and the turf. In addition, weekly sporting papers circulated such as *Pierce Egan's Life in London* and *Bell's Life in London*, its celebrated successor, which commenced publication in 1822.[33]

Nothing remotely like this existed in America, though newspapers sometimes printed accounts of horse races and boxing matches, while weekly magazines, including William T. Porter's *Spirit of the Times: A Chronicle of the Turf*, which was modeled on *Bell's Life in London*, began to appear in the early 1830s. Sports news in the United States was generally deemed to be of lesser interest, and this continued to be the case for much of the century, even after baseball began to be played professionally in the 1870s. Still, Bennett was among the first journalists in the transatlantic world to make the reporting of sports a regular feature of the daily press. He hired a writer ("Old Turfman") to cover racing news and employed journalists specifically to write about boxing and other sports. As if to signify the uncharted waters in which he was setting out, the *Herald* also printed accounts of dubious "sporting" events such as cockfighting. Predictably, this brought down upon Bennett the wrath of religious moralists, who took advantage of his controversial reputation to launch a general attack against the sinful proclivities of popular journalism.

Bennett was a pioneer in at least one further area that was to become a central feature of mass circulation newspapers. This was his use of pictures, which until the 1830s had not been integrated into the structure of daily journalism. He published woodcuts in the *Herald* to illustrate some news stories, notably the "Great Fire" of 1835, which burned down a portion of his own newspaper's building on lower Broadway. At first he printed old cuts to "match" current news, a dubious practice that remained a common feature of American and British journalism until later in the century. But the use of "faked" pictures was less important than Bennett's recognition of the potential lure of a pictorial press. In 1837 he published a war map of sites of the Canadian rebellion. Eight years later he printed a full page of wood engravings of Andrew Jackson's funeral based on original sketches, which has been pinpointed as a breakthrough in pictorial journalism. And in more than one instance he published titillating pictures to illustrate the scene of a murder or other crime. Despite incessant grumbling by a small number of the paper's more traditional readers the *Herald* produced an average of about 20 woodblock engravings a year by 1840, which placed it well ahead of any other daily newspaper in the United States. In the 1850s it began to publish pictorial sketches of living people on a routine basis, as well as the occasional political cartoon.

To a degree British models influenced Bennett's visual innovations, notably the *Penny Magazine*, published by Charles Knight and the Society for the Diffusion of Useful Knowledge beginning in 1832. The *Penny Magazine* (as is true of other British illustrated magazines in the 1830s) did not disseminate any hard news. It featured miscellaneous subject matter that lent itself to illustration, including descriptions of churches, landscapes and ancient monuments. Like the *Herald*, it often used old prints to illustrate more recent events, though Knight, a pioneer in the area of pictorial journalism, emphasized the need to produce "real illustrations of the text, instead of fanciful devices-true eye-knowledge, sometimes more instructive than words."[34] For technical reasons it was difficult to engrave original drawings to match current news events in a weekly magazine (let alone in a daily newspaper). Therefore, while many of its illustrations did not, admittedly, correspond to the text, the *Penny*

Magazine became one of the first successful illustrated periodicals in the world. It greatly stimulated the penchant for cheap pictorial journalism in America as well as in Britain. Both Bennett and Day of the *Sun* were strongly influenced by it.[35]

Bennett, Day, William M. Swain of the Philadelphia *Public Ledger*, Arunah S. Abell of the *Baltimore Sun* and other newspapermen who created a penny press in New York and elsewhere in the 1830s were part of an artisan culture that was permeated by democratic aspirations. Many of these men were printers by training. They formed the nucleus of an evolving middle class whose ideals were rooted in visions of commercial freedom and economic equality, what Michael Schudson has described as a "democratic market society." Several printer-editors had links to radical workingmen's associations and political organizations, though most can effectively be characterized as non-political because they were more concerned with the form of the journalistic product than its content.[36] A "democratic market society" of the type described by Schudson did not exist in Britain at the time because workingmen were locked into more constrained political and class relationships. Yet, to an extent, a trans-atlantic parallel existed in the artisan/middle class collaboration that produced Britain's War of the Unstamped, an event with a considerable impact on popular journalism.

The War of the Unstamped has been the subject of two books and many articles, focusing primarily on its central role in the agitation for radical reform in Britain.[37] It involved the printing and distribution of hundreds of unstamped, illegal newspapers between 1830 and 1836, the chief aim being to compel the Whig government to repeal its unpopular taxes on newspapers, advertisements and pamphlets. These duties pushed up the price of newspapers, effectively extending them beyond the reach of poorer readers. As a result of the taxes, daily news-papers in Britain generally sold for seven pence, which was approx-imately half the hourly wage of an average worker in Britain. The repeal movement led to the reduction of the newspaper duty to a penny in 1836 and the partial removal of the other taxes. The remaining penny duty was eliminated in 1855, while in 1861, the last of the taxes on knowledge, which was levied on paper, was removed. Not until the 1860s therefore was the British press freed from financial restraints and estab-lished on a legal par with the American press.

A key feature of the War of the Unstamped was that it was fought in the streets of London and other leading British cities and towns. Before the 1830s the bulk of newspapers in Britain and the United States were sold by subscription. Purchasers of these papers did not buy them directly from vendors or distributors. There were no newsboys in existence to hawk "extras," or retail shops to sell morning and evening editions of newspapers.[38] Instead subscribers paid an annual sum for delivery, usually 15 dollars in the United States (though from the outset the *Herald* charged its subscribers only three to five dollars, depending upon the place of residence). Newspapers were customarily distributed by wholesale agents or forwarded by post if the purchaser resided beyond the environs of a town. When the latter method was employed delivery was by means of a coach or, commencing in the 1840s, by rail. Either way, the subscription system, based upon traditional modes of communication, meant a relatively inelastic, if stable, circulation for newspapers.

The War of the Unstamped altered this format by transferring distribution methods into the streets. It integrated into the newspaper business the cries and shouts of impecunious hawkers who had sold cheap serial fiction and itinerant street literature to the public for decades. For the first time vendors began to be employed to sell papers. Some of them opened shops. Others purchased a day's supply of a paper from the publisher/printer for cash or credit, and then sold it in the streets, usually for a penny or a halfpenny per number, though the price might be increased at moments of political excitement. These vendors often competed vigorously for business. A large number were financially destitute and engaged in the trade solely to eke out a bare living; others sought to disseminate the radical political convictions of the newspapers they handled.

This "London Plan" of distribution (as it came to be known in America) was not, paradoxically, to be widely used again in Britain until the 1880s and 1890s, when newsboys took over street sales of halfpenny evening papers such as the *Star* and of some mass circulation newspapers, including the *Daily Mail*. Until then (after the suppression of unstamped newspapers between 1836 and 1855) only Sunday papers and halfpenny papers like the *Echo* were sold on the streets as well as by subscription. But in the United States street sales caught on rapidly during the 1830s. Day and other proprietors of penny papers imitated the distribution methods of the unstamped press by hiring vendors (many of them children) at the rate of two dollars a week to sell their newspapers publicly or deliver them to the homes of subscribers. For a time New York, Philadelphia and other cities were alive with the buzz of street sellers thrusting their printed items into the hands of hesitant customers. The increase in circulation of penny papers, including the *Herald*, was based, at least in part, on the unpredictable success of such street sales. This early instance of consumer choice in transatlantic journalism was a harbinger of the aggressive competitive tactics of the modern press and it prefigured an enormous increase in circulation.[39] Yet even in the United States, most newspapers continued to rely predominantly upon traditional subscription methods for their sales, at least until the second half of the century. For the most part publishers chose to play it safe, concentrating on secure markets rather than seeking out random purchasers.

Britain's War of the Unstamped influenced popular journalism in ways other than the street sales of newspapers. Although its overarching aims were political, in contrast with the penny press in America in the 1830s, the very act of bringing illegal newspapers into existence to battle against state power gave a fillip to experimentation. The artisans and laborers who led this movement introduced "human interest" stories into their periodicals. Several of the journalists involved had published street literature prior to establishing their links to the agitation. They now negotiated the transition to a more stable form of print, albeit one whose legality was clearly in question. Others perceived the commercial possibilities inherent in cheap publishing and sought to increase their profits by offering "entertainment" as an integral part of the packaging. An increasing number understood (as labor and socialist movements in both countries mostly failed to do throughout the century) that serious ideas could sometimes be presented more effectively if they were clothed in the outer raiment of sensational journalism.[40]

Crime stories, sports news, pictorial biographies and penny fiction therefore came to be interspersed with radical commentary in many of Britain's unstamped penny papers. A few periodicals were openly marketed as suppliers of amusement, such as the *Sporting Courier* and *Cleave's Weekly Police Gazette*. These papers made fumbling efforts at typographical boldness to denote news of special interest, as in the use of occasional double or triple decked single column headlines. They also purveyed more than the usual quantity of scurrilous political gossip. This had the twofold advantage of enhancing the political convictions of their readers while, at the same time, appealing to their prurient tendencies, as in the revelations that reactionary clergymen and aristocrats routinely engaged in sexually immoral behavior. In tandem with the reforming tendencies of American penny journalism, some unstamped newspapers also pursued investigations into factory and poor law abuses. Two Manchester papers, the *Voice of the People* and the *Poor Man's Advocate*, specialized in exposés of this kind, with the latter featuring a popular weekly column entitled "Beauties of a

Cotton Factory."[41] Overall, these represented more minor efforts at investigative journalism than those of Bennett's *Herald* because lacking adequate financing they were compelled to forego even minimal attempts at documentation. But they exemplified a notable shift towards press initiative in this area.

More striking in its effects on transatlantic journalism than the War of the Unstamped, which was specific to its political terrain, was the popularity of Sunday and illustrated papers in Britain beginning in the early 1840s. In the United States weekly editions of daily news-papers (some of them published on Sundays) began to circulate in the first half of the nineteenth century. Several of these papers amassed large readerships and became fixtures of American journalism, notably Horace Greeley's weekly *Tribune*, which amassed a national circulation of about 150,000, the largest for any edition of an American newspaper before 1850. Others fared less well due in part to religious opposition, including Bennett's *Sunday Herald*, which commenced publication in 1841 but did not gain traction among readers until later in the century. Weekly editions like the *Sunday Herald* adopted magazine formats and for the most part were variations of well-tested daily products. In tone and content, they resembled the newspapers that produced them.

British Sunday papers, on the other hand, had no ties to daily news-papers, and were considered to be "non-respectable," including the ear-liest newspapers, the *Observer* and the *Weekly Dispatch*, which began publication in, respectively, 1791 and 1801. Religious sabbatarianism was a powerful force in Britain, and Sunday newspapers were con-demned for luring workingmen away from churchly pursuits on their single day of leisure. From the outset these newspapers sold at cheap prices and catered to a poorer class of readers whose tastes were rooted in popular culture. They gave extra space (together with extra spice) to crime, sports and gossip, three ingredients of modern tabloid jour-nalism. They frequently illustrated their news stories with crude woodcuts and sometimes decorated them with crossheads and bold headings like "Incest at Reading" or "Atrocious Burglary." In short, Britain's Sunday newspapers were associated with a down-market "Sunday-paper look," which repelled readers who were comfortable with a more traditional product.[42] In the words of a historian of Sunday journalism, such papers merged "old non-political traditions of chap-book and last dying speech and the political radicalism of the unstamped and the Chartist papers."[43]

From the early 1840s, in the aftermath of the unstamped press cam-paign (which witnessed the temporary demise of a radical penny press), Sunday newspapers began to increase in number and circulation. Three journals emerged as successful competitors to the *Observer* and the *Weekly Dispatch*. These were *Lloyd's Weekly Newspaper* (1842), which described itself as the "cheapest, largest, and best family newspaper"; the *Weekly Times* (1843); and *Reynolds's Weekly Newspaper*, established in May 1850 (the title was changed to *Reynolds's Newspaper* in 1851). A fourth newspaper, the *News of the World* ("NEWS FOR THE MILLIONS"), commenced in 1843, had less immediate impact, though in the twentieth century it was to become the leading Sunday newspaper of all time in terms of circulation. (In July 2011, Rupert Murdoch shut it down precipitately during the hacking scandal.) All of the Sunday papers of the 1840s were London-based but attracted networks of readers in different regions of the country, notably Lancashire, and amassed circulations that extended into the hundreds of thousands. After the removal of the final penny of the newspaper tax in 1855, the Sunday papers reduced their price to a penny, which effectively guaranteed them a mass market that comprised large numbers of artisans and lower middle-class workers.[44]

Even by the standards of the mid-Victorian decades, these Sunday newspapers were not as "sensational" as the penny dailies being published at the time in New York. The only hard news they carried was ephemeral, "scissor and paste" items slapped together by sub-editors. Their emphasis was entirely on light entertainment. *Reynolds's Newspaper* was especially popular among workingmen because it featured substantial dollops of sports news along with some bloodcurdling popular fiction. It enunciated radical positions on many of the leading political and economic issues of the day, as did other Sunday papers. But it did so, seemingly, with greater conviction (and ability as well) because its editor, George W. M. Reynolds, was a prolific author of popular fiction and a passionate advocate for political democracy. Reynolds edited many successful periodicals and newspapers, and was vilified by conservatives and radicals alike, including Karl Marx, who accused him of permitting commercial considerations to trump ideological conviction. In short, he was contemned for selling out to sensationalism, a charge frequently leveled against popular journalists during the nineteenth century. However, as Anne Humpherys has perceptively noted, his motives were undoubtedly complicated since profit seeking (that is, viewing news as a commodity for sale) and political passion are by no means incompatible.[45] Edward Lloyd, the founder of *Lloyd's Weekly Newspaper*, was another pioneer of popular Sunday journalism, though he lacked the political convictions of Reynolds. He was steeped in elements of popular culture having launched his career in journalism as a formula writer of "penny bloods" before moving into mainstream popular journalism.

The rise of sixpenny illustrated weekly newspapers in Britain, epitomized by the justly celebrated *Illustrated London News*, founded in 1842, was an additional shaping force in transatlantic journalism. One of a number of pictorial magazines launched during that decade, the *Illustrated London News* drew inspiration from earlier attempts at illustrated caricature in comic periodicals like *Punch* (1841), newspapers such as the *Weekly Chronicle*, which used woodcuts to illustrate crime stories, and established papers like the *Morning Chronicle*, which occasionally complemented news events with pictures, including the opening of the new London Bridge in 1831.[46] As was true of Bennett's *Herald*, the *Illustrated London News* derived a portion of its nourishment from the *Penny Magazine*. It made effective use of woodblock engravings, a technique revived in the 1820s that subsequently became a core ingredient in the success of pictorial newspapers. Furthermore, Herbert Ingram, the proprietor of the paper, quite possibly had a transatlantic model in mind because by the early 1840s American pictorial journalism, including that on display in Bennett's *Herald*, was beginning to make its way across the Atlantic.

The potential advantages of disseminating news in pictorial form are obvious. A melding of words and pictures sharpens news coverage (at least for the consumer) because, in the words of Henry Vizetelly, who was an innovator in this area, it has the ability to "instruct and refine as well as convey information."[47] However, in the early nineteenth century technical problems handicapped pictorial journalism because of the difficulty in making wood engravings from original sketches in time to meet speedy deadlines. At first, illustrated newspapers fudged this process (as the *Herald* and the *Penny Magazine* had done), and usually got away with it. The first number of the *Illustrated London News*, for instance, employed a generic woodblock of a fire to "illustrate" a conflagration in Hamburg. Numerous other examples of this type can be culled from pictorial papers of the 1840s, and, clearly, a true match between words and pictures was rarely consummated during these years. Slowly, however, the technical blockage was overcome, and by 1844 it was possible to prepare wood engravings from sketches in less than two days, more than sufficient time for inclusion in a weekly newspaper.

The *Illustrated London News* and its leading rival, the *Pictorial Times*, commenced by Henry Vizetelly in 1843, filled a significant niche in popular journalism. Ingram was a newsagent and investor in miscellaneous projects whose chief aim was to turn a quick profit. Initially he wanted to publish a crime gazette; then Vizetelly, a wood engraver whose brilliant career as a journalist and publisher extended into the late 1880s, persuaded him to establish a "family" newspaper that would enable readers to see, as well as read, the news. The result was the *Illustrated London News,* which broke new ground.[48] Its earliest numbers were taken up with rusty "news items" from exotic locales like China and India, included solely for the opportunity to parade attractive visuals. Soon the newspaper began to pay good money for talented artists to compose sketches and make up engravings, including John Gilbert, who later became a celebrated painter. Among the earliest successes of the *Illustrated London News* were pictures of the Scottish tour of Queen Victoria and Prince Albert in 1842, the "first known double spread of a word-and-picture story to be used by either a newspaper or magazine."[49] Likewise, Vizetelly's *Pictorial Times* made a splash the following year with its front page engraving of an "Explosion at the Oil and Turpentine Works, Blackwall Railway."[50]

Illustrated news quickly attracted a large readership. By 1850, several weeklies employed "Pictorial Correspondents" based in European capitals who sent sketches of the news to London by express. These were worked into wood engravings and published as speedily as possible. Crimean War wood engravings during the 1850s (some accomplished from sketches copied from photographs taken on the spot) added to the fame of the *Illustrated London News* and other pictorial newspapers, including a host of new rivals. The combination of improved pictures and enhanced journalistic initiative brought these papers an increasing number of readers, so that their circulations began to reach into the hundreds of thousands and to rival that of the Sunday newspapers.

For the most part American illustrated journalism took its cue from British developments. In 1851, *Gleason's Pictorial Drawing-Room Companion,* the "first picture weekly" to be published in the United States, was commenced in Boston by Frederick Gleason and Maturin Murray Ballou ("Captain Ballou"), a writer of sensational fiction. It imitated the format of the *Illustrated London News* but with a distinctly "American" flavor, in that it was more of a magazine than a purveyor of news. (The line between these two versions of print journalism was generally more clearly etched in the United States.) Its expressed purpose was to become an "ornament for the centre-table, and a valuable record of all that is interesting and worthy of note." It featured illustrations of tales, pictures of buildings and landscapes, and portraits of celebrated individuals such as the abolitionist reformer Wendell Phillips.[51] *Gleason's* occasionally provided topical renderings of news stories for its readers, as in December 1851, when Louis Kossuth, the Hungarian nationalist, visited London with a large entourage. On this occasion it published a wood engraving of the group entering Hyde Park. For the most part, however, it followed an attenuated magazine format, failing to utilize the word-picture combination to maximum effect. Key members of the paper's staff included "Frank Leslie" (Henry Carter), an English engraver who had worked for the *Illustrated London News* for several years before immigrating to the United States. During the following decades he was to become the true creator of pictorial journalism in America, at which time illustrated journals began to flourish on both sides of the Atlantic.[52]

Notes

1 Sean Wilentz describes New York in the 1830s as a "metropolitan labyrinth of factories and tiny artisan establishments, central workrooms and out-workers' cellars, luxury firms and sweatwork strapping shops." *Chants Democratic*, 107.
2 There were 65 daily newspapers published in the United States in 1830 with an average circulation of 1,200.
3 On copyright protection, see Jeremy Tunstall and David Machin, *The Anglo-American Media Connection* (Oxford: Oxford University Press, 1999), 105–6, and Mike Ashley, *The Age of the Storytellers: British Popular Fiction Magazines, 1880–1950* (London: The British Library, 2006), 270.
4 Wilentz's discussion of the tavern culture of New York in the 1830s makes clear that many of the broadsides and tracts in circulation were imported from Britain (*Chants Democratic*, 53–5). Iain McCalman brilliantly explores the fine line between bawdiness and politics in *Radical Underworld: Prophets, Revolutionaries and Pornographers in London, 1795–1840* (Cambridge: Cambridge University Press, 1988). The element of fanciful belief in aspects of popular culture has not been adequately studied, though it helps to explain the credulous quality of early popular journalism, which prepared the way for compilers of curiosities like P. T. Barnum.
5 See Louis James, *Fiction for the Working Man, 1830–1850: A Study of the Literature Produced for the Working Classes in Early Victorian Urban England* (London: Oxford University Press, 1963). For brief histories of 45 publishing companies that helped to shape a popular literary taste in nineteenth-century America, see Madeleine B. Stern (ed.), *Publishers for Mass Entertainment in Nineteenth-Century America* (Boston: G. K. Hall, 1980).
6 These included G. W. M. Reynolds, Thomas Prest, and in the United States, Maturin Murray Ballou. See James, *Fiction for the Working Man*, chapters 4–5; George Everett, "Maturin Murray Ballou," *Dictionary of Literary Biography*, LXXIX (1989), 43–50.
7 There is a wealth of material on British popular culture, including studies by Richard Hoggart, Raymond Williams, Louis James, Richard Altick and, more recently, Ian Haywood, *The Revolution in Popular Literature: Print, Politics and the*

People (Cambridge: Cambridge University Press, 2004). Karen Roggenkamp, *Narrating the News: New Journalism and Literary Genre in Late Nineteenth-Century American Newspapers and Fiction* (Kent: The Kent State University Press, 2005), analyzes the ways in which the genres of journalism and fiction shaded into each other.

8 Richard D. Brown, *Knowledge is Power: The Diffusion of Information in Early America, 1700–1865* (New York: Oxford University Press, 1989). Gunther Barth makes the compelling point that the urban press gave a stimulus to cultural change by providing unifying information about the nineteenth-century city. *City People: The Rise of Modern City Culture in Nineteenth Century America* (New York: Oxford University Press, 1980). An analogous interpretation – that the rise of a "commercial press" enabled residents of a city to adapt to it more effectively – is presented in William R. Taylor, *In Pursuit of Gotham: Culture and Commerce in New York* (New York: Oxford University Press, 1992).

9 Andie Tucher, *Froth and Scum: Truth, Beauty, Goodness, and the Ax Murder in America's First Mass Medium* (Chapel Hill: The University of North Carolina Press, 1994), maintains that the penny press of the 1830s reflected "the social and economic turmoil of the Jacksonian age (and) the clashing of the interests of the rising classes with those of the entrenched elite" (p. 16).

10 See Joel H. Wiener, *The War of the Unstamped: The Movement to Repeal the British Newspaper Tax, 1830–1836* (Ithaca: Cornell University Press, 1969) and Patricia Hollis, *The Pauper Press: A Study in Working-Class Radicalism of the 1830s* (Oxford: Oxford University Press, 1970).

11 See John D. Stevens, *Sensationalism and the New York Press* (New York: Columbia University Press, 1991). Mitchell Stephens maintains that sensationalism is endemic to the presentation of news and that, inevitably, "journalists' tastes … run towards the unnatural, the extraordinary." *A History of News: From the Drum to the Satellite* (New York: Penguin Books, 1988), 136.

12 Crouthamel, *Webb*, 16. By 1837 the advertising income of the *Sun*, drawn largely from "small ads," was more than 200 dollars per day.

13 Alexander Saxton, "Problems of Class and Race in the Origins of the Mass Circulation Press," *American Quarterly*, XXXVI (1984), 217–18. Between 1834 and 1840, 35 daily newspapers priced at a penny were launched in New York City alone. Barth, *City People*, 70–1.

14 Isabelle Lehuu, *Carnival on the Page: Popular Print Media in Antebellum America* (Chapel Hill: The University of North Carolina Press, 2000), 37. Jeffrey L. Pasley "The Tyranny of Printers": *Newspaper Politics in the Early American Republic* (Charlottesville: University Press of Virginia, 2001), provides an interesting link between parties and printers, who are seen as embodying elements of cultural democratization.

15 For a detailed account of this hoax, one of the most famous in American journalism, see Matthew Goodman, *The Sun and the Moon: The Remarkable True Account of Hoaxers, Showmen, Dueling Journalists, and Lunar Man-Bats in Nineteenth-Century New York* (New York: Basic Books, 2008). Edgar Allen Poe described the moon articles as the "greatest hit in the way of sensationalism – of merely popular sensation – ever made by any similar fiction either in Europe or America." Nickieann Fleener, "Benjamin Day," *Dictionary of Literary Biography*, XLIII (1985), 143.

16 The most scholarly account of the Burke-Hare murders is in Ruth Richardson, *Death, Dissection and the Destitute* (London: Routledge & Kegan Paul, 1987).

17 The quote by the vendor is taken from Victor E. Neuberg, "The Literature of the Streets," in H. J. Dyos and Michael Wolff (eds), *The Victorian City: Images and Realities* (London: Routledge & Kegan Paul, 1973), I, 194. Asa Greene, editor of the *New York Transcript*, a rival of Day's *Sun*, wrote: "Dreadful dull times at the Police Office, just now: no murders – hardly any burglaries – a surprising diminution in the article of drunkards – and, considering all things, not many brought up for beating their wives." *New York Transcript*, 27 May 1834. In 1845, George Wilkes founded the weekly *National Police Gazette & Police News*, an enormous success for many years due to its aggressive coverage of crime and sports.

18 John Wight, *Mornings at Bow Street: A Selection of the Most Humorous and Entertaining Reports Which Have Appeared in the Morning Herald* (London: Charles Baldwyn, 1824), iv–v.

19 See James Stanford Bradshaw, "George W. Wisner and the New York Sun," *Journalism History*, VI (1979–80), 112, 117–21. Frank M. O'Brien describes Wisner as the "Balzac of the daybreak court." (*Story of "The Sun,"* 17.)

20 *New York Transcript*, 26 March 1835. Horace Greeley described "Oily Attree" as "a shrewd, active and unprincipled penny-a-liner." (Tucher, *Froth and Scum*, 214.)

21 William A. Croffut, "Bennett and His Times," *Atlantic Monthly*, CXLVII (1931), 203.

22 *Ibid*, 105. It has been argued, in my opinion unpersuasively, that Bennett's independent politics shaped his journalism rather than the other way around. Douglas Fermer, *James Gordon Bennett and the "New York Herald": A Study of Editorial Opinion in the Civil War Era, 1854–1867* (Woodbridge: The Boydell Press, 1986).

23 Quoted in James Parton, *Famous Americans of Recent Times* (Boston: Ticknor and Fields, 1867), 292.

24 The phrase is to be found initially in Will Irwin, "American Newspapers," *Collier's*, XLVI, 4 February 1911. Don C. Seitz describes the *Herald* as "the only non-partisan paper in an extremely partisan age." *The James Gordon Bennetts, Father and Son: Proprietors of the New York Herald* (Indianapolis: Bobbs-Merrill, 1928), 96.

25 Bennett's self-assessment was grandiose if not entirely amiss: "It is my passion, my delight, my thought by day, and my dream by night to conduct the Herald, and to show the world and posterity, that a newspaper can be made the greatest, most fascinating, most powerful organ of civilization that genius ever yet dreamed of."

26 For details of this case, see Patricia Cline Cohen, *The Murder of Helen Jewett: The Life and Death of a Prostitute in Nineteenth-Century America* (New York: Alfred Knopf, 1998).

27 For a brief discussion of the importance of the case to Bennett's career, see James L. Crouthamel, *Bennett's New York Herald and the Rise of the Popular Press* (Syracuse: Syracuse University Press, 1989), 28–31.

28 Bennett was the object of numerous attacks during his years as owner of the *Herald*, which lasted until 1867. For example, Charles Mackay, a London

Times correspondent during the Civil War, described him as "rowdy, unscrupulous, scurrilous, and unrespectable." *Through the Long Day, or, Memorials of a Literary Life During Half a Century* (London: W. H. Allen 1887), II, 225. A biographer of Bennett has described the *Herald* as "the most sensational, salacious, and sardonic newspaper in the world." Oliver Carlson, *The Man Who Made News: James Gordon Bennett* (New York: Duell, Sloan and Pearce, 1942), 146.

29 The murder is described in a contemporary pamphlet as follows: "In the annals of crime, for many years past, no act is related that has created such a universal thrill of horror." *The Paddington Tragedy* (London: Orlando Hodgson, 1837), 3.

30 *New York Herald*, 21 September 1835. For Harry Marks, see the article by Dilwyn Porter in the *New Dictionary of National Biography*.

31 For example, see Renton Nicholson, *Rogue's Progress: The Autobiography of "Lord Chief Baron" Nicholson*, ed. John L. Bradley (London: Longmans, 1965), chapter 24; David E. Latane, Jr., "Charles Molloy Westmacott and the Spirit of the Age," *Victorian Periodicals Review*, XL (2007), 44–71. For information about American periodicals of a similar type that circulated at the same time, see Patricia Cline Cohen, Timothy J. Gilfoyle, and Helen Lefkowitz Horowitz, *The Flash Press: Sporting Male Weeklies in 1840s New York* (Chicago: The University of Chicago Press, 2008).

32 The statement by Bennett is in the *New York Herald*, 23 November 1835.

33 On the Regency passion for sports, see John Ford, *Prizefighting: The Age of Regency Boximania* (Newton Abbot: David and Charles, 1971), chapter 10.

34 Charles Knight, *Passages of a Working Life During Half a Century: With a Prelude of Early Reminiscences* (London: Bradbury & Evans, 1864), II, 262. A recent study is Valerie Gray, *Charles Knight: Educator, Publisher, Writer* (Aldershot: Ashgate, 2006).

35 The *Penny Magazine* claimed to have created a genre of illustrated journalism that "had previously been considered to belong only to expensive books." *Penny Magazine*, preface to volume 1 (1832).

36 Schudson characterizes the penny papers as "spokesmen for egalitarian ideals in politics, economic life, and social life." *Discovering the News*, 60. In *The Creation of the Media: Political Origins of Modern Communications* (New York: Basic Books, 2004), Paul Starr expertly sets these events within the framework of a revolution in communications.

37 The books are Wiener, *War of the Unstamped* and Hollis, *The Pauper Press*, both previously cited. I confess that when writing my book I failed to make explicit "popular" connections between the unstamped agitation and general press history.

38 "Extras" were not customarily printed in America where, according to one observer, "an occurrence after the printing of a paper which seemed worthy of especial advice was put in a slip ... and posted on a bulletin." Charles H. Haswell, *Reminiscences of an Octogenarian of the City of New York (1816 to 1860)* (New York: Harper & Brothers, 1897), 108.

39 Edward Dicey, a British correspondent, reported that in 1862 he witnessed boys hawking newspapers everywhere he visited in America. *Six Months in the Federal States* (London: Macmillan, 1863), I, 43.

40 On the difficulties faced by the organized labor movement in producing successful popular newspapers, see Deian Hopkin, "The Left-Wing Press and the

New Journalism," in Joel H. Wiener (ed.), *Papers for the Millions: The New Journalism in Britain, 1850s to 1914* (New York: Greenwood Press, 1988), 225–41.

41 Wiener, *War of the Unstamped*, 189.

42 The phrase "Sunday-paper look" is in Richard Hoggart (ed.), *Your Sunday Paper* (London: University of London Press, 1967), 14. The headings are taken from Brian Lake, *British Newspapers: A History and Guide for Collectors* (London: Sheppard Press, 1984), 127.

43 Virginia Berridge, "Popular Sunday Papers and Mid-Victorian Society," in Boyce, *Newspaper History*, 254.

44 Virginia Berridge, "Popular Journalism and Working Class Attitudes, 1854–1886: A Study of *Reynolds's Newspaper, Lloyd's Weekly Newspaper* and the *Weekly Times*" (University of London Ph.D. thesis, 1976), 39–45.

45 On this point, see Anne Humpherys's fine essay, "G. M. W. Reynolds: Popular Literature and Popular Politics," in Joel H. Wiener (ed.), *Innovators and Preachers: The Role of the Editor in Victorian England* (Westport, Connecticut: Greenwood Press, 1985), 3–21. See also Anne Humpherys and Louis James (eds), *G. W. M. Reynolds: Nineteenth-Century Fiction, Politics and the Press* (Aldershot: Ashgate, 2008).

46 C. N. Williamson, "Illustrated Journalism in England: Its Development–I," *Magazine of Art*, XIII (1890), 297–301; Charles Mackay, *Forty Years' Recollections of Life, Literature, and Public Affairs: From 1830 to 1870* (London: Chapman & Hall, 1877), II, 64–5.

47 *Pictorial Times*, conclusion to volume 2.

48 Ingram made a small fortune by marketing "Parr's Life-Pills" and founded *Old Moore's Almanack* to advertise them. For Vizetelly, see his *Glances Back Through Seventy Years: Autobiographical and Other Reminiscences* (London: Kegan Paul, Trench, Trubner, 1893), 2 volumes; Joel H. Wiener, "Vizetelly and Company," *Dictionary of Literary Biography*, CVI (1991), 314–20.

49 R. Smith Schuneman, "Art or Photography: A Question for Newspaper Editors of the 1890s," *Journalism Quarterly*, XLII (1965), 44. For the early history of the *Illustrated London News*, see Mason Jackson, *The Pictorial Press: Its Origin and Progress* (London: Hurst and Blackett, 1885), chapter 8.

50 The issue of the *Pictorial Times* (22 July 1843), in which this wood engraving appears, includes an accompanying news article describing the damage. On 5 November 1842, the *Illustrated London News* congratulated itself for having "discovered and opened up the world of *Illustration* as connected with *News*."

51 The quotation is from *Gleason's Pictorial Drawing-Room Companion*, 25 October 1851. The paper lasted until 1859. Almost any number of the *Illustrated London News* offers more news and is more impressive. For example, the issue of 19 July 1851 includes excerpts from parliamentary debates, a smattering of foreign and colonial news, obituaries, reports of meetings, court news and a complement of pictures.

52 A fine study of American illustrated weeklies during these decades is Joshua Brown, *Beyond the Lines: Pictorial Reporting, Everyday Life and the Crisis of Gilded Age America* (Berkeley: University of California Press, 2002).

3
The Democratization of News

The middle years of the nineteenth century were a period of expansion in both Britain and the United States. During these decades Britain commenced its unexampled rise to economic power and became the industrial and trading center of the world. Its manufacturing base increased exponentially. Its working classes, partly reconciled to sharing in the material comforts of a rapidly developing economy, ceased to agitate for reform to the extent they had done previously. Most of the political penny papers disappeared in the aftermath of the War of the Unstamped. Other movements for radical reform, including Chartism, had a diminished impact on the public consciousness. By mid-century, political and administrative changes were gradually taking hold in Britain. These included an extension of the parliamentary franchise, an economic system constructed around the principles of free trade and the beginnings of factory and public health legislation.

The United States proceeded along broadly parallel lines. It began to establish an industrial foundation and its population shifted increasingly westward, strengthening a process of territorial expansion that was to culminate in the nation's rise to great power status by the end of the century. Immigrants flocked to America in increasing numbers, primarily from Western Europe and Asia. The literacy level for both sexes increased at a more rapid rate than in Britain and state education took further root in many sections of the nation. The "chants democratic" of the 1830s, the dissonant attempts by urban artisans and workingmen to give effect to aspirations for social and political change, began to be heard less frequently. On the surface, the divisive national issues of slavery and sectionalism marred what otherwise appeared to denote a collective sense of purpose and achievement.

But if developments in the two countries appear to be roughly similar, this was somewhat less true concerning journalism. In the United States, press innovations were bolder and more radical. As the outlines of a democratic society began to take shape, it became ever more clear that a newspaper-oriented culture was integral to it. The statistics of press expansion in America during the middle decades of the century exceed anything comparable in Britain. Between the 1830s and the 1860s, the number of newspaper titles published in the United States tripled, outpacing the growth of population, which increased about 2.6 times.[1] More dramatic was the proportionate increase in the overall number of daily newspapers. It has been estimated that in the 1840s alone the number of daily newspapers published in the United States increased by more than 84 per cent.[2] The statistical indices for individual papers were in many instances even more impressive. The *Herald*, for example, claimed a combined daily/Sunday readership of over 150,000 in 1861. Allowing for a degree of hyperbole (in the absence of independent auditing procedures), the actual figures were probably not significantly below this.[3] Likewise impressive was the growth of advertising, and again the *Herald* offers a useful illustration. It printed an estimated three to six columns of advertising per issue in 1848; within a decade these figures had increased by about four times.

By contrast, the expansion of a daily press in Britain was held in check until after the repeal of the penny stamp duty in 1855. Popular Sunday papers gained large circulations, as did "useful knowledge" miscellanies such as the *Penny Magazine*, serialized popular fiction and pictorial weeklies like the *Illustrated London News*. Many of these periodicals (or segments of them since they were sometimes sold in parts) sold for three pence or less and attracted a large readership. But daily newspapers remained a scarce item in Britain, one that relatively few people could afford. With the exception of the *Times*, whose circulation in 1850 hovered in the range of 50,000, no daily newspaper regularly sold more than a few thousand copies. In fact, less than 20 newspapers were published every weekday morning in Britain in 1850 (compared with 254 in the United States), all of them in London. Provincial newspapers, including several that were subsequently to be among the most illustrious in the history of journalism, such as the *Scotsman* (1817) and the *Manchester Guardian* (1821), appeared only two or three times weekly.

Innovations in technology, especially in America, created a secure foundation for print expansion during these years, without which it would have been impossible to meet increased reader demand. In 1814 steam presses were employed for the first time on the *Times*, and by the 1830s they were in widespread use in both countries. Another critical breakthrough in technology occurred in the mid-1840s, when type-revolving, or rotary presses, which greatly speeded up production, were applied to newspaper production for the first time. As with other technical advances in the nineteenth century, these rotary presses were initially manufactured in quantity in the United States, principally by the Hoe Company in New York, and were then imported into Britain. By mid-century, New York had come to be recognized as the print capital of the United States and the Hoe Company, based on Broadway in lower Manhattan, was key to its reputation.

Rotary presses speeded up production by turning curved plates of type at high speed and holding them in place. These presses, which had the capacity to generate several thousand copies an hour, were first used by the Philadelphia *Public Ledger* in 1846, and then widely adopted by other newspapers. When multiple cylinders were applied to the rotary presses several years later, productivity began to increase at a spectacular rate. One ten-cylinder press, for example, could generate a minimum of 20,000 impressions an hour. Proprietors of American newspapers, stimulated by the prospect of massive increases in circulation, invested heavily (and expensively) in these "lightning presses," which made their way slowly across the Atlantic in the following decade. By 1857, Bennett could boast of his ability to turn out 150,000 copies of the *Herald* within a few hours, representing the entire run of the edition of the paper.[4] Newspaper proprietors in Britain may have lacked a comparable incentive to invest heavily in technology, in part because their readership base was more limited, at least until after 1855. In that year *Lloyd's Weekly Newspaper* imported the first Hoe "lightning press" into Britain. The *Times* followed the next year, and soon these and other advanced presses began to be commonly used in printing London and provincial papers. In 1870 the *Daily Telegraph* boasted that with the aid of its "lightning presses," it was able to distribute and sell thousands of copies of the newspaper every morning.[5]

Facsimile molds mounted on rotary presses were another aspect of mechanization that greatly speeded up newspaper production and its capitalization during these years. This stereotyping process replaced the need to set individual type for each press. The technique was invented by a London printer and first used by publishers of cheap fiction ("dime novels") such as Beadle & Company in America and Tillotson's in Britain. Initially facsimile molds were distributed in the form of "readymades," but publishers soon began to cut and print their own plates. In the early 1860s, the Hoe Company developed a web perfecting press that enabled stereotype plates to be used on both sides of a sheet of newsprint, which could then be folded and trimmed mechanically. This facilitated the inclusion of late-breaking stories, an enormous advantage when rapid news was at a premium, as was, notably, the case during the American Civil War.[6] Stereotyping quickened the distribution of a wide range of standardized printed matter, including fiction serialized in parts, multi-column display advertising and miscellaneous political features such as "Washington Letters," which began to appear in American newspapers for the first time in the late 1860s. By the third quarter of the century, press agencies in both countries as well as individual newspapers were making regular use of stereotyped material and syndicates were being established to distribute and sell it on a commercial basis.[7]

During the mid-century decades, America's experience with local journalism was more striking than that of Britain. The nation's size and diversity was a contributing factor; so, too, was the absence of a single certifiable political and intellectual center such as London. (Washington and New York tended to split these functions, as they still do today.) "National" newspapers could not be distributed rapidly enough throughout the country to satisfy divergent local needs, unlike Britain where "special trains" were employed as early as the 1840s to distribute London papers to provincial cities. Nor was it possible to encompass regional variations of the news within the limits of a "national" paper (as it was with the London press), though weekly "country editions" of newspapers like Greeley's *Tribune* successfully attracted many thousands of distant readers.[8]

As cities and towns sprang up overnight across America a semi-mythical personage emerged: the small town newspaper editor who was prepared to uphold an isolated battle for individual rights against entrenched interests. Regional newspapers flourished to a degree unimaginable in Britain. A few examples should suffice to make this clear. In the middle decades of the century, rapidly growing metropolises such as New Orleans, Chicago, Baltimore and Cincinnati each had six to 12 daily papers, as well as weekly and monthly periodicals, a distant cry from today's rapidly diminishing numbers. San Francisco, founded in the midst of the gold rush of the 1840s, boasted 12 daily newspapers by 1853, a remarkable accomplishment that demonstrates the intricate linkage between press expansion and economic change. The construction of railway and telegraph lines in the 1850s and 1860s coaxed hundreds of additional newspapers into existence, as did a burgeoning appetite for self-promotion and regional influence on the part of diverse local entities.[9]

At times competition was intense because it was possible for an unsubsidized printer/editor of modest means to launch a paper and achieve a successful career in journalism. Likewise, fashions in reading tastes were undergoing rapid change. As with Britain's unstamped press, some penny newspapers in the United States were only as long-lived as the endurance and commitment of the journalists who held them together. Yet other local papers launched during these years were to become ornaments of transatlantic journalism. The *Public Ledger*, commenced in Philadelphia in 1836 by a trio of printers headed by William M. Swain, is a notable example. Like the *Herald* in New York, it trod a path of independence from political parties and provided energetic local news coverage. George W. Childs, Swain's successor as editor, created the paper's motif around two principles that became central to journalism: that he "knew his people ... (and) gave them what they wanted."[10]

Arunah S. Abell, originally a partner with Swain on the *Public Ledger*, carved out an even more impressive career in journalism. In 1837 he founded the penny *Baltimore Sun*, which rapidly became one of the most highly respected newspapers in the country. Initially the *Baltimore Sun* purveyed mostly city news, some of it having to do with crime and written initially in the old "Bow Street" style. Although early issues of the paper were "fabulously bad," according to its own assessment, it satisfied the cravings of its readers for novelty, while making a "vigorous effort to inform Baltimoreans of what was going on in their own town."[11] Abell emulated Bennett, Day and other journalists in launching investigations of corrupt local practices and publishing the results. The *Cincinnati Commercial*, established in 1843, was another local paper that achieved a large circulation based primarily upon its dissemination of municipal news. It secured national recognition and increased its readership base considerably during the 1860s, when Murat Halstead, who acquired a reputation as an outstanding war reporter, became its editor.[12]

Beginning in the 1830s, a "news revolution" took place in America that was not to be emulated in Britain until several decades later. Throughout the century transformations in journalism reflected a tension between two of its central elements: opinion and news. Prior to the 1830s, opinion easily triumphed over news in both countries. Newspapers were conceived primarily as forums for influencing people's minds and dominated by editorials and leading articles, which meant that news was largely relegated to the inside pages. (The British word "leader" is instructive in this context since it evokes the predominant role played by an educated class.) Most newspapers had strong connections to political parties. And in both countries the front pages of newspapers offered little more than a potpourri of classified advertising and "soft news," with only an occasional special dispatch making its way to a prominent position.

Although the placement of news did not begin to undergo a decisive shift in the United States until the 1860s when important news started to gravitate regularly towards the right hand column of the front page (it did not reach the front page of British newspapers until more than 30 years later), the "news revolution" of the 1830s and 1840s generated significant changes in content, which for all practical purposes meant giving ordinary readers a franchise in determining what appeared in the paper. News coverage might one day emphasize a local crime or fire and the next a political upheaval or diplomatic squabble. Readers of the *Herald* and other daily newspapers could still anticipate being able to peruse the traditional nuggets of information that had been the mainstay of journalism for decades. But coverage of everyday (or ordinary) news on a regular basis began to increase at a rapid rate, a process that in the opinion of one historian reflected, "not just commerce or politics but social life."[13] News was being redefined as the nature and size of the readership that consumed it underwent a makeover. And "sensational" news was coming to be featured, as to some extent was its opposite: objective, value-free information. Bennett, Day, Abell, Swain, John Wentworth of the *Chicago Democrat*, Kendall of the *New Orleans Picayune*, even the characteristically fusty Horace Greeley of the *Tribune*, were all pioneers in a wide variety of news. In so doing, they fundamentally reshaped not only the American press but, to an increasing degree, the course of transatlantic journalism.[14]

Greeley is an apposite example of this key development in press history because he is almost invariably perceived as a writing editor. To be sure, he was a stylist of uncommon ability who wrote powerful editorials on subjects personally dear to him, including temperance, antislavery and, in the words of Sean Wilentz, the "search for a democratic solution to exploitation that would preserve the supposed harmony between employer and employee and the benefits of capitalist growth."[15] He has been described as "a publicist, not a newspaper man," an accurate observation in the narrow sense that he was less concerned with the tastes of his readers than the propagation of ideas.[16] Yet such a characterization misses a dimension of Greeley the journalist that is critical to an understanding of the larger changes under way in journalism. For an indelible feature of the *Tribune* was its ability to cement the ties between a teaching press and one that disseminated news. Like Bennett and Day, Greeley began his career as a reporter, and from the outset he venerated solid news coverage even if it was communicated in a partisan guise. During his editorship, the *Tribune* met the needs of its expanding readership, which was increasingly middle class, while claiming (not always persuasively) to eschew sensationalism and give publicity solely to moral causes.[17] It printed city news and accounts of crime, though neither of these were its chief focus. At the same time it imparted a central role to newsgathering by establishing a corps of permanent correspondents in Washington, Albany, Boston and, subsequently, London and other European capitals. Interestingly, in 1851 when Greeley visited London for the first time he criticized that city's newspapers because they did not cover the news in "New York fashion," by which he meant informing it with a more coherent narrative structure.[18]

Henry Raymond, Greeley's assistant during the first two years of the *Tribune*'s existence (1841–3), was committed even more urgently to the importance of news, as was Charles A. Dana, who labored for 15 years as the managing editor of the *Tribune*. Raymond and Dana were newshawks by instinct, though Dana lacked Raymond's background as a reporter. Both men subsequently edited newspapers that sparkled by virtue of their news coverage: the *New York Times*, founded by Raymond in 1851, and the *Sun*, edited by Dana from 1868 to 1897. Raymond's uncompromising commitment to news was evident from his earliest days on the *Tribune*. He believed that the "proper business (of a newspaper) was to publish facts, in such a form and temper as to lead men of all parties to rely upon its statement of facts."[19] And to a greater extent than Greeley, he was responsible for the comprehensive news coverage, local and national, provided by the *Tribune*. From the outset he likewise established a tradition of newsgathering on the *New York Times* that enabled that newspaper to present itself in later years as a paper of record. Raymond's faith in the power of news is evident in an instruction he gave to a reporter shortly after founding the paper: "Get all the news; never indulge in personalities ... and remember that a daily newspaper should be an accurate reflection of the world as it is."[20]

Dana was also persuaded of the central importance of news (though not of accompanying pictures). "Get the news, get all the news, get nothing but the news," was one of one of his mantras. He applied the formulations of Greeley and Raymond to the *Sun*, converting it into a "newspaper man's paper" that, in the words of an observer, "rarely overlooks anything." Dana had a more democratic conception of news than Greeley or Raymond. He believed that every kind of news was intrinsically important, "whether in a prize-fight or in theological controversy, in satire or in serious argument," so long as it was "concise and entertaining" and reflected "what the great mass of the people want." His chief aim was to make the presentation of news vigorous and interesting. He encouraged *Sun* reporters to inject a dollop of sensationalism into their dispatches if that was likely to enhance their news value. As a result, the *Sun* under Dana, like the *Tribune* and the *New York Times*, made an enormous contribution to an evolving news revolution in America.[21]

A crucial feature of this mid-nineteenth century "news revolution," contemned by many of its critics, was its increasingly strong links to commercialism. It made economic sense to diversify and increase news coverage because profits were often dependent upon it. American readers, seemingly, longed for news and the existence of improved technology established the conditions for meeting this demand. Ephemeralness was central to this development since speed-driven news might be discarded within hours if it did not generate a favorable response from its readers. As with other commodities, a fine-tuned ability to anticipate consumer demand was a necessary ingredient for success in the publication of news. Bennett, Greeley, Dana and other American editors, powerfully influenced by a cultural belief in the dissemination and consumption of news as the indispensable nexus of press expansion, cultivated this ability in a way that few of their predecessors had done.[22]

The manufacture of news involves a dual process of collecting and distributing it. Both were critical elements in the transformation of transatlantic journalism during the nineteenth century, though new methods for collecting news possessed, at least initially, the more revolutionary implications. The latter involved a paradigmatic shift in organizational structure, whereas enhanced speed and efficiency in news distribution signified incremental change. Before the 1830s most newspapers on both sides of the Atlantic relied upon a polymorphous presentation of news based primarily on whatever information happened to be available. Reports culled from mail packets and rival papers (including news from abroad) provided the bulk of what they offered, together with random letters from correspondents. Absent from this equation were paid reporters, whose initial appearance in American journalism by mid-century marked the commencement of a new profession as well as a core motif in the history of the press.[23]

The emergence of the reporter in America reflected both an increased enthusiasm for news and the diminishing influence of the editorial page. In Britain, "special correspondents" (those hired on a freelance basis to report on individual events) dominated the coverage of foreign and domestic news reporting until the 1870s. Even when paid reporters began to be hired by newspapers such as the *Daily Telegraph* and the *Daily News* in the second half of the century, the connections of "specials" to customary forms of journalism remained powerful, and they continued to file dispatches on an irregular timetable. The differences in transatlantic terminology are illuminating in this regard. In Britain, "reporters" were regarded as mere summarizers of facts allegedly devoid of imagination and creativity, while "correspondents" and "specials" were given the prestigious tasks of analyzing and interpreting the facts. From the outset of the century the *Times* and other London newspapers hired "reporters" to transcribe verbatim accounts of parliamentary debates, the law courts and public meetings, while "correspondents" shaped these unvarnished reports into "news," and thereby gained a requisite degree of social and journalistic respectability.

More than any other journalist, Bennett helped to create the profession of reporting in America, by eliminating the artificial distinction between these two types of newspapermen and giving pride of place to the collection of news. As his sometime rival, Greeley, noted in an obituary notice written in 1872: "(Bennett) had an unerring judgement of the pecuniary value of the news. He knew how to pick out of the events of the day the subject which engrossed the interest of the greatest number of people, and to give them about the subject all they could read."[24] It should be noted that during the *Herald*'s early years, Bennett did much of his own legwork, including firsthand reporting of the Robinson-Jewett murder case. At the same time, he hired what was generally considered to be the best staff of reporters available and by the standards of the time paid them well. In the 1840s, "Herald men" (as they were commonly referred to) were said to be visible almost everywhere.[25]

Raymond resembled Bennett in many ways. Before founding the *New York Times*, he had gained editorial experience on both the *Morning Courier* and the *Tribune*, and had also worked as a reporter. He covered political and other news for both papers, sometimes in unlikely and difficult situations. On one occasion, in 1843, he reported for the *Tribune* news of an agricultural fair in Rochester, New York, whose featured speakers included Martin Van Buren, the former President, and Daniel Webster. A contemporary account follows: "Low water and fog delayed (Raymond's) steamer to Albany so that he missed his train, and when he finally did set out (for Rochester), it was for thirty hours of railway torture, twelve hours more than the advertised time."[26] The effort more than repaid itself. The *Tribune* beat its rivals to the story handily and devoted nine columns of space to what was regarded as a major political scoop. Raymond also reported on numerous criminal trials and police hearings, and, like Bennett, developed a vivid prose style that incorporated elements of narrative realism. He introduced heightened personal terms into his writing, as in this depiction of a defendant in a criminal trial: "He was without gloves, was dressed in a frock coat of blue beaver cloth with a velvet collar, his hair was well brushed, his whiskers were neatly trimmed."[27] Reporting of this type, with its overlay of human-interest journalism and patina of voyeurism, led to significant increases of circulation for the *Tribune* and the *New York Times*, the newspapers with which he was connected.

By the 1840s, there was an increased interest in publishing news quickly and efficiently in both Britain and the United States. But Americans seemed to develop a particular passion for news. Their absorption in local and national news stories arguably reached the level of a near mania by the latter part of the decade, when it became a common practice for newspapers to publish late-breaking editions on a regular basis. Readers interested in business news yearned for commercial information, while the general public seemed to crave a more robust kind of excitement. Moreover, these years were (or so it seems in retrospect) especially newsworthy. In addition to the predictable surfeit of murders and political crises, the financial panic of the late 1830s and early 1840s generated widespread news interest. And public violence, invariably a predictable stimulus to journalism, provided a fillip to the newspaper industry in the 1840s with the war against Mexico, which effectively introduced the practice of war reporting. The California Gold Rush of the same decade also spawned a crescendo of interest in the news.

An increased enthusiasm for news appeared in Britain as well at about this time, with the *Times*, the *Morning Chronicle* and the *Daily News* (among other newspapers) competing vigorously and in conditions of increasing speed to get news to their readers. Reporters who worked for these papers used horse expresses, "extraordinary" dispatch steamers that intercepted the Indian and Continental mails, and "special trains" to transmit news to their London offices. Carrier pigeons were also extensively employed in these pre-telegraph years, more commonly, it seems, than in the United States. Bennett made use of pigeons to send news in the late 1830s, as did the *Sun* several years later. But by then, the London *Times* had created an effective "Pigeon Express" that transmitted messages regularly (and reliably) from Paris to Boulogne, from where they were taken by boat to Dover and pack-horse to London.[28] Interest in local news seems to have been more circumscribed in Britain than in America, however, and relatively little attention was paid to news from America. The focus remained overwhelmingly on national political and international news with a pronounced emphasis given to the Continent and empire.

In America, the competition among newspapers for speedy news collection and distribution became intense during the 1840s. Bennett was the primary initiator of this situation, though many others joined in the fray. Colonel Webb, who was generally less innovatory, prided himself on his ability to get news to his readers before upstart competitors such as Day and Bennett could do so. As early as 1829, his *Morning Courier* began to hire packet boats to intercept copies of European newspapers and dispatches as these approached American shores. For a time he joined with the owners of a rival newspaper, the *Journal of Commerce*, to establish a pony express service between Washington and New York. One of his objectives was to transmit summaries of congressional debates to New York as quickly as possible. Like other proprietors of New York papers he bypassed the Post Office, which offered cheap rates in exchange for a relatively slow, inefficient service.

In 1835, shortly after founding the *Herald*, Bennett plunged headlong into the competition for news. He wrestled with established broadsheets ("blanket papers") such as the *Morning Courier*, which had more space available for news coverage. Bennett made use of steamboats and railways in the late 1830s and 1840s, and, increasingly, on the electric telegraph. Beginning in 1846, a telegraph wire was constructed linking Boston to Jersey City (directly across the Hudson River from Manhattan); a connection to New York by ferry was then established. At stake in this and other complicated maneuvers, which involved legions of newspapermen and evolved over a period of years, was the perceived advantage of a few hours, or possibly a day. Yet such a seemingly small period of time meant the difference between a news story conceived as a success and one that was regarded as a flop. The pressure to beat one's rivals, to "scoop" them, had become intense in America by mid-century, as it continues to be today on both sides of the Atlantic.

A key development took place in 1838, when for the first time steamboats began to ply regularly across the Atlantic. These reduced the time lag between London and New York from an average of 30–39 days to about half that time. In 1840, the Cunard Line began to make scheduled fortnightly crossings from Liverpool to Boston, with stopovers in Halifax, Nova Scotia. This engendered a bustling rivalry among American newspapers, involving metropolitan stalwarts such as the *Baltimore Sun* and the Philadelphia *Public Ledger*. "Steamer nights" in American newspaper offices became deliriously rowdy occasions, as editors and printers vied ceaselessly to collate European news and print it in fast-breaking editions, often setting it in the right hand column of the front page underneath multiple decks with captions such as "BY EXPRESS, IN ADVANCE OF THE MAILS" or "BY SPECIAL AND EXTRAORDINARY EXPRESS."[29]

Bennett initially hired special express trains to meet these Cunard steamships at Boston. As his rivals (including the recently established New York Associated Press) became increasingly daring in their moves, however, he began to charter "Halifax Expresses," which established contact with the ships as soon as they arrived in Nova Scotia. Pilot boats then transported to New York dispatches written by American reporters while the steamers were docked in Nova Scotia, together with copies of British and Continental newspapers and other materials that were sifted for interesting news. To expedite this arduous process with its overriding emphasis on speed, teams of compositors worked with reporters on the steamers, and trains brought the news from Halifax or Boston to New York as soon as the stories were set into type.[30] During the Mexican War (1846–8) attention shifted southward with newspapers like the *New Orleans Picayune* becoming essential cogs in the supply of news. Bennett, Arunah Abell, Greeley and other northern journalists participated in elaborate schemes for conveying news from Mexican War battle sites to New Orleans, Washington, Baltimore and, above all, New York. They made use of pony expresses, although these were technically illegal at the time because private carriers were not allowed to transport mail in direct competition with the Post Office. Nonetheless, pony expresses usually bested the postal service by several days and for the most part managed to avoid prosecution. A portion of the Mexican War news that reached Washington was sent to New York by telegraph, the first recorded instance anywhere in the transatlantic world of military accounts being transmitted in this way.

The application of the electric telegraph to journalism beginning in the 1840s is one of the supreme milestones in press history. Among other things, it broke down existing temporal barriers to news acquisition and transmission, nurtured wire agencies into existence, and accelerated stylistic and typographical changes in reporting. It also gave a pronounced impetus to uniform, "objective" news reporting since most of the early dispatches sent by wire had necessarily to be shorn of all excess. The effects of these changes were not felt instantly, because this expensive, complex piece of technology was applied only intermittently to journalism in the early decades. In the words of a historian: "Delays, line disruptions, inept transmitting and copying, experimental and inadequate equipment – all remained endemic to early telegraphy."[31] Several decades passed before newspaper proprietors and governments were able (and willing) to sort out competing claims of access to telegraph lines. Likewise, the substantial expense of transmitting copy by wire needed to be balanced against the public interest in rapid news flow. Political, cultural and mechanical obstacles intersected in many ways, making telegraphic journalism problematic for several decades. Yet no other breakthrough in technology has affected the press as profoundly, prior to the Internet revolution of our own age.

The first dispatches to be sent by telegraph appeared in newspapers in the mid-1840s, at roughly the same time in Britain and the United States. By the following decade, though, most leading American cities were linked by wire ("the electric power of journalism"), whereas it took significantly longer for this to be accomplished in Britain. A New York-Washington line, completed in late 1846, was critical to news flow since it ensured the speedy transmission of information from the nation's capital to its foremost urban publishing center. In the same year President James Polk's message to Congress calling for war with Mexico was sent by wire to several American newspapers, making it the "longest document ever so transmitted (by telegraph) up to that time."[32] Even more decisive was the publication in the *Herald* of the full text of Henry Clay's speech on the Mexican crisis in 1846. This oration was delivered in Lexington, Kentucky, forwarded at high speed by pony express to Cincinnati, and then wired to the *Herald* office in New York, which ran it as an "extra." In the following year Bennett virtually reduplicated this feat when he published the text of another speech by Clay announcing his candidacy for president. On this occasion he hired a private train to run from Lexington to the telegraph office in Cincinnati.[33]

During the Mexican War Bennett and Greeley made sporadic use of the telegraph as did other American journalists, and by the early 1850s, railways, pony expresses and, with increasing emphasis, telegraph lines were employed in shifting combinations to convey news as rapidly as possible. Several milestones are worthy of note: the establishment of a New York-Chicago telegraph connection in 1848 and of a series of wires erected between the east and west coasts of North America in 1861. Perhaps most significant was the laying of a permanent under-water cable between Europe and the United States in 1866, an event that forecast resplendent possibilities for the future of transatlantic journalism. By mid-century routine political news was being trans-mitted by wire; then, in the 1860s, the Civil War became the first mil-itary conflict anywhere in the world to be systematically reported on in this way. Although the cost of transmission by telegraph remained relatively high by comparison with other means of communication (in part because a single company, Western Union, controlled most of the privately owned wires), the generic front-page caption, "LATEST BY TELEGRAPH," began to appear with increasing frequency in American newspapers.[34]

The telegraph had considerably less of an immediate impact on journalism in Britain in part because London newspapers such as the *Times* and the *Daily News*, while seeking to disseminate news at speed, were not engaged in as intense a competitive rivalry for control of the print market. For the time being the dominant position of the London press over its provincial competitors remained assured, and it was the latter who stood ultimately to gain most from the telegraph. Furthermore, though readers in London were closely attuned to the politics of Manchester, Leeds, Sheffield and other northern cities an interest in provincial news in Britain was generally less evident than in the United States. A seminal difference between the United States and Britain is that the critical Washington-New York axis (politics and journalism) has no precise equivalent in the latter country. London was (and continues to be) at the convergence of both press and politics. As late as the 1980s most newspaper offices were located in the vicinity of Fleet Street, which is only about a mile from Westminster. Foot messengers were able to carry parliamentary and other reports to newspaper offices for a fraction of the expense of the telegraph. The building of a submarine cable between Dover and Calais in 1851, and of a similar line from Dover to Ostend two years later, were of great significance because they made possible the transmission of speedier news reports from the Continent. But the extension of telegraph wires to other parts of Europe and portions of the empire was a slow, unwieldy process, and not until the Franco-Prussian War of 1870–1 (shortly after the British government nationalized the telegraph system and American journalists began to arrive in London in force) did the British press become effectively wired. Until then railways remained the most effective means for disseminating news from distribution points both to London and provincial newspaper offices.[35]

One of the key events following upon the rise of the telegraph in America and Britain was the commencement of news agencies. The New York Associated Press, begun in 1848, and the Press Association, established in Britain in 1868, became the chief suppliers of domestic news in their respective countries. From the 1840s on, freelance "telegraph reporters" in the United States, working for private companies, supplied news on an *ad hoc* basis, while in Britain telegraph companies similarly organized "Intelligence Departments" to provide parliamentary news, stock exchange prices and other information to newspapers.[36] In both countries proprietors of newspapers regarded this situation as unsatisfactory since it did not enable them to control the flow of news, a process at the very core of journalism.

In 1848 several leading New York papers decided to create a more efficient system of news collection and distribution. They founded the New York Associated Press, the forerunner of the modern Associated Press. From the outset the New York AP employed a combination of horses, railways, steamships and telegraph wires to bring news to New York as speedily as possible. Only newspapers that were members of the organization were entitled to receive its services (which assured a steady outward flow of news from New York), though an exception was made for the *New York Times*. By the 1860s, the New York AP had set in motion franchising arrangements with newspapers in other cities that agreed to receive AP news in exchange for exclusive reciprocal rights to the distribution of their own news. An increasing number of papers became affiliated with the New York AP in this way, although non-New York newspapers began to protest vigorously against the "monopolistic" nature of this arrangement.[37] Repeated challenges to the New York AP took place, with offshoots and rival organizations springing up in different sections of the country. After several decades of uncertainty, the modern Associated Press came into existence in 1900 as a cooperative, non-profit newspaper service.[38]

Attacks upon the New York AP characterized much of its half century of existence because it undoubtedly represented an attempt by a powerfully concentrated group of newspaper owners to command the increasingly profitable market in news. Yet a considered analysis of this organization engenders a more benign interpretation. For it represented the interests of journalists – New York journalists, to be sure – who adhered for the most part to an evolving ideal of news objectivity and neutrality, and rebuffed efforts by non-press interests, whether these be economic, political or cultural, to control it. Among the founders of the New York AP were Bennett, Greeley, Gerard Hallock, who owned the New York *Journal of Commerce*, and Moses Y. Beach, the proprietor of the *Sun*. (Beach was Benjamin Day's son-in-law). All of these men believed that news possessed an intrinsic value that transcended partisan bickering. Melville E. Stone, who edited the *Chicago Daily News* and later became general manager of the Associated Press, commended the New York AP for its zeal in "the business of newsgathering" and its adherence to a doctrine of "strict accuracy, impartiality, and integrity."[39] In forming such a cooperative service, the New York newspapers were making a professional and commercial judgment as to how best to shape and distribute news. They were not willing to permit government to intervene for fear of censorship; nor were they prepared to accept the control of news flow by employees of private companies. The establishment of regional offshoots of the New York AP, six of them by the late 1860s, including a Western AP, was a salutary indicator of the shift towards a more open, flexible system of disseminating information.

In Britain the Press Association began to function effectively in 1870, two years after it was formally established, when the government placed the existing private telegraph companies under the control of the Post Office. The Central Press, a small organization founded in 1863, took the lead in circulating stereotyped parliamentary reports and "London Letters" but had only a limited impact on news distribution. (A third organization, the Central News Agency, was founded in 1870 and remained in existence for more than 80 years.) In a partial reversal of the American situation, provincial newspaper owners established the Press Association in reaction against the dominance of the London press. Among them were the owners of the *Manchester Guardian* and other northern newspapers, who were in the vanguard of a flourishing daily and weekly press that began to take root after the removal of the fiscal imposts on newspapers.[40]

Unlike the New York AP, the Press Association did not operate as a monopoly. It sold news to every prospective purchaser willing to pay the price. But it maintained tight controls on the use of its news services. Newspapers carrying Press Association dispatches were not allowed to buy news from other sources. Furthermore, the Press Association collected and distributed only domestic news, while limiting the sale of overseas news to its non-London subscribers by means of the dispatches of Reuters, a private company that for all intents and purposes performed the functions of a press agency. (London newspapers were permitted to purchase their non-British news directly from Reuters.) National and overseas news services in Britain were therefore linked in a tenuous, evolving relationship. In contrast to the policies of the New York AP, whose presence temporarily accelerated the fragmentation of newspaper services in other parts of the country, the Press Association strengthened the position of Britain's provincial newspapers for a time, though London papers continued to retain their dominance.

The establishment of Reuters in 1851 is of considerable importance in the history of transatlantic journalism.[41] Unlike both the New York AP and the Press Association, Reuters was a private company from the outset, one that sought to make a profit from the sale of news. It was established after two other celebrated European press agencies had already been born: Agence Havas in Paris (1832) and Wolff's Bureau in Berlin (1849). At first Reuters sold financial information to the London Stock Exchange and commercial businesses, and had no independent ties to journalism. Only in 1857–8 did it commence the practice of selling news directly to newspapers and other press agencies. The *Times* began to buy Reuters news in 1858, despite its belief that its own correspondents did the job better. Within a short time Reuters employed stringers in Continental cities and, from the 1870s on, it made effective use of a network of expanding telegraph and cable lines. By the final decades of the century, Reuters boys in gray uniforms (subsequently blue) were to be seen delivering the agency's "flimsies" (thin duplicates of news reports) to press offices in the neighborhood of Fleet Street. These dispatches assumed a prominent place in Britain's morning press and became synonymous with speedy, factual news coverage throughout the transatlantic world.

Reuters adopted the American concept of news objectivity ("speed and accuracy") from the outset, which meant that it rigidly separated news from views. Its reports were devoid of literary excess, as were those of most of the press agencies, primarily because of the heavy expenses incurred in using the telegraph but also because of the need to satisfy diverse consumers of news. Only in the 1890s, with the increase of commercial pressure from American-influenced rivals, such as Dalziel's News Agency, with their reputation for lighter news coverage, did Reuters begin to introduce stylistic brio into its dispatches.[42] Even then, it followed the practice of distributing primarily "hard" news, while the New York AP and the Press Association began to provide specialized news services, including political letters, racing results, wood engravings, serialized fiction and a potpourri of human-interest "fillers." An increasing amount of this material was not time-specific. Like the stereotyped feature articles and serialized fiction sold by Tillotson's Literature Syndicate and other literary agencies it was distributed in advance to newspapers, which could use all or a portion of it depending upon their needs. In effect, the modern practice of news syndication with its tendency towards non-political stylistic grayness and economic concentration was being launched. By the late nineteenth century, additional news agencies had come into existence, including influential ones established in the United States by Edward W. Scripps and Arthur M. Laffan.[43] It was commonly remarked that the newspaper reading public in both countries "lived upon the wires."

During these years speed in the collection and distribution of news was the most striking feature of American journalism, while in Britain both newspapers and magazines demonstrated a greater predilection for experimentation in the area of pictorial journalism. The 1850s represented a watermark of pictorial journalism in Britain. Two outstanding illustrated weekly papers, the *Illustrated London News* and the *Illustrated Times*, won considerable popularity as a result of their intensive coverage of the Crimean War. "Special artists" effectively visualized the war for British readers. They made firsthand sketches of battle scenes, sometimes amidst conditions of enormous personal hardship, and transmitted these to their Fleet Street offices where they were converted into wood engravings as rapidly as possible. These engravings were usually complemented by descriptive accounts of the battles, sometimes transmitted by the artists themselves. The quality of the engravings was steadily improved by means of electrotyping, a costly reproductive process using copper that was first employed on *Gleason's Pictorial Drawing-Room Companion* and other American magazines in the early 1850s before being widely adopted by London publications.[44]

Full-sized, or double-paged, engravings were published in the *Illustrated London News*, the first newspaper to develop a successful technique for dismantling and reassembling engravings by means of bolts, which enabled several artists to work on them simultaneously. Coverage of sporting events, especially boxing matches, attracted numerous readers to the weekly pictorial press and helped to increase its circulation. In 1860, the English-born engraver, Frank Leslie (now settled in the United States), gained renown by printing an illustrated "extra" edition of his American journal, *Frank Leslie's Illustrated Newspaper*, which reported extensively on a boxing match in London. A week later he repeated the feat in reverse by providing an account of a similar pugilistic encounter held in New York. As Thomas Leonard has noted, readers began for the first time during these years to "see" aspects of a world that until then had only been conceived in their imagination, including the facial features of politicians and sports heroes.[45] The wood engravings in these illustrated papers were cobbled together in miscellaneous ways and were not always true to life. Yet they came reasonably close to portraying a kind of objective visual truth. They enabled growing numbers of readers of newspapers and magazines on both sides of the Atlantic to organize their politics (and, to some degree, their lives) pictorially.

Although America witnessed major changes in its illustrated press during these years, it seems to have been a less "visual" country than Britain, one more oriented to the world of print. American popular culture appeared to be less richly impregnated with visual memorabilia, and both political caricatures (dating from the eighteenth century) and illustrated comic periodicals were more abundant in Britain. Likewise pictorial technology was less developed in the United States, where there were many fewer trained artists. In the late 1840s, only about 20 skilled wood engravers were thought to be working professionally there, whereas the number in Britain was considerably higher. By mid-century no successful American illustrated newsweekly had been established, despite the efforts of Frederick Gleason and others. It seemed that even military conflicts were incapable of stimulating a decisive pictorial breakthrough. American reporters entered into elaborate schemes to transmit battle accounts of the war with Mexico to northern cities, but with the exception of a handful of maps of war sites, little effort was made to recreate the conflict pictorially. Not until the Civil War of the 1860s did illustrated journalism begin to take off in a meaningful way in the United States.

On the other hand, from the early 1840s on, artist-reporters ("news illustrators," as they were sometimes called) were hard at work in Britain, composing accounts of notable events and making drawings on boxwood in preparation for their translation into wood engravings. Some of these sketches were drawn in advance and culled from news clippings rather than direct observations. But the special artists who worked in the field during the Crimean War in the 1850s provided a breakthrough for British journalism. They transformed the press into an institution of popular visual communication and created "a new pictorial vocabulary for battle art."[46] Special artists on both sides of the Atlantic covered every subsequent nineteenth-century war down to 1914 – a few were still employed productively in the trenches of France in the early stages of World War One – and some went on to become famous journalists in their own right.

The *Illustrated London News,* in the forefront of many aspects of pictorial journalism, took the initiative in hiring these special artists. It broke new ground in its saturation coverage of the Crimean War by publishing nearly 1,000 wood engravings of the conflict.[47] Yet, in some ways, the *Illustrated Times,* a two-penny weekly paper that appeared initially in June 1855 and has been largely overlooked by historians of the press, was equally important. The first editor of the paper was Henry Vizetelly, a talented newspaperman and publisher who constructed a formula of success out of the twin themes of war and crime. Crimean War battle scenes and violent murders were profusely illustrated in the pages of the *Illustrated Times* and, not surprisingly, several issues of the paper garnered a circulation in the hundreds of thousands of readers.[48]

The newspaper's leading special artist was Julian Portch, whose sketches exceeded in quality those of most of the other artists covering the war. He reported from Crimean battle sites, including Sebastopol in September 1855, which provided the newspaper with its first great foreign scoop. (Portch died in the Crimea in the final stages of the conflict.) Henry Sutherland Edwards, a well-known journalist who was to work on the weekly *London Graphic* from its inception in the early 1870s, was another renowned sketch artist who reported on Crimean battles for the *Illustrated Times*. Other artists and engravers of ability toiled in the paper's London office, making drawings and wood engravings out of sketches sent in from the field and, whenever necessary, "doctoring" these to suit the paper's commercial and political objectives. For example, as the *Illustrated Times* began to veer towards a pro-French position during the Franco-Prussian War, it "borrowed" engravings from journals like *Monde Illustré* in support of its stance.[49]

Several of the draftsmen and engravers employed by the *Illustrated Times* worked from photographs taken at Crimean battle sites, which were among the earliest to be used in journalism.[50] The practice of utilizing single photographs as raw material for engravings was to be expanded during the American Civil War and remained commonplace until the 1890s, when the invention of the half-tone process enabled proprietors to bypass engravings altogether and reproduce the tone and likeness of photographs directly into their newspapers. The *Illustrated London News* maintained at least 20 artists on its staff during the Crimean War, including wood engravers and sketch artists. American illustrated magazines, including *Frank Leslie's Illustrated Newspaper,* also printed Crimean War engravings. But these were copied from London papers such as the *Illustrated London News* and the *Illustrated Times*. American journals did not employ their own artists to cover this conflagration, because it was not considered to be of sufficient interest to their readers to justify the large expenditures involved.

Crime was the other great focus of pictorial news in Britain and, to a lesser extent, in the United States. The spectacular Palmer murder case of 1856, involving the poisoning of several people by a surgeon who intended to collect insurance money, became a cause célèbre among newspaper readers in Britain. It was reported on in voluminous detail by the *Illustrated Times*, which described it, immodestly, as "the crime of the age." The paper published a sensational complementary pamphlet illustrating the murder that, in the coruscating words of Vizetelly, was "hastily hashed together" by "half-a-dozen young literary ghouls."[51] The reporting of this murder case by British journalists (including the well known Henry Mayhew) was a landmark in transatlantic press history, because it successfully merged American-style investigative techniques with an evolving interest in "human interest" narration in Britain. As part of its coverage, the *Illustrated Times* interrogated several of the chief protagonists of the drama, and in imitation of Bennett's methods 20 years earlier in the *Herald*, produced one of the first formal interviews to appear in a British newspaper.

Daily newspapers such as the *Morning Post* also covered the Palmer murder case extensively, converting it into an approximate British equivalent of Robinson-Jewett. It helped to establish a paradigm for illustrated crime coverage in Britain, with intensive print reporting being complemented by pictures. In later years, the balance in the mass circulation press shifted much further from words to pictures, as improved technology was developed. But the Palmer story, the "Northumberland Street Affair" of 1861 and several crime cases that taken together connoted Britain's "sensation mania" of the 1860s (when for a time garroting became the favored method of street assault), dramatized the gradual shift away from traditional forms of pictorial journalism dependent upon conventional narrative technique, to a journalism more robustly American in tone.[52]

Frank Leslie is the central personality in American pictorial journalism during the nineteenth century, though he was born in Ipswich and did not immigrate to the United States until he was in his twenties. For several years, Leslie managed the engravings department of the *Illustrated London News*, and when he came to the United States in 1848, he brought innovative pictorial ideas with him, including knowledge of the divided wood-block technique that had been successfully employed on that newspaper. This enabled illustrated weekly magazines to complete large wood engravings speedily by employing several engravers to work on them simultaneously. An engraving of full-page size could now be completed in less than eight hours. Leslie became a dispenser of popular culture as well as a skilled engraver. He contributed to diverse facets of popular pictorial journalism, including the publication of comic periodicals, potted illustrated biographies, women's and children's magazines, and a journal entitled the *Illustrated News*, in collaboration with the entrepreneur and showman, P. T. Barnum, which appeared briefly in New York in 1853 and was one of America's first pictorial news magazines. The *Illustrated News* amassed an estimated circulation of 50,000 readers before being merged with *Gleason's Pictorial Drawing-Room Companion* at the close of the year. Then, in 1855, Leslie founded *Frank Leslie's Illustrated Newspaper*, America's celebrated complement to the

Illustrated London News and the *Illustrated Times.* This ten-cent paper (subsequently reduced in price to six cents) described itself as "the leading Illustrated Newspaper of America."[53] It featured extensive news reporting and was livelier and more "Americanized" than its British counterparts. It gained an enormous circulation during the Civil War.

Leslie mixed together many of the same ingredients as the British illustrated weeklies. He emphasized crime, paying particular attention to the Burdell murder case in February 1857, which involved the gruesome killing of a prominent dentist. He also initiated a type of journalism best characterized as illustrated news investigation, or to use a more modern phrase, pictorial muckraking. In his best-known investigation, featuring lurid pictures of the alleged malefactors, Leslie denounced the "swill milk" interests of New York for endangering the health of the city's residents by selling adulterated milk.[54] Another notable success for *Frank Leslie's Illustrated Newspaper* was its pictorial coverage of the sanguinary Harper's Ferry incident of 1859, led by John Brown, involving an attempt to initiate a slave insurrection in Virginia. This famous occurrence melded the public's interest in radical politics and cheap sensationalism, a news formula that won favor in the nineteenth century and continues to have powerful journalistic appeal. The circulation of Leslie's newspaper in both Britain and America soon reached a plateau of nearly 150,000 readers weekly. It established a competitive goal for its less flamboyant, literary-oriented competitor, *Harper's Weekly*, founded in 1857, which emerged in the vanguard of pictorial journalism during the Civil War and maintained its position throughout the 1870s. It was then that the United States began to attain a competitive level with Britain in the area of pictorial journalism.

Notes

1 Frank Luther Mott, *American Journalism: A History of Newspapers in the United States Through 250 Years; 1690–1940* (New York: Macmillan, 1947), 303–4. Bernard Weisberger maintains that the total number of newspapers published approximately doubled between 1830 and 1914. *The American Newspaperman* (Chicago: The University of Chicago Press, 1961), 65.

2 Richard A. Schwarzlose, *The Nation's Newsbrokers*, vol. I: *The Formative Years, From Pretelegraph to 1865* (Evanston, Illinois: Northwestern University Press, 1989), 162.

3 Carlson, *Man Who Made News*, 300. A contemporary writer estimates a combined total of more than 170,000 for the daily/Sunday circulation. James D. McCabe, Jr., *Lights and Shadows of New York Life; or the Sights and Sensations of the Great City* (Philadelphia: National Publishing Company, 1872), 250–1.

4   On changes in typography during this period, see Allen Hutt, *The Changing Newspaper: Trends in Britain and America, 1622–1972* (London: Gordon Fraser, 1973), chapter 4. A British journalist described the Hoe rotary press as "the most imposing of all the printing presses which have assisted in the advance of journalism." T. Wemyss Reid, "Some Reminiscences of English Journalism," *Nineteenth Century*, XLII (1897), 57.

5   Henry R. Fox Bourne, *English Newspapers: Chapters in the History of Journalism* (London: Chatto & Windus, 1887), II, 254–5. In 1868 the *Daily News* reduced its price to a penny and purchased two "Eight-Feeder" Hoe presses from New York that could produce 7,500 copies per hour. *The "Daily News" Jubilee: A Political and Social Retrospect of Fifty Years of the Queen's Reign* (London: Sampson Low, Marston and Company, 1896), 139.

6   The *Tribune*, the first American newspaper to make regular use of stereotyping, introduced the process in 1861. During the Civil War it employed five of these duplicate presses. J. Cutler Andrews, *The North Reports the Civil War* (Pittsburgh: University of Pittsburgh Press, 1955), 33.

7   T. Wemyss Reid, "Modern Newspaper Enterprise," *Fraser's Magazine*, XIII (1876), 712–14. The best source for information about early newspaper syndicates is Charles A. Johanningsmeier, *Fiction and the American Literary Marketplace: The Role of Newspaper Syndicates in America, 1860–1900* (Cambridge: Cambridge University Press, 1997), 34–98. See also Graham Law, *Serializing Fiction in the Victorian Press* (Basingstoke: Palgrave, 2000).

8   Richard B. Kielbowicz, *News in the Mail: The Press, Post Office, and Public Information, 1700–1860s* (New York: Greenwood Press, 1989), 62. For information about the "special trains," see Jack Simmons, The *Victorian Railway* (London: Thames and Hudson, 1991), 238–45.

9   Mott, *American Journalism*, chapter 16; Michael and Edwin Emery, *The Press and America: An Interpretive History of the Mass Media* (Englewood Cliffs: Prentice Hall, 1992, 7th edition), 115–17.

10   John Russell Young, *Men and Memories*, ed. May D. Russell (New York: F. Tennyson Neely, 1901), 414.

11   Gerald W. Johnson, Frank R. Kent, H. L. Mencken and Hamilton Owen, *The Sunpapers of Baltimore* (New York: Alfred A. Knopf, 1937), 6, 37.

12   See Donald W. Curl, *Murat Halstead and the "Cincinnati Commercial"* (Boca Raton: University Press of Florida, 1980).

13   Schudson, *Discovering the News*, 22.

14   For an excellent analysis of the redefinition of news in Britain in the 1870s, see Lucy Brown, *Victorian News and Newspapers* (Oxford: Clarendon Press, 1985), chapters 5, 9–11.

15   Wilentz, *Chants Democratic*, 338.

16   Will Irwin, "The American Newspaper: A Study of Journalism in Its Relation to the Public," *Collier's: The National Weekly*, 4 February 1911, 15. A recent biographer describes Greeley as "a kind of international switch-board for a trans-Atlantic conversation about liberty and freedom." Robert C. Williams, *Horace Greeley: Champion of American Freedom* (New York: New York University Press, 2006), vii.

17   One of Greeley's stated aims in starting the *Tribune* was to "embody in a single sheet the information daily required by all those who aim to keep 'posted' on every important occurrence." Greeley, *Recollections of a Busy Life*

(New York: J. B. Ford, 1869), 142. He sought to exclude from the paper "immoral and degrading Police Reports, Advertisements and other matter which have been allowed to disgrace the columns of our leading Penny Papers." Quoted in Henry Luther Stoddard, *Horace Greeley: Printer, Editor, Crusader* (New York: G. P. Putnam's Sons, 1946), 61.

18 Horace Greeley, *Glances at Europe: in a Series of Letters from Great Britain, France, Italy, Switzerland, etc. During the Summer of 1851* (New York: Dewitt & Davenport, 1851), 54.

19 Francis Brown, *Raymond of the Times* (New York: W. W. Norton, 1951), 317.

20 Quoted in Augustus Maverick, *Henry J. Raymond and the New York Press for Thirty Years: Progress of American Journalism from 1840 to 1870* (Hartford: A. S. Hale, 1870), 220. For its early history, see Meyer Berger, *The Story of the New York Times, 1851–1951* (New York: Simon and Schuster, 1951), chapters 1–2.

21 O'Brien, *Story of the "Sun,"* 154. John L. Given, *Making a Newspaper* (London: Williams & Norgate, 1907), 162.

22 Baldasty, *Commercialization of News*, provides a fine analysis of this development.

23 For a key facet of reporting, see Thomas C. Leonard, *The Power of the Press: The Birth of American Political Reporting* (New York: Oxford University Press, 1986).

24 *New York Tribune*, 3 June 1872.

25 Fermer, *Bennett and the New York Herald*, 21–4.

26 Brown, *Raymond*, 39.

27 The description of John C. Colt, a prominent defendant in a murder case, is taken from Brown, *Raymond*, 35.

28 Pigeons were used by the *Times* in the early 1830s. (Sir Joseph Crowe, *Reminiscences of Thirty-Five Years of My Life* (London: John Murray, 1895), 8.)

29 T. H. Giddings, "Rushing the Transatlantic News in the 1830s and 1840s," *New York Historical Society Quarterly*, XLII (1958), 47–59. In the 1840s, British journalists waited at the Mersey River for the arrival of American steamers with news from New York. H. Findlater Bussey, *Sixty Years of Journalism: Anecdotes and Reminiscences* (Bristol: J. W. Arrowsmith, 1906), 30.

30 "Steamer news" from Halifax was transported by sea to Portland, Maine, and then by rail to Boston. Johnson, *Sunpapers*, 66.

31 Schwarzlose, *Nation's Newsbrokers*, I, 67. For the early history of the telegraph, see Robert Luther Thompson, *Wiring a Continent: The History of the Telegraph Industry in the United States 1833–1886* (Princeton: Princeton University Press, 1947). Neil Postman maintains (if with a degree of exaggeration) that the telegraph created "a world of fragments and discontinuities." *Amusing Ourselves to Death: Public Discourse in an Age of Show Business* (London: Heinemann, 1986), 70.

32 Johnson, *Sunpapers*, 71.

33 Carlson, *Man Who Made News*, 219. Howe, *What Hath God Wrought*, 828.

34 On the expense of sending news reports by wire, see George W. Smalley, *Anglo-American Memories* (London: Duckworth, 1911), 145.

35 Michael MacDonagh, "The Wires and the Newspapers," *Sell's* (1906), 30–6; William Hunt, *Then and Now: or, Fifty Years of Newspaper Work* (Hull: Hamilton, Adams, 1887), chapters 5, 10. Two fine books discuss telegraphic links between

the London press and the Empire: Potter, *News and the British World* and Kaul, *Reporting the Raj.*

36   Jeffrey Kieve, *The Electric Telegraph: A Social and Economic History* (Newton Abbot: David and Charles, 1973), 70–2.

37   Schwarzlose, *Nation's Newsbrokers*, I, 233; Melville Stone, "The Associated Press," *Century: Illustrated Monthly Magazine*, XLVIII (1905), 299–310.

38   For a history of the Associated Press, see Oliver Gramling, *AP: The Story of News* (New York: Farrar and Rinehart, 1940) and Alfred McClung Lee, *The Daily Newspaper in America: The Evolution of a Social Instrument* (New York: Macmillan, 1937), 476–575. An organization called the United Press existed from 1882 to 1897, but the modern United Press Association was created in 1907. See Edward Porritt, "The Largest Agency in the World for the Collection and Distribution of News," *Sell's* (1894), 98–103.

39   Gramling, *AP*, 123.

40   For a history of the Press Association, see Chris Moncrieff, *Living on a Deadline: A History of the Press Association* (London: Virgin Books, 2001) and George Scott, *Reporter Anonymous: The Story of the Press Association* (London: Hutchinson, 1968).

41   The best accounts of Reuters are Donald Read, *The Power of News: The History of Reuters, 1849–1989* (Oxford: Oxford University Press, 1992) and Graham Storey, *Reuters' Century, 1851–1951* (London: Max Parrish, 1951).

42   Read, *Power of News*, 44–5. A competitor to Reuters was the Exchange Telegraph Company, chartered in 1872, which specialized in financial and sporting news. See J. M. Scott, *Extel 100: The Centenary History of the Exchange Telegraph Company* (London: Ernest Benn, 1972).

43   An excellent summary of the rise of news agencies is to be found in Robert W. Desmond, *The Information Process: World News Reporting to the Twentieth Century* (Iowa City: University of Iowa Press, 1978).

44   *Gleason's Pictorial Drawing-Room Companion*, 25 October 1851, announced the introduction of electrotyping so as to "render our cuts as fine as copperplate printing." See also Jackson, *Pictorial Press*, chapter 2.

45   Leonard, *Power of the Press*, chapter 2.

46   Matthew Paul Lalumia, *Realism and Politics in Victorian Art of the Crimean War* (Ann Arbor: UMI Research Press, 1984), 57.

47   The best study of the work of special artists is Paul Hogarth, *The Artist and Reporter* (London: Gordon Fraser, 1986). See also Pat Hodgson, *The War Illustrators* (New York: Macmillan, 1977) and Peter Johnson, *Front Line Artists* (London: Cassell, 1978).

48   T. H. S. Escott has described the *Illustrated Times* as follows: "It sowed in the journalistic soil of the middle Victorian Age the seed of ideas that were to become powerful growths a little later and whose fruit is still being gathered in the twentieth century's present years." *Masters of English Journalism*, 225. For the origins of the paper, see George Augustus Sala, *The Life and Adventures of George Augustus Sala Written by Himself* (New York: Charles Scribner's Sons, 1896), I, 269–70.

49   Michele Martin, *Images at War: Illustrated Periodicals and Constructed Nations* (Toronto: University of Toronto Press, 2006), 174.

50   Philip Knightley, *The First Casualty: From the Crimea to Vietnam: The War Correspondent as Hero, Propagandist and Myth Maker* (New York: Harcourt Brace Jovanovich, 1975), 15.

51 *Illustrated Times*, 2 February 1856; Vizetelly, *Glances*, I, 418–19. The coverage of the Palmer murder case has been described as a "representative cause of a new journalism," by Thomas Boyle in *Black Swine in the Sewers of Hampstead: Beneath the Surface of Victorian Sensationalism* (London: Hodder & Stoughton, 1990), 63. See also Dudley Barker, *Palmer: The Rugeley Poisoner* (London: Duckworth, 1935).

52 According to Richard Altick, the press could "speculate, report rumors, assess character, (and) decide guilt untrammeled by law or any canon of journalistic ethics." *Evil Encounters: Two Victorian Sensations* (London: John Murray, 1986), 28. See also Rob Sindal, *Street Violence in the Nineteenth Century: Media Panic or Real Danger?* (Leicester: Leicester University Press, 1990).

53 *Frank Leslie's Illustrated Newspaper*, 21 September 1861.

54 Budd Leslie Gambee, Jr., *Frank Leslie and His Illustrated Newspaper, 1855–1860* (Ann Arbor, Michigan: University of Michigan Department of Library Service, 1964), 69–72.

4
The Stimulus of War

The passion for war news was a leading feature of the 1850s and 1860s, and it further transformed the nature of transatlantic journalism. War correspondents ("specials") dominated these decades, with military news taking precedence over more commonplace kinds of information. In the United States the Civil War marked a decisive turning point in the history of journalism. It propelled the American press into new areas, including the regular use of wired news, the beginnings of the front-page news spread and the introduction of the inverted pyramid. At the same time, war correspondents injected an aura of romance into the "sensational" side of journalism, in a seeming challenge to the increased tendency towards "objective" press writing. These twin poles of diversity and sameness were to become complementary integuments of journalism in both Britain and America during these crucial years of transition.

Most historians of the British press are in agreement that William Howard Russell, the special correspondent who reported on the Crimean War, the Indian Mutiny of 1857–8 and several other international conflagrations in spectacular fashion for the *Times*, was the outstanding war reporter of the nineteenth century. One writer has characterized his dispatches as "unprecedented in the history of (press) enterprise"; another offers the opinion that "few journalists in history can claim to have exerted such a direct influence on great events."[1] Russell has been credited with placing journalism at the fulcrum of public consciousness and subverting the military reputation of Lord Raglan during the Crimean War, and of undermining the government of Lord Aberdeen, which fell from power in 1855 after questions were raised in Parliament about its mismanagement of the war effort. Tennyson's "The Charge of the Light Brigade" could not have been written in the absence of Russell's impassioned account of the ill-fated British cavalry charge at Balaclava in 1854. Nor would the *Times*, a newspaper of enormous influence, have been able to sustain its dominant position as readily without Russell, whose reports from the scenes of battle helped to triple the paper's circulation.

An analysis of transatlantic journalism must therefore pay inordinate attention to Russell. He wrote the first series of consecutive dispatches from any theater of war in the nineteenth century and was the first journalist to whom the epithet "war reporter" can accurately be applied. It was Russell who placed the Crimean War on the daily map of journalism, attracting competitors to the scene from other London and Continental newspapers, though none, it would appear, from the United States.[2] Russell began his press career as a non-military "special" who accepted miscellaneous assignments on a freelance basis.[3] Initially he worked for the *Times* in Ireland and as a parliamentary reporter. At the beginning of 1854, the newspaper's editor, Delane, sent him to the Crimea, and from that point on he began to enjoy a celebrity status vouchsafed to few other journalists during the century.

For 15 months Russell remained in the Crimea, where he came to be known as "Our Special Correspondent" to *Times* readers, who devoured his dispatches with unflagging zest. Previously, many of the paper's reporters and correspondents had transmitted summaries of domestic or foreign news, or verbatim accounts of speeches made in Parliament or at public meetings. Russell, on the other hand, composed lengthy "descriptive letters" of 6,000 words or more, whose frequency depended upon the ebb and flow of military action. Whenever possible, he provided a narrative account of a battle, seated as he was on the sidelines with a table and writing implements nearby, behaving much like a spectator at a football match. In an era when traditional courtesies still prevailed, he was sometimes accompanied in these endeavors by groups of fashionably attired ladies who sat nearby. (The *Times* offered to let his wife and children join him in the Crimea but he declined the offer.) What Russell did not directly observe, he did his best to reconstruct through an elaborate process of taking testimony from people who were present. For the most part he passed along to *Times* readers a powerfully written overview of events, both critical and informed, rather than a "snapshot" of a fixed moment in time.

Much of Russell's writing was suffused with literary drama, as in the opening lines of his famous description of the defeat at Balaclava: "There was a clash of steel and a light play of sword-blades in the air, and then the Greys and the redcoats disappeared in the midst of the shaken and quivering columns."[4] His judgments were often censorious, even when describing a victory. His insightful conclusion regarding the professed "success" of the British army at Inkermann, in November 1854, is suggestive of this: "A heavy responsibility rests on those whose neglect enabled the enemy to attack us where we were least prepared for it."[5] When covering the Crimean War Russell wrote prodigiously, experiencing a significant amount of physical and mental discomfort in the process, including denunciations from persons who felt threatened by his determination to publish the truth as he saw it. In a distinctive methodological way he helped to professionalize journalism and give it a standing – in America as well as Britain – that it previously lacked.

This brief conspectus of Russell's accomplishments, while acknowledging his considerable importance, is intended to suggest that he was a transitional figure in the history of journalism. For his career as a war reporter, which lasted until 1879, reveals as much about the attenuating strengths of traditional journalism as it does about the energizing transformations under way. By the time of the Franco-Prussian War, 15 years after the conflict in the Crimea ended, Russell had become rather old-fashioned in his methods, unable to compete successfully with younger pressmen on both sides of the Atlantic, such as Archibald Forbes and Januarius MacGahan, who were equipped with modern tools of the trade, notably a penchant for speed. Russell's resistance to the increasing Americanization of journalism, faltering and ineffectual as it was, signifies the presence of a fault line in the structure of press history. If this outstanding war correspondent, at the peak of his powers as a journalist in the mid-1850s, could not hold back the transformative power of change, driven primarily by the dual engines of commercialism and speed, it is evident that others of lesser ability would be unable to do so. In a sense, therefore, with the gradual supplanting of Russell as a preeminent war reporter, American journalism began to carve out for itself a more consequential role in transatlantic journalism, or at the least to anticipate a future built around such a role. The weapons with which it accomplished this were principally forged during the Civil War.

Before focusing in detail on this moment of transition in press history, it is helpful to set Russell's achievements as a war reporter in context. The best starting point for this is the Mexican War (1846–8), when American special correspondents prefigured some of his exploits by reporting directly from the battlefields for the first time. In the northern states, there was considerable interest in this war. Nationalistic feeling was aroused, as heroic Texans were perceived to be waging a defensive stand against their barbarous neighbors to the south. Newspapers like the *Herald* and the *Baltimore Sun* aimed to satisfy the clamor of their readers for war news by establishing cooperative distribution networks. New Orleans, the fourth largest city in the United States, became a hub of information, and the first regular war reporters anywhere in the world took residence there, seven years before Russell set out for the Crimea.

Prior to the 1840s, war news in both Britain and the United States was collected haphazardly and informally. War reporters as such did not exist. During a military conflict army officers or private soldiers would sometimes send accounts of battles to newspapers. The acquisition of military news in this fashion was, to say the least, unpredictable. Dispatches of this type might produce news reports of exceptional quality; more often than not, they were less than satisfactory. Furthermore, newspapers lifted from their competitors whatever war news they could acquire without corroboration, as was the customary practice in other areas of reporting.

Press historians who maintain that the reporting of war news was gradually becoming more systematic generally cite two examples before the 1840s: the dispatches of Henry Crabb Robinson, sent from Spain to the *Times* in 1808–9, in the midst of Britain's struggle against the armies of Napoleon, and the work of Charles Lewis Gruneisen, who reported on the Carlist Wars in Spain for the *Morning Post* in 1837–8. Gruneisen, who subsequently achieved fame as a music critic, has a better claim to be considered Russell's forerunner than does Robinson, who did not witness any of the battles he described.[6] Gruneisen's observations were firsthand, though tainted by partisan loyalties. He traveled with the rebel Carlist army (nearly losing his life on one occasion) and was more of an enthusiastic camp follower than an independent professional journalist.[7]

The proper beginnings of a shift in transatlantic war reporting took place therefore during the Mexican War, an event mostly overlooked by British press historians and, to an extent, even by some who have written about American journalism. For in a tentative way at least, it was George W. Kendall, preceding Russell by nearly a decade, who initiated the modern profession of war reporting. Kendall, the editor of the *New Orleans Picayune*, intuited the insatiable interest of the American public in speedy military news, at a time when telegraph wires were beginning to connect American cities, though not as yet much of the South. "Kendall's Expresses," sponsored by the *Picayune*, carried exciting news in record times from the battlefronts to New Orleans, where they were taken by steamer and horseback to northern cities. But it was his own reporting from Mexican locales such as Buena Vista and Monterrey that broke new ground in the history of journalism.

Kendall attached himself to American troops stationed in Mexico and reported directly on what he observed, much as Russell was to do. As with the latter's Crimean accounts, Kendall's lengthy, impassioned summaries of events were clothed in extended prose that occasionally achieved a peak of eloquence. Like Russell, he drew unflinching conclusions about the events he described. After one battle he commented typically that a "bold feint or demonstration sufficient to have held the enemy in this quarter and prevent them from sending reinforcements ... was all that was required."[8] Other Mexican War reporters imitated Kendall's example, including stringers and enterprising freelancers who were attracted to a possible career in journalism. Some of these writers were "embedded" in regiments (to use a modern term), so as to be able to witness the fighting firsthand. They made coverage of the Mexican War, in the words of a historian, "far more copious than that of any previous war in any part of the world."[9] They paved the way for Russell's exploits and those of other Crimean War specials, such as Edwin L. Godkin, a young journalist of Irish background who reported vigorously from the Turkish side of the line for the London *Daily News*.

What Kendall, Russell, Godkin and other war reporters failed to do was to make effective use of the telegraph. Although Kendall grasped the revolutionary potential of this instrument and tried to do his best with it under the circumstances, he was handicapped by the absence of telegraph wires south of Richmond, Virginia. His pony expresses carried news from Mexico to New Orleans, and then to Baltimore or Washington, from where it was transmitted by a combination of telegraph and ferry to New York. Russell and other specials confronted similar handicaps during the Crimean War because telegraph wires had not yet been extended to the area of most of the fighting. At the beginning of the conflict, a commercially run system stretched only as far to the east as Vienna. By 1855, a combination of submarine cables and overhead wires reached Bucharest and Varna, on the Black Sea, which still placed them at a considerable distance from the front lines. Only a single telegraph wire reached as far as Balaclava, the site of one of the key battles of the war. Understandably, British military authorities maintained tight control of this line and did not make it available to journalists.

Of greater relevance is that American journalists like Kendall and Bennett, whose *Herald* cooperated with the *Picayune* in collecting and disseminating news from Mexican war sites, were prepared to sacrifice accuracy for speed in many instances. They welcomed the telegraph and sought to use it whenever and wherever they could. On the other hand, Russell, Godkin, Mowbray Morris, the manager of the *Times* in London, and other newspapermen involved in covering the Crimean War were skeptical of technological innovation of this type, both on grounds of expense and because they were reluctant to become engaged in the frenetic American practice of chasing after "scoops." Godkin, who was to become an outstanding journalist in the United States as editor of the New York *Evening Post* and the weekly *Nation* after he emigrated from Britain in 1856, maintained that the primary obligation of journalists was to write "as good descriptive letters as we knew how, which might cover not only warlike operations, but anything that interested us."[10] Russell wholeheartedly agreed. He observed to one of his editors in London: "I cannot describe to you the paralysing effect of sitting down to write a letter after you have sent off the bones of it by lightning."[11] Russell did send a small number of short dispatches by telegraph from Bucharest and Varna during the war. But Godkin, who adhered to a more traditional conception of journalism, refused to make any use of the telegraph. On average, therefore, the Crimean letters of Russell and Godkin reached London two to three weeks after the events being described took place; to make matters worse, they were often published out of sequence. None of this was regarded as of critical importance to them or their London editors. For their primary objective was to convey information with a measured degree of accuracy as well as a recognized standard of literary competence.

Two spectacular wars in the decade and a half after the Crimean conflict shattered this complacent view of journalism and transformed the Anglo-American press in ways that Russell and others did not foresee. The first was the American Civil War (1861–5), a four-year conflagration between North and South that was primarily fought over the issues of states' rights and slavery. This war created a "wonderful greed for news," in the words of an observer. Among other things, it increased the size and visual appearance of American newspapers; generated significant stylistic changes; and made war reporting an integral facet of modern journalism. Equally important, it secured a permanent niche for speed, particularly in conjunction with the greatly increased use of the telegraph. In journalistic terms the Civil War also linked the Crimean War to the Franco-Prussian War of 1870–1, a conflict that reconfigured the structure of war reporting in Britain. Russell reported on all three wars for the *Times*, a marker that helps to pinpoint his diminishing effectiveness as a journalist, and to make clear the pointed changes in the press unleashed during these years.

Russell's involvement in the Civil War was curtailed shortly after it began. In March 1861, while at the apex of his popularity, he was sent to the United States by the *Times* in the expectation that he would be able to recreate his Crimean escapades, a reminder that the "Great Thunderer" continued to regard itself (and was regarded by many people even in America) as the most important newspaper of the age. Observers looked initially to Russell for a definitive analysis of this conflict. He sought to fulfill public expectations, though absent an underwater cable, his dispatches to the *Times* did not reach Britain until several weeks after they were written. This was the case with his famous account of the first Battle of Bull Run in July 1861, which unpredictably turned into a disorderly rout for the Northern armies in Virginia.

On the day of the battle Russell arrived late and was unable to witness it. He made no pretense that he had. What he saw and wrote about with his usual aplomb in seven columns in the *Times*, were Union soldiers engaged in a "cowardly" retreat. As a result of this news report – slow to be circulated in America, factually unassailable (based as it was on the testimony of firsthand observers) and expressed with stylistic brio – Russell was unfairly pilloried for his alleged pro-Confederate views and, under pressure, compelled to leave the country. "I fear I'm the best abused man in America," he plaintively told his readers in August 1861.[12] He was removed as *Times* correspondent by Mowbray Morris, who believed him to be in physical danger, and replaced by Charles Mackay, a journalist more innovative in his methods as well as more sympathetic to the northern cause. Other British pressmen soon began to dominate coverage of the war, including Godkin, who again represented the *Daily News*; the irrepressible George Augustus Sala ("carefree, reckless, even daring") bearing the standard of the *Daily Telegraph;* and Frank Vizetelly, a celebrated sketch artist for the *Illustrated London News*, who was to endure a violent death in the Sudan in 1883.[13] Reporting circumstances had changed hugely in the five years since the Peace of Paris had ended the Crimean War, and Russell's inglorious departure from the United States signified this, if only problematically. His successors from the London press, even the traditionalist Godkin (who, as it turned out, did not file any dispatches from the field), were younger and better able to adjust to the chief ingredients of American-style journalism: speed, versatility and a stylistic rhythm in tune with an expanding readership.

More than any other single event, the Civil War placed a definitive imprint on transatlantic journalism. For one thing, it was reported on with unexampled thoroughness and intrusiveness.[14] American newspapers assigned between 300 and 400 correspondents to cover the Union armies alone. This does not include representatives of press agencies, who remained mostly based in Washington; reporters covering the war from the vantage point of the South; correspondents from British and Continental newspapers; and, equally important, about 50 special artists. Additional penny-a-liners, stringers, "occasionals" (who worked exclusively on space-rates) and telegraph reporters joined the swelling ranks of pressmen. As the journalist Franc Wilkie cogently observed: "You meet newspaper men at every step ... They are constantly demanding passes, horses, saddles, blankets, news, copies of official papers, a look into private correspondence, and things whose use and extent are only appreciated by conscience."[15] Edmund Stedman, a 27-year-old self-described "green horn," who was a member of this horde, wrote somewhat triumphantly: "We pioneers were creating the profession of the War Correspondent in America, and this, in spite of the sensation which it produced, was prentice work."[16]

Readers, both North and South, could not, it seemed, get enough news during the four years of this fratricidal conflict. In normal times, crime is often the biggest seller of papers, as Bennett had intuited in the 1830s. But at moments of crisis war transcends it, especially when the sectarian passions of a nation are fully aroused. The Civil War was such a moment in the history of the United States, exacerbated by the fact that it was an internal conflict in which friends and families occasionally took sides against each other. Casualty lists were scoured closely by voracious readers, as were detailed accounts of the fighting. Not surprisingly, the assassination of President Lincoln in April 1865 was the most publicized news story of the century up to that time.[17]

The newshounds of the 1860s took full advantage of their opportunities: Bennett of the *Herald*, whose energy remained steadfast after 30 years of press battles and whose newspaper tripled its circulation during the war; Greeley of the *Tribune*, supported by his influential managing editor, John Russell Young; Raymond of the *New York Times*, still in indefatigable pursuit of a good news story; Frank Leslie, whose illustrated newspaper finally gained the laurels it sought so strenuously. Editors of regional newspapers seized the moment as well, notably Wilbur F. Storey of the *Chicago Times* and his chief rival, Joseph Medill, who owned the *Chicago Tribune*.[18] These men and other editors and proprietors sent reporters and artists into the field, and in some instances went themselves to observe and write. Or they shuttled journalists ceaselessly in and out of Washington, where news could be extracted from political and military sources, at least until Lincoln instituted a partial censorship of the press in 1862.

During the war, *Herald* writers were to be espied everywhere, an estimated 63 strong, keeping up with companies of troops and rushing to battle sites in the hope of gaining an edge on their competitors. A confidential memo sent by Bennett to his reporters stated: "In no instance and under no circumstances must you be beaten."[19] His journalists were better paid than others and their compensation was sometimes determined by the speed with which their stories were filed. The competition for scoops was intense, with regional reporters like John Russell Young, who wrote on Bull Run for the *Philadelphia Press*, Whitelaw Reid ("Agate") of the *Cincinnati Gazette* on Shiloh and Carleton Coffin ("Carleton") of the *Boston Journal* on Gettysburg, sometimes outmaneuvering and outperforming correspondents of national reputation. Young and Reid were among a group of exceptionally fine writers who launched brilliant careers in journalism during the Civil War.[20]

Some Civil War reporting was surprisingly good, considering the difficult circumstances in which it was carried out. Reporters observed, wrote and transmitted dispatches in conditions ranging from the mildly uncomfortable to the perilously intolerable. In the absence of a formal system of accreditation journalists were at the mercy of military commanders. When things went well, they fared as decently or better than ordinary soldiers. At other times, they were compelled to endure the discomforts of rancid food, substandard lodging, the risks of incarceration and, less easily delimited, episodes of psychological and physical harassment initiated by the military.[21] Field commanders could be expected to provide comfort and support to reporters who wrote positive assessments of their military deeds. Less compliant journalists tended to fare poorly. Their difficulties were compounded by Lincoln's telegraphic and postal censorship, which varied in its effectiveness, but made it difficult for some journalists to function effectively.

Sketch artists confronted similar obstacles. Many of them worked for the two leading British pictorial weeklies, the *Illustrated London News* and the *Illustrated Times*. But *Frank Leslie's Illustrated Newspaper* and *Harper's Weekly*, the foremost American illustrated periodicals, dispatched the largest number of artists into the field. Leslie's paper built steadily upon the support it had won during the antebellum years and enhanced its reputation by reporting on the war with a degree of objectivity, though its proprietor's sympathies lay with the South. Its dozens of sketchers covered the conflict from both sides of the line and the newspaper acquired additional drawings from soldiers in the field. To his credit, Leslie did his best to authenticate these sketches before converting them into wood engravings, of which he published about 3,000 during the war. *Harper's Weekly* was a formidable competitor because of the better quality of its illustrations, although its reputation for reliability was sometimes called into question. It strongly endorsed the policies of the government in Washington, and several times was accused of "faking" illustrations for political ends. Thomas Nast, its leading staff artist, joined the magazine in 1862 after working for Leslie for several years and helped to enhance its reputation.

This frenzied Civil War reporting is closely linked to a key aspect of Americanization: the increased emphasis on speed. Americans wanted news, and they wanted it as quickly as possible. This sense of urgency was palpable to British journalists covering the war, such as Godkin and Sala, as well as to the noted American war reporter, George Smalley of the *Tribune*, who was to have an enormous influence on the nature of transatlantic journalism. Speed became the overriding goal of American journalists, one result being that dispatches came to be written in a pithier style. As the British journalist, William Beatty-Kingston, noted: reporters were compelled to "bolt (their) information down to a mere skeleton and pack the dry bones into a small parcel." The Washington agent of the New York AP, Lawrence Gobright, complained about this: "My dispatches are merely dry matters of fact and detail. My instructions do not allow me to make any comment upon the facts which I communicate." Given these circumstances, it is not surprising that the inverse pyramid (the "who, what, why, how and when" of modern journalism) came into use for the first time during the Civil War.[22] This stylistic innovation represented a radical departure from the prevailing mode, epitomized so effectively by Russell, of constructing a logical narrative account in measured, cadenced prose. These "summary leads" did not become a regular feature of American journalism until the early 1890s, when Pulitzer began to employ them regularly in the pages of his *World*. But their initial appearance in the 1860s was a significant portent of change in the discourse of journalism.

The most positive feature of the Americanization of transatlantic journalism during these years was its vitality and increased conformance with the likes and dislikes of its readers. The least appealing side of it – singled out for condemnation by its critics – was its unreliability. Russell made it a policy to validate his sources whenever he could and, regardless of the intensity of the competition, to return to the scene of the battle to attempt to get his story right before transmitting it to his office. He had the leisure to do this because speed was not at a premium in the British press during the Crimean War. But the pressures of the Civil War in America were intense and, consequently, some reporters made up stories, rushed ahead with accounts of battles before the outcome could be verified, or indulged in prose so excessive that it was often unreadable. Their aim was to gain a few hours on a rival. Junius Henri Browne of the *Tribune*, a reporter whose reputation withstood the pressures of the time, admitted that he wrote a "firsthand" account of the Battle of Pea Ridge, Arkansas, while in St. Louis, Missouri, many miles from the front. He got away with it by weaving an "authentic" story out of a mélange of rumors and scuttlebutt.[23] Raymond, a brilliant journalist in so many ways, was pushed into errors by the pressure of speed. He significantly misreported the outcome of the second Battle of Bull Run, to the detriment of the *New York Times* and its readers.

At the core of the Americanization of journalism, with its emphasis on speed, was the telegraph. From the beginning of the war, more than 50,000 miles of telegraph wire crisscrossed the United States, a considerable advancement upon the previous decade. But it was not yet the practice for newspapers to use the telegraph routinely. Private companies controlled the bulk of the wires, and costs remained high. Before the 1860s an increasing amount of agency news was transmitted by wire; however, reporters working for individual papers transmitted most of their dispatches by rail or other means of overland communication.

The Civil War fractured this dual system. Whenever reporters had access to wires and support from their editors they began to forward news by telegraph. Competition for proximity to wires became intense, especially among New York reporters. (Headings like "The Latest News Received by Magnetic Telegraph" filled front-page columns of both the *Herald* and the *Tribune*.) Some dispatches were transmitted to New York so rapidly that readers of newspapers in that city knew the outcome of a battle before word of it reached Washington or Richmond, Virginia, the capital of the Confederacy. Telegrams were often followed by detailed narrations forwarded by other means. Frederic Hudson, the managing editor of the *Herald*, instructed his Washington reporters to send every dispatch to New York by telegraph; for reasons of economy he subsequently altered this policy and directed them to transmit only the first 600 words by wire. It has been estimated that during the war Bennett spent the phenomenal sum of 525,000 dollars on the *Herald*'s news coverage, the bulk of it for wire reporting. Regional papers such as the *Chicago Tribune* also expended large sums of money in reporting the war.[24] The farther the distance a newspaper was located from the site of combat, the more likely it was to instruct its representatives to transmit their stories by wire.

Two additional factors helped to increase the use of the telegraph. The first was that some reporters, such as Raymond, were also editors of their newspapers, which meant that they had the power to authorize large expenditures on short notice. A second factor was that the New York AP, the leading news agency, did relatively little independent reporting during the war. The federal government effectively commandeered its facilities and, to a degree, converted them into a conduit for official statements emanating from Washington.[25] This encouraged reporters who worked for independent newspapers to chase after stories aggressively and send them by wire. Ironically, a negative feature of this increased use of unregulated telegraph wires was that it provoked a strong governmental response. From 1862 on, when the partial censorship of the press was imposed, federal rules permitted telegrams to be sent only with the concurrence of local military commanders, which deterred objective reporting. According to Gobright of the New York AP, if the censor "did not like the dispatch, he would assassinate it, or so maim it as to destroy its original features."[26]

Notwithstanding numerous difficulties, thousands of dispatches were sent by wire between 1861 and 1865, making the telegraph an indispensable tool in the hands of journalists. Accounts of military events appeared in newspapers within a day or two of their occurrence. Many of these reports were printed on the front page, so as to command an immediate reaction from readers. The New York *World*, for example, devoted all six columns of its front page to its reporter's account of the Battle of Bull Run. The practice of placing news on the front page had been introduced by a small number of newspapers in the 1850s, including the *Herald*, which had also tried it out for several months in 1836 without any apparent success. But it became a regular feature of journalism during the Civil War. This innovation was not, however, to be adopted in Britain until near the end of the century and, interestingly, after the war the *Herald* returned to its traditional format of placing small ads on its front page and relegating news to the inside pages.

During the war some newspapers abandoned the conventional "blanket" format of four pages and doubled or tripled their size to handle the increased flow of news. Decked headings, used before 1861 though restricted to a single column for technical reasons, became more widespread. The *Herald* and several competitors used headings with as many as ten decks to introduce some military news. This typographical efflorescence was intended to provide a brief narrative of the event for readers, since elaborate multi-decks were in effect little more than inverse pyramids. Sunday editions of newspapers also began to be published with greater frequency, as did "extras," which now appeared on a regular basis. Likewise, the price of newspapers was raised due to the increased cost of paper. Led by the *Herald* and the *Tribune*, the penny press quadrupled its selling price during the war, resulting in one of the few "anti-democratic," if short-term, changes in journalism to be provoked by the conflict.

The effects of the Civil War on American journalism are evident. Yet its consequences for the press in Britain were also significant. Journalists like Sala returned to London during and after the war with enthusiastic accounts of what they had observed. Sala, who helped to shape a New Journalism in Britain during his stint of more than 30 years on the *Daily Telegraph*, was greatly influenced by the Americanizing techniques of the journalists with whom he had worked. His social leaders in the *Daily Telegraph*, characterized by an elaborate personal style of expression, were light and gossipy in tone and, to a degree, bore the imprint of American journalism.

More important in the long term were those American pressmen, invigorated by their Civil War experiences, who conveyed "new style" methods of speed in journalism to Britain in the years after 1865. They included Raymond, who had also reported for the *New York Times* on the Austro-Italian War of 1859, and two correspondents who were to subsequently cover the Franco-Prussian War: Murat Halstead of the *Cincinnati Commercial* and Moncure Conway of the *World* (who also worked for the London *Daily News*). Halstead was at bottom a political writer, while Conway, a rising star in the profession, lived in London for a many years beginning in 1863 and became an influential freethinker. Another key American journalist resident in London after the war was Colonel Finley Anderson of the *Herald*, who made extensive use of the Atlantic cable between 1868 and 1871.[27] An additional cluster of journalists manned the permanent bureaus that were being opened abroad by American newspapers and press agencies. In 1866 the New York AP established a bureau in London and in the following year the *Tribune* became the first newspaper to set up a permanent London office. The journalist who organized and managed this office for almost 30 years was George Smalley, a seminal figure in the history of transatlantic journalism and a close friend of Sala, Edmund Yates and other British writers who were to be integrally linked to the New Journalism.

Smalley played a critical role in bringing American ideas about journalism to Britain, especially between 1867 and 1871. He had been an outstanding war reporter, notably in fashioning an account of the Battle of Antietam for the *Tribune* in September 1862, which has been described by Henry Villard as "the best piece of the work of the kind produced during the Civil War." Smalley was placed in charge of the *Tribune*'s London office and soon became an influential figure in London press circles. As much as any newspaperman of the age, he believed that the future of journalism was integrally linked to speed and, specifically, to the impact of the telegraph. "Whether we like it or not, the telegraph is our master," Smalley pointedly observed. That conviction became a reality for him after the construction of an Atlantic cable in 1866.[28]

During the Franco-Prussian War Smalley and a group of American and British correspondents made ample use of this cable and, in so doing, brought about a revolution in transatlantic journalism. Almost from the time the *Tribune* bureau was established, Smalley used the cable extensively. He transmitted news from London that appeared the next morning in New York, helped along by the favorable time lag. He directed the *Tribune*'s European reporters to send their dispatches to the paper's London office first, an initiative that derogated from the authority of John Russell Young, the manager of the newspaper in New York, and created organizational tensions. But it ensured that the cable became a central factor in strengthening the international reputation of the *Tribune*, since it became the practice for dispatches to be bundled together and sent to New York as a package. When Smalley forwarded these reports to New York he used "cablese," a truncated, linguistically neutral version of the dispatches, which enabled drastic economies to be made in transmission. After the story reached New York it was usually re-expanded to its original size.[29]

The Franco-Prussian War, beginning in July 1870 and ending with the siege of Paris and a brief experiment with a Commune in the spring of 1871, was more thoroughly covered by journalists than any previous European war. And during this conflict American press methods, resisted until then by many British journalists, began to be vigorously used. Russell, now in his 50s, covered the war in conventional fashion for the *Times*. However, he was consistently beaten in the field by a young Scotsman, Archibald Forbes of the *Daily News*, a friend of Smalley, who became the foremost war reporter of the period and one of the most "Americanized" British reporters in the second half of the nineteenth century. The *Daily News* consistently scooped the *Times* because it spent heavy sums of money on wired dispatches. Its circulation tripled during the war and reached a temporary peak of 150,000.[30] Smalley was also a friend of Russell, and he helped to broker a competitive relationship between Forbes and Russell by accelerating the substitution of quicker methods of disseminating news in place of more traditional ones. He inspired Forbes to execute sensational feats of journalism by demonstrating clearly the value of the telegraph.

Smalley and his *Tribune* associates scored notable "beats" during the war, a circumstance magnified in importance when the *Tribune* and the *Daily News*, Forbes's paper, began to collaborate in news sharing. One beat occurred when an American reporter, Joseph Hands, forwarded a concise account of the decisive Battle of Gravelotte (1870) by wire to Smalley in London, who then cabled it to New York. This was the first time a newspaper anywhere in Europe (the *Daily News*) reported firsthand the outcome of a military engagement by telegraph, making it in the words of Forbes, a "cheap pioneer achievement."[31] A second *Tribune/ Daily News* scoop was even more spectacular. An English journalist, Holt White, a "short-lived but brilliant star" who had worked previously for the *Pall Mall Gazette*, sent a full account of the Battle of Spicheren (in place of a summary) to London by telegraph. It was then forwarded by cable to New York at considerable expense. The *Tribune* printed it the following morning, and the morning after that it appeared in London in the *Daily News*, which received a copy of the report under the terms of its news sharing agreement. The incident demonstrated that news could be more quickly cabled back and forth across the Atlantic than transmitted by ordinary post from anywhere on the Continent to London.[32]

Perhaps Russell concluded that his career was effectively nearing its termination when a *Tribune/Pall Mall Gazette* combination (again involving Holt White) beat him by a full day in reporting the outcome of the Battle of Sedan (1870), the climactic encounter of the war. By the time Russell had rechecked his notes, returned to Sedan to verify some critical firsthand information, gone back to his quarters to write a "full and detailed" descriptive narrative account of the battle and then carried it personally to London, newspaper readers almost everywhere were familiar with what had transpired. Sedan, as one of Russell's biographers quaintly expressed it, had become "ancient history."[33] Too late, Mowbray Morris in London begged Russell to make use of the telegraph in future. In what was, inadvertently, a fitting gesture, Russell chose to make this the last European war he covered for the *Times*.

Forbes, Russell's best-known successor among the specials, and Januarius MacGahan, an American reporter who worked for the London *Daily News* and died of typhus fever at the age of 33 after brilliantly documenting

Turkey's "Bulgarian atrocities" in 1876, represented the future. And that future, journalistically speaking, was almost wholly inspired by American methods. The "tall, tough, and ugly" Forbes had a distinguished career in journalism that commenced in the 1860s on Justin McCarthy's *Morning Star*. It culminated in 1879 in his sensational reporting of the Zulu War, when he rode unaccompanied for 14 hours on horseback to the nearest telegraph station to provide an account of the British victory at Ulundi. It has been observed that Forbes composed this and other dispatches, "sitting, standing, or lying down, with a drum-head for a table, or at need the saddle of his horse." According to the sketch artist, Frederic Villiers, a close friend, his overarching aim was "to get off the first and best news of the fighting; and he never spared himself till that was done."[34] MacGahan, who frequently wrote descriptively in the first person, was motivated by a temperamental sympathy for the underdog. He championed the Balkan peoples who, he believed, were the victims of persecution at the hands of the Turks. In an early dispatch from the war zone, he wrote: "I fear I am no longer impartial and I am certainly no longer cool."[35] Both Forbes and MacGahan preferred speed (the "earliest intelligence") to felicity of expression. They wanted to be first with the news and were determined to get their stories to London and New York as quickly as possible, notwithstanding adverse conditions. Customarily this meant riding horseback to the nearest telegraph office, which was often at a considerable distance, and in the case of the Turkish War, being able to surreptitiously bypass the intrusive and sometimes brutal Russian censorship.

Forbes bested Russell during the Franco-Prussian War because he wrote much more rapidly and used the wire to transmit his reports. He defined a successful war reporter not in terms of accuracy or quality of composition, but "who can get his budget of dry, concise, comprehensive facts into print twenty-four hours in advance of the most graphic description that ever stirred the blood."[36] On the other hand, the resourceful MacGahan beat Forbes repeatedly in the Turkish War, which they jointly covered for the *Daily News* and the *Herald*. MacGahan devised clever shortcuts such as hiring "gallopers" to carry segments of a story to the nearest telegraph office every 20 minutes or so, while he was still in the process of composing it. In the opinion of Stephen Bonsal, an outstanding American special, MacGahan had "lightning flashes at his command." Forbes paid him the ultimate tribute when he died, describing him as "the most brilliant correspondent I have ever known."[37] The point of recapitulating these journalistic feats is not to burnish the romantic image of the Victorian war correspondent, which continued to fascinate the public during the imperial wars of the late nineteenth century. Rather it is to emphasize that a new era of journalism was emerging, one that reified speed. "It is an age of hurry," commented Bennett Burleigh, a reporter for the *Daily Telegraph*, "and the war correspondents are in the running."[38] An enormous number of newspaper readers yearned for military news during these decades, and the daily newspapers with their quotient of wired dispatches and agency reports provided it.

The increased use of the telegraph accelerated the trend towards stylistic uniformity and standardization in journalism. To be sure, there was more than enough to read, but much of what there was lacked "color and incident." "Remember that telegrams are for facts," affirmed Moberly Bell, in a memorandum to reporters on the *Times*, "appreciation and political comment can come by post." The need for economy when using the telegraph led to the drastic pruning of words. So too did the elevation of news agencies and the increased practice of sharing news reporting, such as the cooperative agreement between the *Tribune* and the *Daily News*, or the *Herald* and the *Daily News*, or a more formal pact between the New York AP and Reuters. Individuals in different parts of the United States (and at different ends of the Atlantic) began to read the same words, which were often dry and neutral in tone. This brought reporting a step closer to the ideal of professional objectivity that came to be highly praised in the twentieth century. Yet, as critics never ceased to point out, uniformity of style at its worst merely produced a series of uninteresting "news machines." Such a trend was apparent as early as 1863 when the New York AP instructed its agents to use "the fewest words compatible with a clear understanding of the correspondent's meaning."[39]

The pioneering breakthroughs of the 1860s and 1870s affected not only war reporting. Other facets of domestic journalism became permeated by an ethos of speed. The use of the telegraph facilitated the communication of financial and sports news. It also gave a fillip to managerial efficiency by centralizing and bureaucratizing the transmission of information through newspapers. The number of editors and reporters holding full-time jobs increased dramatically on both sides of the Atlantic, in part to cope with the rapid flow of news. Sections of newspaper offices were given over in entirety to the receipt and handling of cables and telegrams. Much like the "steamer nights" of the 1840s, the clicking sounds of the telegraph (and the jarring rings of the telephone several decades later) signified that journalism was being transformed and reshaped, sometimes in profound ways.

Changes ushered in by the telegraph also helped to transform the relationship between metropolitan and regional journalism, though this process sometimes operated in unpredictable ways. For example, notwithstanding the alacrity with which the telegraph was adopted in the United States, domestic news continued to be less commonly transmitted by wire than in Britain. A key factor is that telegraph rates were approximately four times higher in the United States between 1870 and 1900. At the same time, American postal rates were much lower, which facilitated the transmission of news by mail.[40] Furthermore, the nationalization of the telegraph system in Britain in 1868 led to a decrease in the cost of transmitting news, which gave a temporary boost to provincial journalism.

By the late 1860s, several British newspapers outside London had begun to lease "special wires" during the off-peak hours of 6 p.m. to 6 a.m., when rates were lower. The *Scotsman* took the initiative in bringing about this system and other Scottish and English provincial papers followed suit. These special wires connected the reporting staffs and London branches of the newspapers to their home offices. News communication could be instantly established with the regions, bypassing the London press. The cost was high, averaging about 500 pounds per wire annually. (Most provincial newspapers leased two wires.[41]) From the early 1880s, when non-London reporters gained access to the parliamentary gallery for the first time, debates in both Houses of Parliament began to be reported by means of privately rented wires. Sports results and market prices were disseminated, too, as was syndicated literary and political material, including "London Letters" and parliamentary sketches. This expanded overall news coverage but, at the same time, accelerated the trend towards uniformity. It meant, for example, that readers of the Newcastle *Evening Chronicle* and the *Manchester Evening News*, both of which made extensive use of private wires, could now receive as rapid and substantial a flow of news as their London counterparts.[42]

American regional city papers continued to feature a larger quantity of local news, a practice accentuated by their reluctance to employ private wires for the transmission of domestic news. In 1875, the New York AP acquired the first privately leased wire in the United States (New York/Washington) and in the following year the *Tribune* followed suit. By the 1880s more newspapers began to lease wires from the private telegraph companies and to connect these to their newsrooms in New York and Washington. Most regional papers in the United States continued nonetheless to purchase summaries of the news from press agencies or to buy "filler" material (fiction as well as non-fiction) from publishing houses like McClure's Associated Literary Press or Bacheller's Newspaper Syndicate, both of which came into existence during the 1880s. As telegraph rates slowly began to fall in America, newspapers made more use of leased wires, particularly in sending dispatches to their home offices from Washington, where every paper with even the slightest pretension to respectability maintained a permanent reporter. This trend strengthened provincial news reporting in the third quarter of the century and coaxed additional regional newspapers into existence, including the *Atlanta Constitution* (1868), the *Boston Globe* (1872), the *Detroit Evening News* (1873), the *Chicago Daily News* (1876) and the *Washington Post* (1877), all of which were to achieve subsequent renown. To a degree, this development counteracted the influence of the powerful New York dailies, though the latter maintained a position of dominance. In both Britain and the United States, a transatlantic press shaped primarily by speed was gaining momentum, a situation that portended a period of subsequent change.[43]

Notes

1   Alexander Andrews, *The History of British Journalism: From the Foundation of the Newspaper Press in England to the Repeal of the Stamp Act in 1855* (London: Richard Bentley, 1859), II, 329; Ray Boston, *The Essential Fleet Street: Its History and Influence* (London: Blandford, 1990), 84.

2   George Kendall of the *New Orleans Picayune* was *en route* to the Crimea when the war began but decided not to report on it. Fayette Copeland, *Kendall of the Picayune: Being His Adventures in New Orleans, on the Texas Santa Fe Expedition, in the Mexican War, and in the Colonization of the Texas Frontier* (Norman: University of Oklahoma Press, 1943), 271.

3   The term "special correspondent" referred to reporters on special assignment, not necessarily those covering foreign news. But during the Crimean War, it came to be used synonymously with "war reporter."

4   W. H. Russell, *The War: From the Landing at Gallipoli to the Death of Lord Raglan* (London: George Routledge, 1855), 228. Rupert Furneaux, one of Russell's biographers, stated that his readers could "hear the thunder of battle and see the details of every tent and bivouac as they read." *The First War Correspondent: William Howard Russell of "The Times"* (London: Cassell, 1944), 11.

5   Russell, *The War*, 247.

6   *The History of The Times: "The Thunderer" in the Making, 1785–1841* (London: The Times, 1935), 143.

7   Desmond, *Information Process*, cites the description of Gruneisen in the *Morning Post* as "the first regular war correspondent for a daily paper." (p. 98) For further information about Gruneisen, see his *Sketches of Spain and the Spaniards during the Carlist Civil War* (London: Robert Hardwicke, 1874).

8 Quoted in Copeland, *Kendall*, 192.

9 Mott, *American Journalism*, 248–9.

10 Rollo Ogden (ed.), *Life and Letters of Edwin Lawrence Godkin* (New York: Macmillan, 1907), I, 101. For Godkin's Crimean War exploits, see William M. Armstrong, *E.L. Godkin: A Biography* (Albany: State University of New York Press, 1978), chapter 2.

11 Quoted in Furneaux, *First War Correspondent*, 202. Another reporter denounced "that pestilent wire, which is utterly destructive of style and too often lends itself to inaccuracy." John Augustus O'Shea, *Leaves from the Life of a Special Correspondent* (London: Ward and Downey, 1885), I, 120.

12 Quoted in Martin Crawford (ed.), *William Howard Russell's Civil War: Private Diary and Letters, 1861–1862* (Athens: The University of Georgia Press, 1992), xli.

13 Vizetelly had an illustrious career as a sketch artist and print reporter. He covered the Confederacy for the *Illustrated London News* and became its foremost visual interpreter of the war. See the fine study by W. Stanley Hoole, *Vizetelly Covers the Confederacy* (Tuscaloosa: Confederate Publishing Company, 1957).

14 Godkin wrote in 1898: "No war since men began to fight has ever been so fully recorded." Quoted in Ogden, *Godkin*, I, 219.

15 Franc B. Wilkie, *Pen and Powder* (Boston: Ticknor and Company, 1888), 82.

16 Laura Stedman and George M. Gould, *Life and Letters of Edmund Clarence Stedman* (New York: Moffat, Yard and Company, 1910), I, 236.

17 The *New-York Times*, 16 April 1865, devoted its entire front-page to this event. "OUR GREAT LOSS" topped the 11 decks in the left column; "THE NATIONAL CALAMITY" headed the nine decks in the right column.

18 Storey was reputed to have instructed his specials as follows: "Telegraph fully all news you can get and when there is no news send rumours." Quoted in Knightley, *First Casualty*, 23.

19 The figure of 63 is in Oswald Garrison Villard, *Some Newspapers and Newspaper-Men* (New York: Alfred A. Knopf, 1923), 274. The Bennett memo is quoted in Crouthamel, *Bennett's New York Herald*, 120.

20 A discussion of Reid's famous account of the Battle of Shiloh is in Royal Cortissoz, *The Life of Whitelaw Reid* (London: Thornton Butterworth, 1921), I, 84–91.

21 A description of some of these adverse working conditions is to be found in Junius Henri Browne, *Four Years of Secessia: Adventures Within and Beyond the Union Lines* (Hartford: O. D. Case and Company, 1865), 17.

22 The comment by Beatty-Kingston is in his *Journalist's Jottings* (London: Chapman and Hall, 1890), II, 360. Gobright's remark is quoted in Gramling, *AP*, 39. The first use of an inverted pyramid has been attributed to Bradley S. Osbon of the *Herald*, in writing about the fall of Fort Sumter. But a quick perusal of the *Herald* during the first half of 1862 reveals few, if any, examples of the use of the inverted pyramid in its news reporting.

23 See Wilkie, *Pen and Powder*, 125–9. "Cairo war correspondent" was the invidious term used for reporters who faked or exaggerated their stories.

24 Louis M. Starr, *Bohemian Brigade: Civil War Newsmen in Action* (New York: Alfred A. Knopf, 1954), 136. The estimate for Bennett is in Richard Kluger, *The Paper: The Life and Death of the "New York Herald Tribune"* (New York:

Alfred Knopf, 1986), 99. The *Chicago Tribune* made a wise investment. In 1861, its daily circulation was estimated at 18,000; by 1864, it had reached 40,000.

25   Schwarzlose disputes this view. He maintains that the New York AP generated a significant amount of independent news during the Civil War. (*Nation's Newsbrokers*, I, 233.)

26   Gobright's comment is in his *Recollection of Men and Things at Washington during the Third of a Century* (Philadelphia: Claxton, Remsen & Haffelfinger, 1869), 318. Henry Villard of the *Tribune* rode on horseback to Washington with his famous account of the battle of Fredericksburg. Unwilling to send his story by wire because of the censorship, he forwarded it to New York by special messenger on the night train. *Memoirs of Henry Villard, Journalist and Financier* (Westminster: Archibald Constable, 1904), I, 388–9.

27   For an account of Conway's experiences in 1870, see his *Autobiography: Memories and Experiences* (London: Cassell and Company, 1904), II, 198–222. For Halstead's career with the *Cincinnati Commercial*, in which he helped to pioneer new methods of news acquiring news, see Curl, *Murat Halstead*. There is a brief summary of Anderson's contribution to journalism in Mitchel P. Roth, *Historical Dictionary of War Journalism* (Westport: Greenwood Press, 1997), 9. Anderson's obituary is in the *New York Times*, 5 September 1905.

28   Villard's statement is in his *Memoirs*, I, 335. For Smalley's comment on the telegraph see Joseph J. Mathews, *George W. Smalley: Forty Years a Foreign Correspondent* (Chapel Hill: The University of North Carolina Press, 1973), 74.

29   H. Findlater Bussey, a British journalist who worked for the *Herald* in Paris during the Franco-Prussian War, stated that his 300-word cables were inflated to fill two to three columns of type in the newspaper. Bussey, *Sixty Years*, 202–4.

30   Forbes has been described as "the first great war correspondent of the penny press." ("Character Sketch: James Creelman, War Correspondent," *Review of Reviews*, XVIII (1898), 340.)

31   Archibald Forbes, *Memories and Studies of War and Peace* (London: Cassell, 1895), 220.

32   Before 1870, only abbreviated dispatches in Europe were sent by telegraph. Frederick Moy Thomas (ed.), *Fifty Years of Fleet Street: Being the Life and Recollections of Sir John R. Robinson* (London: Macmillan, 1904), 164–5. See also George W. Smalley, *Studies of Men* (New York: Harper & Brothers, 1895), 344–5. Henry M. Stanley, the great *Herald* special, became famous in 1868 when he sent an account of a battle fought in Abyssinia to New York by telegraph and cable from where it was cabled back to London ahead of the competition. Frank Hird, *H. M. Stanley: The Authorized Life* (London: Stanley Paul, 1935), 55–6.

33   The quote is in Furneaux, *First War Correspondent*, 103.

34   Richard Whiteing, *My Harvest* (New York: Dodd, Mead & Company, 1915), 282; Frederic Villiers, *Villiers: His Five Decades of Adventure* (New York: Harper & Brothers, 1920), II, 185. The "tall, tough, and ugly" reference is in R. J. Wilkinson-Latham, *From Our Special Correspondent: Victorian War Correspondents and Their Campaigns* (London: Hodder & Stoughton, 1979), 117. For Forbes's feat at Ulundi, see the *Illustrated London News*, 9 August 1879 (book cover).

35 Dale L. Walker, *Januarius MacGahan: The Life and Campaigns of an American War Correspondent* (Athens: Ohio University Press, 1988), 175. MacGahan's dispatches from the Balkans inflamed public opinion in Britain, as is evident from a reading of R. T. Shannon, *Gladstone and the Bulgarian Agitation 1876* (London: Thomas Nelson and Sons, 1963).

36 Forbes, *Memories*, 225.

37 Stephen Bonsal, *Heyday in a Vanished World* (New York: W. W. Norton and Co., 1937), 413; Forbes, *Memories*, 234. Interestingly, the *Times* turned down a job application from MacGahan because Mowbray Morris, its managing director, feared his "sensational proclivities." *The History of The Times: The Tradition Established, 1841–1884* (London: *The Times*, 1939), 465.

38 Burleigh's quote is in Wilkinson-Latham, *From Our Special Correspondent*, 107.

39 The *Times* memorandum is in E. H. C. Moberly Bell, *The Life & Letters of C. F. Moberly Bell* (London: The Richards Press, 1927), 160. The AP circular is cited in Schwarzlose, *Nation's Newsbrokers*, I, 180.

40 For information on telegraph costs, see Kieve, *Electric Telegraph*, 218, and Schwarzlose, *Nation's Newsbrokers*, II, 112. In an interesting book David M. Henkin maintains that "a new culture of national ... connectedness emerged in the nineteenth century around a cheap and comprehensive postal system." *The Postal Age: The Emergence of Modern Communications in Nineteenth-Century America* (Chicago, Illinois: The University of Chicago Press, 2006).

41 For a detailed account of this system, see Charles A. Cooper, *An Editor's Retrospect: Fifty Years of Newspaper Work* (London: Macmillan, 1896), chapter 16; "Private Wires," *Sell's* (1903), 153–4.

42 T. Wemyss Reid, who worked on the *Northern Daily Express* in Manchester, estimated that in 1870 a provincial daily newspaper included about half a column of telegraphed news on average, and that by 1877 the amount had increased by approximately 24 times. (Reid, "Some Reminiscences," 59.)

43 Private wires continued to be used infrequently in the United States up to the first decade of the twentieth century. (Given, *Making*, 227.)

5
Expansion of the Press

The third quarter of the nineteenth century witnessed an unparalleled expansion of the press. In Britain, the increase in the number of daily newspapers considerably outstripped per capita growth in population. The repeal of the remaining penny duty on newspapers in 1855 (coinciding with the end of the Crimean War) brought scores of new papers into existence. Only 14 daily papers existed in 1846, all of them in London; by 1890, the number had jumped to nearly 200, with well over half published in provincial cities and Scotland. It has been estimated that 50,000 copies of newspapers were printed daily in Britain in 1854 and about one million 15 years later.[1] The expansion of the press was even more notable in the United States. Reliable statistics are harder to come by because of significant regional variations. But the figures for daily newspaper consumption per capita continued to be much higher than in Britain. The overall growth in circulation exceeded 250 per cent between 1850 and 1870, while the number of daily newspapers published soared from 387 in 1860 to 1,731 in 1890.[2]

To some degree the continuing gap in newspaper circulation between the two countries reflected differing levels of literacy. If for purposes of statistical comparison the large African-American population is excluded from consideration, the United States had achieved nearly total adult literacy by 1870, for women as well as men, a considerable feat when compared to Britain, where the percentage of literate women in the population was much lower. Literacy levels in Britain are a source of continuing disagreement among historians (as is the precise definition of literacy). The Education Act of 1870, which created the first formal system of state primary education, undoubtedly provided an impetus to literacy. At best, though, estimates for adult literacy in the late nineteenth century rarely exceed 75 per cent of the population, with somewhat better figures generally accepted for Scotland. According to John Vincent, as late as 1914 a noticeable intergenerational gap existed in Britain, where residual illiteracy remained a persistent problem among adults.[3] Nonetheless, in both Britain and the United States literacy claims are subject to misuse, misinterpretation and, above all, exaggeration, as is evident from the acrid comment of a journalist who heaped praise on Americans for being "the best half-educated lot in the world."[4]

As indicated, the increase in British daily newspaper production and circulation was disproportionately greater in provincial and Scottish cities than in London. Between 1855 and 1870, 78 dailies (including 17 evening papers) were founded in English provincial cities, predominantly in Lancashire and Yorkshire. During these years, newspapers such as the *Birmingham Daily Post*, the *Sheffield Daily Telegraph*, the *Liverpool Daily Post* and the *Leeds Mercury* commenced publication, while journals established earlier in the century, including the *Manchester Guardian*, the *Glasgow Herald* and the *Scotsman*, began to appear on a daily basis. A telegraph system that provided access to agency news and placed these newspapers on an even keel with their London competitors, acted as a spur to expansion. According to an observer in Scotland, a "very marked ... stir" was in the air, which seemed for a time likely to shift the balance away from the London press.[5] The restless energy of a newspaper such as the *Newcastle Daily Chronicle*, founded in 1858 and edited for several decades by the radical M.P., Joseph Cowen, exemplifies this trend. By 1870 the *Newcastle Daily Chronicle* had amassed a circulation of 35,000, the largest of any provincial newspaper up to then. This resulted primarily from its extensive news coverage, including a focus on sports reporting. At the outset, Cowen's newspaper had only two journalists on its staff, both of them untrained; by 1871, it was able to gain credit for a minor press sensation when it scooped other newspapers by publishing a lengthy cabled dispatch from Canada describing the result of an Anglo-Canadian boat race.[6]

Even in the "Golden Age" of the 1860s and 1870s, however, when prospects for the future of the provincial press in Britain seemed brighter than ever, these newspapers came up short when compared with the strength of regional newspapers in the United States. From the 1830s on, American local journalism displayed a considerable vitality, which was accentuated by the outstanding contributions many papers made to coverage of the Civil War. Due to the enormous distances involved, regional newspapers in the United States had a powerful advantage over their New York competitors, much greater than that enjoyed in Britain, where provincial cities were never more than hours away from London by rail. In the United States this was true only of a cluster of metropolises along the eastern seaboard, such as Baltimore, Philadelphia and Boston. The *Manchester Guardian,* for example, had at best a four to five hour edge over the *Times* in disseminating local news by rail, while a comparable gap between readers of the *Chicago Tribune* and the *New York Times* was nearer to 25 hours. In such circumstances, regional press strengths inevitably came to the fore in many sections of the United States.

The dissemination of news was a critical factor in the success of American regional journalism, even on newspapers owned and edited by influential pedagogical voices such as Murat Halstead of the *Cincinnati Commercial* and Henry Watterson of the *Louisville Courier-Journal.* Halstead became a champion of the Republican Party nationally after 1865 and transformed his Cincinnati paper into a powerful organ at a key economic junction of the nation. He was the equivalent of a formidable British writing editor like Alexander Russel of the *Scotsman* or, at a later date, C. P. Scott of the *Manchester Guardian.* Yet Halstead's news instincts were more finely honed than those of many British editors. By experience and instinct he was a reporter, who personally covered national political conventions and other major events for his newspaper while serving as editor. However, he kept news and views rigorously apart in the pages of the *Cincinnati Commercial* because he believed that it was essential to examine news in an unblemished form. "Our citizens have no guardians," Halstead stated. "They are responsible for themselves to themselves ... It is information, rather than instruction, that they demand."[7] To this end, he made frequent use of the telegraph, and has been described as a journalist who led the way in objective news reporting and "the creation of the modern newspaper we know today."[8]

Watterson was another influential regional editor who nurtured his career as a reporter by working in the press gallery of the House of Representatives in Washington. A gifted writer, he supported the Democratic Party, though from the perspective of a liberal Southerner. Yet, "Marse Henry," to employ his affectionate nickname, kept the *Louisville Courier-Journal* in the forefront of journalism for half a century through a judicious blend of solid news coverage and impassioned editorializing. As with Halstead, the reputation of the paper derived from the persuasiveness of its leaders, which were quoted and paraphrased in newspapers throughout the country. At the same time, Watterson emphasized the importance of reporting news accurately and possessed the ability to intuit precisely where the interests of his readers lay. His commonsensical definition of a successful editor has been much quoted: somebody who knows "where all hell is going to break loose next and (has) a man there to report it."[9]

During these important decades of press expansion Chicago emerged to play a seminal role in the transformation of journalism. Its newspapers mirrored the bustling pace of economic change in the Midwest, which was becoming a transportation hub as well as a magnet for immigrants from Eastern and Central Europe. By the 1870s, several of Chicago's newspapers had become well known nationally, including the *Chicago Tribune* and the *Chicago Herald*, which had the largest circulation of any morning newspaper in the city. Both papers combined extensive local and national news reporting with a popular editorial page. However, two other newspapers, the *Chicago Daily News* and the *Chicago Times*, which led the way in press innovation, soon surpassed them.[10]

The *Daily News*, an evening penny paper founded in 1876, promoted "sensational and intensely personal reporting," a phenomenon to which Melville Stone, its part proprietor and editor, who subsequently became general manager of the Associated Press, attached the label "detective journalism." (In 1893, the *Daily News* merged with the *Chicago Morning News* to form the *Chicago Record,* a widely respected morning paper.) Not only did the *Daily News* energetically attack "public plunderers," it literally hunted them down. On one occasion, Stone's reporters located a fugitive bank president who had decamped to Germany and extracted a confession of embezzlement from him. Published accounts of this escapade had a sensational impact in Chicago's press wars. Another time, Stone pursued a Chicago official who had absconded to Canada with thousands of dollars of public money. He gave this case a huge amount of publicity; then, in a turnabout that befuddled his readers, helped the man to repay the money and get the original indictment dismissed.[11] Less creditably, Stone was an arch-conservative who instructed his reporters to infiltrate labor unions in order to uncover information damaging to them. He defended this public exposure of "corruptionists and revolutionists" by stating: "We must with single-mindedness accept as our only masters our readers."[12] Whatever his motives, there is little doubt that the publicity value of Stone's exploits, amounting in effect to the creation of news by journalists, considerably boosted the circulation of his newspaper.

Wilbur F. Storey of the *Chicago Times*, Stone's chief rival, had fewer inhibitions. He specialized in gossip, while espousing a press philosophy of reporting every scrap of news, irrespective of its reliability or importance. Much of the news that the *Chicago Times* printed consisted of reports of crimes and sex-related incidents, "the juiciest and spiciest accounts of mayhem and scandal." Storey gained an unsavory footnote in press history when he instructed one of his reporters to "telegraph fully all news, and when there is no news, send rumours."[13] The extravagant headlines appearing in the *Chicago Times*, succeeded by multiple decks, were unusually daring for the time. "RAMPANT RAPE" and "THE ARSENIC FIEND" are two examples; another is "JERKED TO JESUS," the caption for a story about the execution of a murderer. These decks (and many other instances of sensationalism) prefigured some of the insalubrious features of American yellow journalism that were to emerge in future decades. There was nonetheless a constructive side to Storey because, as with Bennett, he helped to bring about an expansion and redefinition of news. During his 23 years with the *Chicago Times*, he was the first Midwestern editor to hire a permanent reporter based in Washington, open a London bureau (staffed by London journalists) and publish detailed accounts of such news events as the sanguinary Plains War of the 1870s. In short, despite his irresponsible ethical sense and ultra-conservative political views, which were similar to those of Stone, his paper offered some of the broadest and best news coverage in America.

Joseph B. McCullagh ("Little Mack") of the St. Louis *Globe-Democrat* was another regional pressman who accelerated the shift towards mass circulation journalism in America. McCullagh, who was born in Ireland, gained a reputation as an intrepid reporter during the Civil War while working for two Cincinnati newspapers. He carried that reputation with him to St. Louis, a city larger than Chicago in the 1870s and home to numerous German immigrants. During his 21 years as editor of the *Globe-Democrat*, he converted that newspaper into one of the foremost products of journalism in the Anglo-American world. A "chill and distant figure," according to Theodore Dreiser, who worked for him as a novice reporter, McCullagh emphasized the overriding importance of news.[14] He established a Washington bureau and hired reporters in European and American cities to collect news for him. By the early 1880s the front page of the *Globe-Democrat* consisted for the most part of wired news stories engendered by the paper's own staff, a comparative rarity in the press.

Unlike Stone and Storey, however, McCullagh had a commitment to accuracy, for which reason he is often cited as an exemplar of a newly developing professional attitude towards journalism. Among the rules he enforced on his staff was this one: "Good news is often scarce. This journal desires no other kind. When there is nothing to send, send nothing." (It should be noted that in a less heartwarming directive to his staff he told them that the "communistic utterances of labor agitators are not wanted.")[15] But while McCullagh cherished "good news," he was not averse to bringing crime and sex stories within that definition, or occasionally "creating" news when a period of undue placidity seemed to require it. He also pioneered the American practice of interviewing, which represented a decisive advance in popular journalism and, at the time, conveyed with it a patina of sensationalism. As part of an evolving conception of the democratization of news, McCullagh asserted: "A good newspaper, like a great hotel, must be conducted on the theory that tastes differ – and the best newspaper, like the best hotel, is that which prepares the largest variety of entertainment for the largest number of guests."[16]

In Britain, popularization to this degree was rarely to be found in the provincial daily press (or for that matter, the London press) until nearer to the end of the century, when halfpenny and penny evening newspapers began to be published in increasing numbers, and typographical and other innovations were adopted. Up to then, even local news was not as extensively covered as in the American press. Residents of Glasgow and Manchester, for example, read the *Glasgow Herald* and the *Manchester Guardian* primarily for their national and international news, and the well-written leading articles accompanying them, which generally supported local interests.[17] As a journalist on the *Guardian* commented: "(The paper was) local only in its place of origin, metropolitan and more in its vision."[18] At the same time, London newspapers maintained a large circulation lead among provincial readers. For the most part they reflected a suitably national perspective in both their news and editorial columns, a situation that strengthened uniformity and most likely hampered the emergence of press innovation.

The development of advertising took on added significance during these decades of transition in journalism. As an improvement in the standard of living occurred on both sides of the Atlantic, the buying power of readers rose proportionately. Furthermore, the excise duty on advertisements, one of the surviving taxes on knowledge, was repealed in Britain in 1853. Subsequently newspaper advertisements "took off," though for the time being they continued to be less of a fixture of journalism than in the United States. By the 1870s American "want ads" were coming to occupy prime space in that nation's daily press, as is evident from a perusal of Bennett's *Herald* or Greeley's *Tribune*, and the overall percentage of column space taken up by advertisements in American daily newspapers (increasingly negotiated by outside agencies) expanded from about 25 per cent in the 1870s to almost 50 per cent by 1914.[19] To accommodate this expansion a doubling or tripling in the size of papers occurred, from four to 12 pages, a practice that gained momentum after 1865. In turn, increased size pushed up the costs of publication as well as the retail price. Profits from advertising in America rose from an estimated 44 per cent of total revenue in 1879 to about 60 per cent in 1909, a predictable development since as early as mid-century there was scarcely a newspaper that was able to support itself solely from the income of its sales.[20]

British newspaper advertising appears to have lagged somewhat behind, though the evidence for this is sketchy and impressionistic. In both countries the rates charged for advertising fell during these decades, and as volume increased, newspapers hired business managers to handle it. The front pages of newspapers were still dominated by advertisements, especially in Britain, where changes in this area are much less visually evident than in America. It is difficult to compare the revenue intakes of individual newspapers, but it is safe to say that the overall margins of profit from advertising were critical to the financial health of the press on both sides of the Atlantic. It has been estimated that by the early 1880s the percentage of revenue derived from advertisements in Britain's Sunday papers (if not in its daily papers) approached 30 to 40 per cent, which may have set the two countries on an approximately even keel.[21]

There are several interesting points of comparison in regard to advertising. In both countries proprietors of newspapers were becoming aware of the financial possibilities inherent in advertising and of the ways in which it could be employed to expand and diversify readership. During the 1860s and 1870s, advertisements began for the first time to be systematically targeted at defined groups of consumers ("consumption communities"), notably women, and increasingly at the middle and lower middle classes, a fluid social grouping later referred to generically by Harmsworth as the "man on the knifeboard of the omnibus." Before the 1890s classified ads, or "smalls" (also known as "want ads"), predominated, as they had done throughout most of the century. This was especially true in Britain, where "agony columns" were regular features of the press. (The phrase "agony column" was first used in reference to the large number of personal advertisements that appeared in the second column of the front page of the *Times*.) In the United States, a stimulus to advertising occurred in the 1870s when the *Herald* and other newspapers began to adopt a single insertion policy, that is, to accept want ads on a daily basis rather than in bulk and for an extended period of time, as had been the practice previously.[22]

In a further break with tradition, American "smalls" began to reflect a shift away from the listing of impersonal items such as publishers' stocks and herbal remedies, and towards the retailing of personal messages. Readers were encouraged to burrow through columns of ads in search of jobs or, reciprocally, to make clear their qualifications for employment by posting such ads. They were enticed into searches for house rentals and, more questionably, into a titillating hunt for abortionists or partners for furtive sexual assignations. Bennett's *Herald*, which rebuffed efforts by churchmen and press rivals to vet its copy for "improper notices," began to solicit advertising of this type in the early 1840s, a policy expressed by the proprietor in a familiar commercial aphorism: "Business is business – money is money."[23]

Until the closing decades of the century, the British press was fettered to some extent in the content of its advertisements. Newspapers hewed to traditional norms of decorum, and with the notable exception of "non-respectable" Sunday papers and a few of the popular weeklies, refused to publish salacious "smalls," of the type routinely accepted by the *Herald*. Newspapermen in Britain tended more readily to look askance at intimations of personal intrusiveness, initially shunning even the practice of assigning anonymous box numbers that was employed in American classified ads. It was generally accepted that the encouragement of dubious advertising would have a deleterious effect on profits by diminishing the "respectability" of the newspaper. The manager of the *Times* expressed this policy as follows: "If the advertiser is unknown by his reputation, the nature of his business can, as a rule, be gauged from the character of his copy and should there be any doubts as to its <u>bona fides</u>, a reputable newspaper ought to refuse it, not only in the interests of its readers, but in those of its other advertisers."[24]

British newspapers also rejected display, or star advertising, a pictorial device that was becoming popular in America by the late 1860s. The use of stereotyping and of folding machines made it easier to break the constrictive single column rule in preparing layout and design. It opened up untested visual frontiers for advertisers. Yet Harmsworth for one refused to sanction such "American abuses," what a British observer described as "sensation typography."[25] He maintained that readers purchased newspapers primarily for their news content, and that "advertisements should not swamp the news, either actually or apparently." Shortly after the first number of his *Daily Mail* appeared in 1896, the paper boasted to its readers that it gave "exactly the same news (as other newspapers), but fewer advertisements." The fact is that it, too, relied heavily on advertising as a source of income and continued to run small ads on its front page until 1939.[26] When the *Times* (which Harmsworth purchased in 1908) began to introduce multicolumn "picture blocks" into its columns in the 1890s, it did so with considerable reluctance, and some of the newspaper's more conservative readers promptly attacked the experiment as misplaced and vulgar.

Notwithstanding resistance to innovation in advertising methods, "Americanization" proceeded apace in Britain in this area. Beginning in the 1870s, the penny *Daily Telegraph* aped the *Herald* by introducing increasing numbers of "personals" into its pages (referred to by critics as "the cries of the lovelorn"). Many were highly suggestive, though their language was attenuated to fit the expectations of discreet British readers. In effect, the *Daily Telegraph* served up an American formula of commercialism and semi-titillation in its columns, while publicly airing homespun tales of personal longings and rejection. It gained a reputation as a kind of vicarious narrator of ordinary events and, by 1880, claimed to have a daily circulation of 200,000. Critics generally agreed that a considerable measure of its popularity derived from the prevalence of these cheap "personals."

The *Daily News*, founded in 1846 as a literary outlet for Charles Dickens and reduced in price to a penny in 1868, was more closely wedded to the formulas of the older journalism. But it also took advantage of the visual incarnation of American-style journalism, when it began to adopt display advertising in the 1870s, emulating the kind of commercialism that was appearing with increasingly regularity in Greeley's *Tribune*. (Interestingly, Bennett's *Herald,* while aggressive in its pursuance of "smalls," continued to follow the more conventional transatlantic practice of single-column advertising in small agate type until the 1880s.) Businesses such as the Singer Manufacturing Company regularly inserted multicolumn advertisements in the *Tribune* to publicize their wares, and in subsequent decades department stores like Marshall Field in Chicago and Wanamaker in Philadelphia did the same on an ostentatious scale. Most display advertisements, including those appearing in the *Daily News*, featured woodcuts and many appeared on the front page. They enhanced the pictorial "look" of newspapers, and in the words of a chronicler of the late nineteenth-century press, represented a decisive break with "the old canons of typographical neatness and artistic effect."[27]

The increased street sale of newspapers was a further indicator of the advancing democratization of the press. By the 1850s, the distribution of newspapers by means of subscription lists had begun to diminish significantly. Improved techniques for distributing papers were now in use on both sides of the Atlantic, and in some instances middlemen began to be bypassed altogether. Speed in delivery was emphasized, and wholesale agencies, special depots, "runners" who carried papers from one newsagent to another and chartered newspaper trains were employed with varying measures of success.[28] Publishers in both countries attempted to build on an increase of circulation. The beginnings of suburbanization gave an impetus to their efforts. By the 1870s, hundreds of thousands of urban residents in Britain and America were commuting to work daily by public transportation and had become potential consumers of newspapers, especially those printed in the late afternoon or early evening. As a journalist noted caustically: "Nothing must seek to hold (these readers') interest for long: it is hard to concentrate attention with passengers getting in and out (of trains and trams), with noise and rattle around one."[29]

Although the "London System" of street sales of newspapers originated in Britain in the 1830s, proprietors in America were quicker to grasp its potential. They continued to make use of a base of subscription readers but encouraged street sales. By mid-century, it was a common practice for newsboys in New York and other cities to be posted near the entrance to train and ferry stations with the objective of selling newspapers to passing commuters. (In London some of these boys were referred to as "Battered Breeches.")[30] Newsstands became an element of the frenetic street life of metropolises like Chicago and New York. Public kiosks lured customers by means of boldly printed signs, while hawkers repeatedly shouted out enticing slogans such as "Shocking Murder" or (in April 1861) "Fort Sumter Bombed." Occasionally these hawkers rang bells or clanged mechanical devices to attract the attention of passersby. One of the classic newsboy shouts of the century, used by sellers working for the halfpenny London *Star* in 1888, was: "The Pope: No News." This stratagem reportedly increased sales.[31]

It became the practice for newspapers to be folded above the crease so as to make their boldly decked headlines visible and for pictorial journals like *Frank Leslie's Illustrated Newspaper* to feature wood engravings on the top half of the front page. When the *New York Times* commenced publication in 1851, it hired "ragged newsboys" to assist it in securing casual purchasers. The implications of this shift towards the street selling of newspapers are evident. Print became more accessible to ordinary people, which represents one of the central democratic transformations in nineteenth-century journalism. The availability of newspapers in public places (a common phenomenon by the late nineteenth century) tapped a rapidly expanding consumer market that shifted unpredictably in response to ephemeral events and the diverse ways in which newspapers reported them. In turn this public culture accelerated typographical and visual changes intended to satisfy the preferences of transient readers, many of them eager to read the latest headlines or sports results.

Street sales in Britain lagged considerably behind those in the United States. After the suppression of the unstamped press in 1836, the vending of newspapers disappeared for several decades, a chief exception being "disreputable" Sunday papers. Higher-priced papers like the *Times* refused to countenance street sales since (as with advertising) they feared this would sully their image among respectable readers. Only during the Crimean War, when "extras" were published with the latest news of fiercely contested battles, were newspapers sometimes hawked in the streets of London. However, the repeal of the newspaper duty in 1855 marked a turning point because several of the cheap daily newspapers that came into existence at around that time sought to boost their readership through the adoption of aggressive American-influenced marketing techniques. The penny *Morning Star*, for example, pioneered in the use of direct street sales. It distributed contents bills and brightly-colored posters, and it hired sandwich men to circulate them. When the *Echo*, a popular halfpenny evening paper, appeared in 1868, a brigade of smartly uniformed boys was paraded through the streets of central London to celebrate its virtues.[32] Still, most newspapers (including those printed in evening editions) eschewed the practice of street sales until the 1880s, when Stead, Harmsworth, George Newnes and other proprietors and editors began to promote the New Journalism, and the bookstalls of wholesale distributors such as Smith & Son assisted in this process. In 1904 Stead organized the ultimate performance in street entertainment when he launched his short-lived *Daily Paper*. He hired 1,000 sandwich men to trumpet its virtues, sponsored a fireworks display on Hampstead Heath and arranged to have five-pound notes dropped from balloons so as to attract a crowd of bystanders.[33] Even so, a class schism of sorts was perpetuated within British journalism, with only cheaper mass circulation papers relying heavily on the practice of street sales.

During these decades, the methods of reporting news underwent important changes. New York papers like the *Herald* and the *Sun*, which sold for two cents, led the way in investigative reporting and stories featuring human-interest. The *Herald* demonstrated a notable penchant for news coverage, as it had done from the outset, and in the 1870s it boasted a circulation of 90,000. Whole areas of news coverage were said to have become "Heraldized," as the newspaper established cooperative undertakings with the *Daily Telegraph* and the *Daily News*, and reported on far-flung overseas adventures, including the participation of British troops in the Ashanti Wars of 1873–4. It created a stir with several

Figure 5.1   Henry M. Stanley at the outset of his Central African expedition;
J. Hall Richardson, *From the City to Fleet Street* (1927)

memorable scoops, including firsthand news accounts of the "last stand" by General George A. Custer at the battle of the Little Big Horn against the Sioux Indians in 1876. Its stories were preceded by sensational single column decked headings like "A Horrible Slaughter Pen," "The Scalping of United States Skirmishers Told by an Eyewitness" and "The Red Man's Treachery."[34] The *Herald* hired many special correspondents and paid them well, among them Henry M. Stanley, a Welshman by birth, who possessed an unerring instinct for the adventurous beat, a talent that matched the whirring tone of the paper. Stanley's search for and discovery of the Scottish missionary, David Livingstone, in 1871–2, along the banks of Lake Tanganyika, a project sponsored and funded by the *Herald* with considerable ballyhoo (and shared with the *Daily Telegraph*), was one of the most thrilling press initiatives of the century. It aroused unprecedented enthusiasm for the paper and has been described as "the first sensational news story to break simultaneously on both sides of the Atlantic."[35]

To the end of his life, Bennett, who was succeeded in 1867 as proprietor and editor-in-chief of the *Herald* by his son, the flamboyant James Gordon Bennett, Jr. ("Commodore"), believed that the printing of news, "full, complete, and without bias," was the essential prerequisite to a successful newspaper.[36] Resources permitting (some of them set aside to pay informants for helpful tips), he preferred to rely upon his own staff of reporters to carry out this policy. He was persuaded that *Herald* readers would forgive the odd indiscretion, including factual inaccuracy, if news values were given primacy. As a result, accounts of news in his paper sought to capture at least the rudiments of a good story; in the view of a historian, they were "immensely more readable than (those of) any other journal issued in America."[37]

Under the editorship of Charles A. Dana, the *Sun* had almost as considerable an impact on journalism as the *Herald*. Whereas the latter enveloped its coverage of the news within a thin patina of sensationalism, particularly after the younger Bennett took over the proprietorship, the four-page tabloid-sized *Sun* developed its own version of an entertainment formula, though from a more restrained model. Led by Dana, who came to be recognized as one of the foremost journalists in the Anglo-American world during the second half of the century, and his acerbic managing editor, Amos J. Cummings, it achieved notable success beginning in the 1870s. With an estimated daily paid readership of 147,000 at the close of the decade (the largest in the United States), it focused on "human interest": concise and accurate news coverage ("condensation, clearness, point"); brief editorials; sharp headlines; snippets of local information; and lightly written, evocative news accounts intended to be readily comprehensible to a miscellany of readers, some of whom were perceived to be ill-educated.

New York intellectuals disparaged the *Sun* as a paper read by "horse car drivers." But Dana aimed to make it a quintessential metropolitan organ, "just what the great mass of the people want." Rejecting the more finicky British approach to journalism, which he derided as "mere perfumeries and pigeon-wings," he instituted a policy of excluding nothing from the pages of the *Sun* that met the twin desiderata of being lively and interesting. "I have always felt that whatever the Divine Providence permitted to occur I was not too proud to report," he wrote.[38] *Sun* journalists were instructed to unearth the inner "truth" of an event as well as its public manifestation. John B. Bogart, the paper's city editor, summarized its populist leanings in a quip that has, perhaps, come to be more widely quoted than any in the entire history of journalism: "When a dog bites a man that is not news; but when a man bites a dog, that is news." This philosophy was to prove immensely attractive to, among others, Hearst, who described the *Sun* as an "intelligently condensed newspaper," Harmsworth, who admired its vitality, and Pulitzer, who characterized it as "the most piquant, entertaining, and without exception, the best newspaper in the world."[39]

Investigative journalism was another area in which the American press operated with greater scope and initiative. In part this resulted from the existence of a less restrictive legal system. The framework of libel law continues to be broadly similar in both countries, yet there are significant differences. For one thing, as a result of the celebrated trial and acquittal of John Peter Zenger, the editor of the *New York Weekly Journal*, for seditious libel in 1735, and the existence of First Amendment press protections, prosecutions for seditious libel had become relatively uncommon in America by the second half of the nineteenth century, whereas they continued to be employed on an intermittent basis by governments in Britain. Likewise, writs for personal libel were not initiated nearly as frequently in the United States. After the termination of Republican-Federalist hostilities in the early years of the century, when political opponents regularly used legal tactics against each other, a tradition of journalistic give and take largely became the norm. American editors were afforded public leeway to make accusations against individuals; on the other hand, British journalists were more likely to have to answer to a personal writ for comments judged to be excessive. The *New York Times* escaped unscathed after its spectacular exposure of the Tweed Ring in the 1870s; whereas insinuating statements about financiers and politicians in British periodicals, such as Henry Labouchere's *Truth* and Edmund Yates's *World*, led to a slew of debilitating libel suits.

At least as important in accounting for the seminal role of investigative journalism in the United States is that country's more aggressive public culture. To be sure, denunciations of aristocrats, clergymen and politicians were rife in nineteenth-century Britain, especially when couched in satirical terms. Such attacks (often in pictorial form) drew upon eighteenth-century political writing, with its fiercely partisan commitments, as can be seen, for example, in the scathing journalism of Jonathan Swift and Joseph Addison. These two combatants attacked the venality of politicians by resort to wit and irony, with Swift advocating for the Tories and Addison staunchly defending the Whigs. During the nineteenth century this combative style of journalism was carried on in the pungent comic illustrations of George Cruikshank and Kenny Meadows, and in periodicals like *Punch*. The technique (lacking a precise counterpart in America) was to aim darts of ridicule, mostly containing personal allusions, at public and private persons deemed to be corrupt or immoral.

By comparison with the United States, though, the investigative side of British journalism was frequently devoid of specificity. As numerous visitors observed, the barrier dividing public and private space in America was fungible. Journalists often forced themselves aggressively into the private lives of individuals, extracting interviews from people against their will and writing about them in offensive terms. They shared information with readers based on exaggeration or hearsay, which was presented in the form of damaging personal barbs. Newspapers like Storey's *Chicago Times* ignored the boundaries of public good taste on numerous occasions and were validly criticized for doing so. Yet, even in its most extreme form, this scattershot approach to journalism (with its creative morality) sometimes had a liberating effect on the press, if only by bringing authority into question more frequently and aiming a spotlight on hidden machinations in government. As Louis Heren has observed: "The archetype (of the questioning journalist) is American. He emerged and developed in the United States ... because that attitude of mind is essentially American."[40]

The exposure of the Tweed Ring by the *New York Times* is a key example of nineteenth-century news investigation, though, ironically, both the editor of the paper and its chief reporter at the time were British. Louis J. Jennings arrived in the United States as a special correspondent for the London *Times* in the aftermath of the Civil War. He went to work for the *New York Times* and edited it for six years before returning to London in 1876. Subsequently he became manager of the American-influenced "City Article" that appeared weekly in Yates's *World*, a popular society journal. (This column was the object of numerous libel suits that eventually threatened the financial viability of the paper.) Likewise, John Foord, the chief reporter for the *New York Times* at the time of the Tweed Ring exposures, was a Scotsman who had worked for several London and provincial newspapers before immigrating to the United States. He succeeded Jennings as editor, a position he held until 1883.

During the post-Civil War decade, the Tammany Hall machine in New York had come to epitomize urban corruption. It controlled jobs and public contracts, and dominated the educational fabric of the city on behalf of its predominantly Irish-Catholic political constituency. Commencing in July 1871, the *New York Times* published detailed information about Tammany Hall's nefarious activities, based partly on purloined City Hall ledger books. For six months it shared information with its readers concerning widespread corruption in the city. The paper featured multicolumned headlines with titles such as "Proof of Undoubted Frauds Brought to Light," along with front-page stories documenting the Ring's illegal activities. Simultaneously, Thomas Nast created a pictorial counterpart to this crusade in *Harper's Weekly*, where in a series of cartoons he depicted the archetypal Tammany boss, William Marcy Tweed, as a manipulator of both the city and state of New York at the expense of millions of hardworking residents. Taken together Jennings, Foord and Nast unleashed a crescendo of literary and visual broadsides against Tammany Hall, until the *New York Times*, which had boasted from the outset of its determination to expose public malfeasance, and *Harper's Weekly*, became jointly identified with this crusading news story.[41]

In 1879–80, the *Herald* launched a similar crusade against the Gas Trust, a corrupt body controlled by the Republican administration in Philadelphia. Bennett, Jr. sent Julius Chambers, his star reporter, to investigate the activities of this public association, which superintended Philadelphia's municipal lighting plant and, it was alleged, controlled its graft. Chambers more than exceeded his brief, in using underhanded methods to gain access to the private letters and vouchers of members of the Trust. Ignoring a crescendo of legal and physical threats, he wrote articles for the *Herald* detailing the pervasiveness of corruption in Philadelphia, including several that focused on the maladministration of Blockley Almshouse, where the city's paupers were housed.[42]

No precise equivalent of Jennings, Bennett or Chambers existed in British press circles in the 1870s. But a handful of journalists earned a degree of notoriety for publicizing alleged financial scandals, among them Henry Labouchere and Edmund Yates. Labouchere, a radical MP, was the more combative of the two men, though he is of lesser importance in the history of journalism. Initially he gained renown as the "Besieged Resident," who reported on events in Paris for the *Daily News* during the Franco-Prussian War. Subsequently he wrote the "City Article" for Yates's *World* that Jennings took over after his return to London. In January 1877, Labouchere launched *Truth*, a weekly featuring gossip, sports and, above all, the exposure of financial malfeasance in the City of London. Having lived in the United States for several years, "Labby" (as he was popularly known) possessed a fondness for the exuberant iconoclasm of American journalism. "It is the business of newspapers to create a sensation," he observed. And with this in mind, he instructed Henry Lucy, a friend and fellow pressman, to "especially study the American papers."[43] But Labouchere's vicious anti-Semitism marred his search for truth, causing him to shine his investigative lantern disproportionately on alleged Jewish financial interests and to employ scurrilous religious epithets, in particular against the Levy family, who owned the *Daily Telegraph*. Anti-Semitism occupied a fashionable niche in radical circles on both sides of the Atlantic during the late nineteenth century, though it was especially sharply delineated in the writings of Labouchere.[44]

Yates was a key figure in transatlantic journalism. Like Labouchere, he specialized in gossip, and while his approach was that of the disengaged man about town, he published the results of financial investigations in the *World*, with the intention of providing "an amusing chronicle of current history."[45] His weekly "In the City" article, appearing in the *World*, aimed to transport readers "behind the scenes" in uncovering a variety of abuses, such as unfairness in tax collection, illegal railway investments, fraudulent dealings in the art market and the baneful activities of life insurance companies. Yates boasted that the publicity he gave to "commercial iniquity and speculative imposture" was "unparalleled in the history of English journalism," an overstatement, to be sure, but one that usefully draws attention to the *World*'s contributions to press history.[46]

At about the same time, a genre of social exploration into the hidden byways of "Unknown England," which drew upon the earlier investigations of street journalists such as Henry Mayhew, began to emerge.[47] This came to be identified with personal descriptive writing, of a kind that had little traction in American urban reporting, where a more forthright style of investigatory discourse was dominant. However, this genre of social exploration was loosely influenced by American journalism, and some of its better examples are to be found in newspapers like the *Daily Telegraph* and the evening *Pall Mall Gazette*, which was founded in 1865 by Frederick Greenwood, a pressman receptive to new ideas.

In 1865 Greenwood's younger brother James published in the *Pall Mall Gazette* a flamboyant, if moralistic, account of the shocking conditions he uncovered in a South London workhouse after spending a night there. He informed readers of the paper that "towzled, dirty, villanous (sic) (casual paupers) squatted up in their beds, and smoked foul pipes, and sang snatches of horrible songs, and bandied jokes so obscene as to be absolutely appalling."[48] Greenwood's "A Night in a Workhouse by an Amateur Casual" became a celebrated nineteenth-century scoop that led to a significant increase of circulation for the *Pall Mall Gazette*. Yet this series of investigative articles (and others of a similar nature, such as "How the Poor Live" by George R. Sims, which appeared in the *Pictorial World* in 1883) stood apart from those in the American press in relying upon "impressionistic" descriptions and not revealing the names of public officials responsible for the abuses. Aaron Watson, who worked on the *Pall Mall Gazette* under Greenwood's two immediate successors, John Morley and Stead, was nearer in temperament to "American-style" journalists. In the early 1880s, he wrote special reports detailing appalling housing conditions to be found in the East End, together with descriptions of adolescent "fighting gangs" active in the area. As with Greenwood's workhouse articles and the peregrinations of Sims through the tenement houses of Southwark, these reports were based on firsthand observations, though Morley diluted their impact by printing them under the innocuous by-line, "A Correspondent Writes."[49]

Stead took the investigative process much further in July 1885, when he published a sensational series of articles in the *Pall Mall Gazette* entitled "The Maiden Tribute of Modern Babylon," which exposed the prevalence of child prostitution in London. Like the Chicago journalist, Melville Stone, Stead "created" this shocking news story by setting a journalistic trap for the malefactors. He "purchased" a young girl from her mother and transported her to a brothel. His objective was to demonstrate that children were the victims of sexual exploitation. In his effort to dramatize a public cause through sensationalism (including the use of bold headings) he owed a debt to Bennett, Pulitzer and a bevy of other American journalists. Yet even in this key example of extreme personalized reporting the British approach to uncovering the existence of a social underworld differed from American reportorial

Figure 5.2   W. T. Stead as editor of the *Pall Mall Gazette*; Estelle W. Stead, *My Father* (1913)

techniques, which probed more aggressively and concretely into layers of events. As a postscript to this incident – culminating in a parliamentary statute that raised the age of consent to 16 – Stead was prosecuted and sentenced to three months at hard labor for "aiding and abetting" an indecent assault on the girl. Whether justifiably or not, such a prosecution reinforced the general impression that press investigations of this type were more likely to be curbed in Britain than in America.[50]

In one important area, the British press underwent a major transformation during the third quarter of the nineteenth century: the creation of a penny press. The repeal of the penny stamp duty made it possible to execute an "internal revolution," that is, to circulate newspapers for a penny or a halfpenny and, in so doing, to reach out to a multitude of new readers. (Ironically, most American penny papers had by now increased their price to two or three cents.) However, cheapness in price brought respectability into question, and it became harder to locate a point of equilibrium between these disparate elements in Britain. When Algernon Borthwick transformed his Conservative *Morning Post* into a penny paper in 1876, and began to extend its reach towards a large middle-class readership, his associates warned him that he risked forfeiting "the political authority which was based on the support of the privileged classes."[51] It was rumored that John Walter III, the owner of the *Times*, would not even read any of the penny papers, let alone sell a newspaper at that price. He did his best to preserve the traditional quality and authority of the *Times*, and believed he could best accomplish this if the price of the paper was not allowed to fall below 3d. In Walter's defense, he was correct to conclude that it would be difficult for the *Times* to maintain its comprehensive news coverage if revenue from sales was allowed to slide. But this ignores the crucial fact that the tenuous link between press reputation and social nexus remained his primary concern.[52]

Among the best-known penny and halfpenny newspapers published in the years after 1855 were the *Daily Telegraph* (1855), the *Morning Star* (1856), the *Echo* (1868) and the Darlington *Northern Echo* (1870). (The *Shields Daily Gazette*, launched in South Shields in 1856, was the first halfpenny evening newspaper to be published in Britain.) These and other cheap newspapers confronted a panoply of obstacles: the scruples of educated readers; an overreliance on press agency dispatches as a means of curtailing expenses; obstreperous news agents and vendors whose income was threatened by a reduction in price; and a need to balance the conflicting pressures of conventional reader expectations and transformative change. On the positive side, the penny and half-penny papers were generally more receptive to testing new frontiers. "London is at length to be upon an equality with New York," the *Daily Telegraph* proclaimed in one of its early leading articles, a statement that established a welcoming mood for many of the substantive innovations to follow.[53]

The *Morning Star*, which was absorbed by the *Daily News* in 1869, led the way in adapting to this new kind of journalism. Together with its stablemate, the *Evening Star*, it hired a brilliant group of journalists, including several who were deeply influenced by American ideas: Justin McCarthy, the editor of the paper for several years; Yates; William Black, a well known writer of popular fiction; Richard Whiteing, the author of a sensational series of articles about London life by "A Costermonger"; and Archibald Forbes, the renowned war correspondent. The *Morning Star* was unostentatious typographically and had only a small circulation, its primary aim being to disseminate Liberal-Radical political ideas. But under the tutelage of McCarthy, it developed a means of communicating with its readers that was "all pictures, suggestion, felicity of phrase."[54] McCarthy maintained close ties with a bevy of American journalists, and for a time considered moving to the United States and becoming a citizen. He introduced gossip columns into the newspaper, including a celebrated one written by Yates ("The Flaneur"). He also featured detailed sports reporting, a departure from mainstream British press tradition.

Both halfpenny *Echoes* (London and Darlington) likewise contributed to the development of mass circulation journalism. T. P. O'Connor, like McCarthy an Irish politician-journalist, joined a "band of young bloods" on the London *Echo* who, in the words of one of them, "drove nails into the coffin of the Old Journalism." In its small-sized format, the *Echo* featured snappy news articles, gossip columns, and crime and sports reporting.[55] Its Darlington namesake, the *Northern Echo*, became even better known because its editor from 1871 to 1880 was Stead, the chief interpreter of American journalism in Britain during the late nineteenth century and a pressman who did as much as any other to bring about a revolution in journalism. Initially the *Northern Echo* exhibited a kind of restrained populism, partly because the prodigiously talented Stead was only 22 years old when he became editor. Yet under his tutelage, the newspaper gained a widespread degree of public recognition by undertaking several American-style crusades, including support for the movement to repeal the Contagious Diseases Acts.

Of the many penny newspapers published in these decades, by far the most Americanized and successful was the *Daily Telegraph*. Established in June 1855, the *Daily Telegraph* claimed to initiate a "new era in journalism" and to extend to the nation the "benefit of a cheap and good Daily Press."[56] It professed to have the "Largest Circulation in the World," a claim abandoned after 1896 when it was overtaken by Harmsworth's halfpenny *Daily Mail*. By American standards, the *Telegraph* was constrained in both typography and sensationalism ("full of raciness and variety," was how the American editor, Henry Watterson, described it). But it made use of suggestive headings, "silly season" stunts intended to provoke controversy, numerous crime stories, an array of colorful narratives (including joint sponsorship with the *Herald* of Stanley's extended second expedition to central Africa in 1874-7) and, perhaps most striking, a famous account by James Greenwood of an alleged fight between a man and a dog, which it printed in 1874.[57] The *Telegraph* represented the lighter end of the journalistic spectrum with its entertaining news coverage, classified ads, "descriptive" sketches of events and pithy leading articles, a large number of them written by Sala, whose sole objective was to provide amusement. In some ways it was a diluted version of the *Herald* – wittier and less news-oriented – "a sort of family paper in excelsis for the comfortable classes."[58] This was even truer of its Saturday edition, which published magazine-style features such as "Holiday Hints."

Joseph M. Levy, the business-minded printer who founded the *Daily Telegraph*, was an unabashed admirer of the *Herald*, as was his son and successor, Edward Levy-Lawson, the first Baron Burnham, who edited the paper for many years. Both men believed that news coverage should focus on its human core and tried to harness to the paper the aspirations of an expanding suburban and lower middle class "cockney" readership.[59] They cobbled together an impressive staff, including Sala and William Wilde, Oscar's older brother, which provided the paper with a dollop of "wholesome literary matter" and a dash of style. "We don't want sound reasoning, we want sound writing," Levy informed one of his reporters."[60] The "magnificent roaring...young lions" of the *Daily Telegraph* created a version of British journalism that was sneeringly castigated by its critics for its "telegraphese," but which played a significant role in the history of transatlantic journalism.[61]

Sala, who wrote about 9,000 "social leaders" for the *Telegraph* during a career that extended to nearly 33 years, was an exemplar of "telegraphese," almost certainly more so than any other journalist of the time. He honed his craft as a correspondent during the Civil War, and like other reporters who spent time in the United States, developed a respect for that nation's energy, what he subsequently described as a "magnificent empire of Democracy turned crazy." While in America, he worked closely with Smalley of the *Tribune* and William H. Hurlburt ("W. H. H.") of the *World*, consummate insiders in New York's press world. Sala's effusions – verbally overheated and self-indulgent to the extreme – are far removed from the compressed urban style being developed in America. Many of the leaders he wrote were coaxed into existence by the joint stimuli of a pressing deadline and a bottle of whiskey. In some ways they are a throwback to Bow Street reporting and a monument to literary bohemianism. But there is in them a vigorous democratic component, even if, as Sala himself admitted, many were "totally destitute of the faculty of imagination."[62]

Sala was in one sense at least a perfect journalist. He was capable of writing on any subject at a moment's notice, and doing it in an immensely readable way. Like Yates, he absorbed a multitude of city experiences and flung them back hurriedly at his readers. "The average public," Sala wrote, "would much sooner read an essay on the last new breach of promise case, the last new fashion, the last new folly, or song, or picture, or society lion, and especially the last new murder, than prosy deliverances on politics, native or foreign."[63] This was the quintessence of "descriptive reporting," intended to interject a picturesque embellishment to the news ("gossiping accounts") in place of a mere summary of it. It differed from the factual timbre of American-style journalism. For the most part Americans liked their news straight up or delivered in blasts of sensationalism (they still do), while Britons preferred it be mixed with a chaser of whimsy. The distinction is important if only because it tended to establish speed and quantity against a form of journalism that continued to set a higher value on literary imagination and pedagogy. Both are legitimate integuments of modern journalism. But at a time of evolving technology, standardizing pressures and, above all, a greatly increased emphasis upon speed, the Americanized version of a culturally democratic press ("news not views") gained more acceptance with an emerging transatlantic mass readership.

Notes

1 Frederick Greenwood, "The Newspaper Press," *Nineteenth Century*, XXVII (1890), 835; Hunt, *Then and Now*, 92.
2 Anthony Smith, *The Newspaper: An International History* (London: Thames and Hudson, 1979), 108.

3 See John Vincent, *Literacy and Popular Culture: England, 1850–1914* (Cambridge: Cambridge University Press, 1989). For Scotland see William Donaldson, *Popular Literature in Victorian Scotland: Language, Fiction* and the Press (Aberdeen: Aberdeen University Press, 1986), 17–18. A solid study of American literacy is Carl F. Kaestle et al, *Literacy in the United States: Readers and Reading Since 1880* (New Haven: Yale University Press, 1991).

4 T. P. O'Connor's quote is in Melville E. Stone, *Fifty Years a Journalist* (London: Curtis Brown, 1921), vi. Curran, *Power*, estimates literacy in Britain at 97 per cent by 1890, which seems much too optimistic.

5 Lee, *Origins of the Popular Press*, 68–9; D. Croal, *Early Recollections of a Journalist, 1832–1859* (Edinburgh: Andrew Elliot, 1898), 114–15. The first daily newspaper to be published in England was Liverpool's *Northern Daily Times* (1853).

6 William Duncan, *Life of Joseph Cowen (M. P. for Newcastle, 1874–86)* (London: The Walter Scott Publishing Co., 1904), 45.

7 Wingate, *Views and Interviews*, 123.

8 Curl, *Murat Halstead*, viii, 142.

9 Quoted in Robert K. Thorp, "Henry Watterson," *Dictionary of Literary Biography*, XXIII (1983), 332. For an account of Watterson's life, see Joseph Frazier Wall, *Henry Watterson: Reconstructed Rebel* (New York: Oxford University Press, 1956).

10 A writer praised the Chicago press in the following terms: "As newspapers, that is, as gatherers of the details of the world's daily history, and its presentation, with fitness and skill, they have no equals on the continent." Z. L. White, "Western Journalism," *Harper's New Monthly Magazine*, LXXVII (1888), 687.

11 Stone, *Fifty Years a Journalist*, 77–82.

12 *Ibid*, 52.

13 Justin E. Walsh, *To Print the News and Raise Hell* (Chapel Hill: The University of North Carolina Press, 1968), 132; Franc B. Wilkie, *Personal Reminiscences of Thirty-Five Years of Journalism* (Chicago: F. J. Schulte, 1891), 114.

14 Dreiser's quote is in *A Book About Myself* (London: Constable, 1929), 172.

15 Both quotes are in Charles C. Clayton, *Little Mack: Joseph B. McCullagh of the St. Louis "Globe-Democrat"* (Carbondale: Southern Illinois University Press, 1969), 92, 95.

16 *Ibid*, 146.

17 On this point, see Andrew Aird, *Reminiscences of Editors, Reporters, and Printers during the Last Sixty Years* (Glasgow: Privately printed, 1890), 36. Maurice Milne has pointed out that in Northumberland and Durham leading articles were mostly indistinguishable from those in the London morning press. *The Newspapers of Northumberland and Durham: A Study of Their Progress during the 'Golden Age' of the Provincial Press* (Newcastle upon Tyne: Frank Graham, 1971), 14.

18 Whiteing, *My Harvest*, 123.

19 The figures cited in Stevens, *Sensationalism*, 65, are 30 per cent in the 1880s and 50 per cent by 1914. For a study of the expansion of advertisements in popular journals and magazines, see James D. Norris, *Advertising and the Transformation of American Society, 1865–1920* (New York: Greenwood Press, 1990).

20 Dane S. Clausen, "Economics, Business, and Financial Motivations," in W. David Sloan and Lisa Mullikin Parcell (eds), *American Journalism: History, Principles, Practices* (Jefferson: McFarland & Company, 2002), 109–10. Horace

Greeley told a British parliamentary committee in 1851 that, however large the circulation, a newspaper's primary source of revenue derived from advertising. Parliamentary Papers, Select Committee on Newspaper Stamps, 1851, XXVII (558), 395.

21 Berridge, "Popular Journalism," 32. Charles Wintour states that in the 1970s 38 per cent of the revenue of British daily newspapers was produced by advertising, and that the figure for the quality Sunday papers was twice as high. *Pressures on the Press: An Editor Looks at Fleet Street* (London: Andre Deutsch, 1972), 35.

22 In 1911, the advertisement manager of the *Times* observed: "The average London daily paper contains only one-tenth of the retail advertising which daily appears in an average Chicago paper." J. Murray Allison, "The Newspaper as an Advertising Medium," in Thomas Russell (ed.), *Advertising and Publicity* (London: Educational Book Company, 1911), 67.

23 Fermer, *Bennett and the New York Herald*, 26.

24 Quoted in Allison, "Newspaper as an Advertising Medium," 78.

25 The phrase is by Edward Dicey in *Six Months*, I, 38.

26 The Harmsworth quote is in T. R. Nevett, *Advertising in Britain: A History* (London: Heinemann, 1982), 82. For the *Daily Mail* statement, see Wareham Smith, *Spilt Ink* (London: Ernest Benn, 1932), 249. Kevin Williams, *Get Me a Murder a Day: A History of Mass Communication in Britain* (London: Arnold, 1998), claims that the "Northcliffe Revolution" was "crucial in establishing advertising as central to the economic structure of the newspaper industry" (p. 60).

27 H. J. Palmer, "The March of the Advertiser," *Nineteenth Century*, XLI (1897), 137. An examination of the *Daily News* for April 1875 reveals display advertising on the front page by companies such as Mappin & Bebs, a large cutlery firm. For an incisive analysis of the impact of display advertising, see William Leach, *Land of Desire: Merchants, Power, and the Rise of a New American Culture* (New York: Pantheon Books, 1993), 40–3.

28 A brief account of some of these developments in Britain is in J. Ewing Ritchie, "Newspaper Distribution in London," *Sell's* (1899).

29 Hamilton Fyfe, *Press Parade: Behind the Scenes of the Newspaper Racket and the Millionaires' Attempt at Dictatorship* (London: Watts & Co., 1936), 76–7.

30 James Greenwood uses the term "Battered Breeches" in *Unsentimental Journeys: or, Byways of the Modern Babylon* (London: Ward, Lock & Tyler, 1867), 229–32.

31 At times newsboys from different papers fought with each other physically for vending rights. Don C. Seitz, *Horace Greeley: Founder of the New York Tribune* (Indianapolis: The Bobbs-Merrill Company, 1926), 88.

32 Simon Nowell-Smith, *The House of Cassell, 1848–1958* (London: Cassell & Company, 1958), 119. The *Illustrated London News* (14 May 1842) claimed that it hired 200 boys to walk through the streets announcing a forthcoming issue. The first number of *Tit-Bits* (30 October 1881) was advertised by a Boys' Brigade that marched along Market Street, Manchester, wearing "Tit-Bits" bands in large letters on its caps.

33 *Review of Reviews*, XXIX (1904), 11–13.

34 On the coverage of Little Big Horn, with its dramatic accounts of the Sioux massacre, see the *Herald*, 6 July 1876.

35 The *Herald* gave Stanley financial carte blanche but he nonetheless voiced the complaint that, "I am at the beck and call of a chief whose will is imperious." (Dorothy Stanley (ed.), *The Autobiography of Sir Henry Morton Stanley* (Boston: Houghton Mifflin, 1909), 244.) For information about Stanley's expeditions, see Beau Riffenburgh, *The Myth of the Explorer: The Press, Sensationalism, and Geographical Discovery* (London: Belhaven Press, 1993), 57–63.

36 Quoted in Carlson, *Man Who Made News*, 286.

37 Kluger, *Paper*, 44.

38 Candace Stone, *Dana and the Sun* (New York: Dodd, Mead & Company, 1938), 55; Dana, "The Newspaper Press," in Frederic Hudson, *Journalism in the United States, from 1690 to 1872* (New York: Haskell House Publishers, 1968; first published in 1873), 680. See also Janet A. Steele, *The Sun Shines for All: Journalism and Ideology in the Life of Charles A. Dana* (Syracuse: Syracuse University Press, 1993), 119–20.

39 The Hearst quote is in Robert N. Pierce, "How the Tabloid was Born," *Journalism Studies Review*, I (June 1977), 2. For Pulitzer's laudatory comment, see Stone, *Dana of the Sun*, 53.

40 Louis Heren, "All Journalists are American," *Journalism Studies Review*, I (June 1976), 6. See James L. Aucoin, *The Evolution of American Investigative Journalism* (Columbia: University of Missouri Press, 2005), especially chapter 1.

41 There is an excellent account of these events in Kenneth D. Ackerman, *Boss Tweed: The Rise and Fall of the Corrupt Pol Who Conceived the Soul of Modern New York* (New York: Carroll & Graf, 2005). The details of Jennings's wide-ranging career in journalism on both sides of the Atlantic can be gleaned in David Morphet, *Louis Jennings MP: Editor of the New York Times and Tory Democrat* (London: Notion Books, 2001).

42 Julius Chambers, *News Hunting on Three Continents* (New York: John Lane, The Bodley, 1921), 234–41.

43 Quoted in Hesketh Pearson, *Labby: The Life and Character of Henry Labouchere* (London: Hamish Hamilton, 1936), 123. A journalist who worked with Labouchere on *Truth* described him as "acute, ready-witted, audacious, irresponsible, intent only upon amusing himself and amusing his readers." Algar Labouchere Thorold, *The Life of Henry Labouchere* (New York: G. P. Putnam's Sons, 1913), 495. See also Gary Weber, "Henry Labouchere, *Truth*, and the New Journalism of Late Victorian Britain," *Victorian Periodicals Review*, XXVI (spring 1993), 36–43.

44 Labouchere's anti-Semitism is analyzed by Claire Hirshfield in "Labouchere, Truth and the Uses of Anti-Semitism," *Victorian Periodicals Review*, XXVI (Fall 1993), 134–42.

45 *World*, 8 July 1874. Henry Lucy, who wrote regularly for the paper, claimed that it had a "spice of devilry" that "shocked good people." Lucy, *Sixty Years in the Wilderness: Some Passages by the Way* (London: Smith, Elder & Co., 1911), 105.

46 *World*, 30 December 1874.

47 See Peter Keating (ed.), *Into Unknown England, 1866–1913: Selections from the Social Explorers* (London: Fontana/Collins, 1976).

48 James Greenwood, *A Night in a Workhouse* (London: Pall Mall Gazette, 1866), 13. T. H. S. Escott claims that these articles marked the beginning of sensationalism in British journalism. Escott, *Platform, Press, Politics and Play:*

Being Pen and Ink Sketches of Contemporary Celebrities (Bristol: J. Arrowsmith, 1894), 219.

49   Aaron Watson, *A Newspaper Man's Memories* (London: Hutchinson and Co., 1925), chapters 11–12; George R. Sims, *My Life: Sixty Years' Recollections of Bohemian London* (London: Eveleigh Nash Company, 1917), 135–6.

50   For accounts of this famous incident, see Raymond L. Schults, *Crusader in Babylon: W.T. Stead and the Pall Mall Gazette* (Lincoln: University of Nebraska Press, 1972), chapters 5–6; Judith R. Walkowitz, *City of Dreadful Night: Narratives of Sexual Danger in Late-Victorian London* (Chicago: University of Chicago Press, 1992), 81–134.

51   Quoted in Smalley, *Anglo-American Memories*, 296.

52   On Walter's alleged sensitivities to the penny papers, see *History of the Times, 1841–1884*, 308.

53   Quoted in *Ibid*, p. 296. W. H. Mudford, the Conservative editor of the penny *Standard*, told his staff to use a clear narrative style as a "corrective to the loose and pretentious diction of the time." Escott, "Old and New in the Daily Press," 359.

54   Whiteing, *My Harvest*, 61.

55   Harry Jeffs, *Press, Preachers and Politicians: Reminiscences: 1874 to 1932* (London: Independent Press, 1933), 43. "E. T. Raymond" (Edward Raymond Thompson) described the *Echo* as "one of the earliest pioneers of popular journalism." *Portraits of the Nineties* (London: T. Fisher Unwin, 1921), 296. A perusal of the *Echo* in 1888 indicates a continuing adherence to old-style typography.

56   *Daily Telegraph*, 29 June 1855.

57   Watterson's comment is in Wingate, *Views and Interviews*, 11. This is the same James Greenwood who had written the sensational workhouse articles for the *Pall Mall Gazette*.

58   Whiteing, *My Harvest*, 74.

59   See Duff Hart-Davis, *The House the Berrys Built* (London: Hodder and Stoughton, 1990), 30. Henry W. Massingham characterized the *Daily Telegraph* as a "cockney" newspaper because it represented "the average thinking and believing of one or two great layers of London life." (*The London Daily Press* (London: The Religious Tract Society, 1892), 91.)

60   *Memoirs of Sir Wemyss Reid*, 134.

61   The "young lions" phrase is in J. W. Robertson Scott, *The Story of the Pall Mall Gazette, of Its First Editor Frederick Greenwood, and of Its Founder George Murray Smith* (London: Oxford University Press, 1950), 152. Viscount Camrose, *British Newspapers and Their Controllers* (London: Cassell and Company, 1947), maintains that the paper "blazed a new trail in its presentation of news, its more humanised grip of life" (p. 28).

62   Sala, *Life and Adventures*, I, 326. See also P. D. Edwards, *Dickens's 'Young Men': George Augustus Sala, Edmund Yates and the World of Victorian Journalism* (Aldershot: Ashgate, 1997).

63   George Augustus Sala, "The World's Press: What I Have Known of It: 1840–1890," in *Sell's* (1891), 24. Sala told J. Hall Richardson, a crime reporter on the *Daily Telegraph*: "I am ready now to write on any subject from the price of beef to a coronation." J. Hall Richardson, *From the City to Fleet Street: Some Journalistic Experiences* (London: Stanley Paul & Co., 1927), 112.

6
Gossip and Other Matters

Personal relationships form a key strand in the evolution of a trans-formed Anglo-American journalism, especially during the 1860s and 1870s. A cosmopolitan literary culture flourished on both sides of the Atlantic. When British pressmen visited America on extended lecture tours or when transmitting stories to their newspapers, they frequently stayed with American writers or journalists, were wined and dined by them, and became part of a transatlantic literary coterie. From these men and women they absorbed rapid-fire techniques of news collect-ing as well as such American press "vulgarisms" as interviewing; some of them returned to Britain suffused with ideas that had a considerable impact on its journalism. The details of this interaction are frequently difficult to trace. But Henry Lucy's observation that the development of a popular press in Britain resulted from "grafting American journal-ism on a British stem," is, undoubtedly, close to the mark.[1]

Several American journalists are repeatedly mentioned in the accounts of British visitors who spent periods of time in the United States, among them Bayard Taylor, William H. Hurlburt and John Russell Young. All three men made important contributions to the American press and helped to expand the speed-driven culture that reshaped it. Yates, Sala, O'Connor, McCarthy, Richard Whiteing of the *Morning Star* and other British journalists got to know them well during extended visits to New York, Philadelphia and Boston, and were drawn into their social circles. Professional camaraderie intensified over shared conversations and drinks, some elements of which took the form of literary bohemianism. Yates and Sala were noted *bons vivants* and scintillating conversationalists, which eased their paths into these coteries, while Whiteing was a gregarious young novelist on the make. All of them cultivated American contacts and were receptive to changes emanating in journalism, or as Thomas Escott expressed it, to a belief in "the superiority of American notions to home grown ideas."[2]

Taylor was the leading member of a "genteel" literary-journalistic set in Manhattan that was a part of some key press transformations. He was a prolific writer who worked for many years on the *Tribune*. His forte was descriptive travel sketches and light essays on subjects of human-interest with the potential for dramatic embellishment, such as the California Gold Rush. Sala and Yates were friendly with Taylor and most likely influenced by his fluid style of composition and proclivity for experimentation, couched as it was in restrained literary terms.[3] Hurlburt moved in the same circle but was a more forceful contributor to the American press, notably in the outstanding editorials he wrote for the *World*. He was not an overt practitioner of the New Journalism (nor, strictly speaking, was Taylor). Yet his bohemian lifestyle and penchant for gathering human-interest news placed him at the epicenter of Anglo-American journalism. Whiteing became well acquainted with Hurlburt while working as a London correspondent for the *World* in the 1870s. He singled him out as a "sort of introducer of celebrities for the dinner parties of Fifth Avenue" and, more emphatically, as "the interpreter of America to England."[4]

Young was undoubtedly more influential than Taylor or Hurlburt. He spent his formative years working on the *Philadelphia Press*, where he wrote a famous description of the Battle of Bull Run. But his key years as a journalist were as managing editor of the *Tribune* from 1866 to 1869, and as London correspondent for the *Herald*, in the late 1870s and again between 1885 and 1890. Young got to know many of the leading British journalists professionally and socially, and became an intimate friend of O'Connor, whose editorship of the halfpenny London *Star*, beginning in 1888, ushered in a decisive phase of the New Journalism. Young personified several of the glaring defects of American journalism, including unrestrained zeal in the pursuit of news that brought about his downfall on the *Tribune* after an incident in which he violated professional ethics while in contact with the New York AP. Yet he was a creative newspaperman who developed a variation on the genre of human-interest: "pen pictures of scenes and conversations" that were based on personal interviews. Both Yates and O'Connor were influenced by him, the former in the important column that he wrote for his weekly journal, the *World*, entitled "Celebrities at Home," which relied heavily upon American-style interviewing; the latter in the "sensational" tone and format of the news-oriented *Star*. According to Young, Yates "created a new field of journalism" and "told me that he found the idea in the United States."[5]

Two other New York literary personalities were notably active in this Anglo-American journalistic set: Sam Ward and George W. Curtis. Ward ("Uncle Sam") was a well-known raconteur, minor poet, government informer and general man about town who did little actual press work, though he contributed occasionally to New York newspapers, including the *Tribune*. He and his London visitors dined frequently at Delmonico's, a celebrated restaurant in the Madison Square section of Manhattan, where they gossiped and exchanged information about recent developments in British and American journalism.[6] Like Hurlburt, Curtis was an imposing press personality. He was the political editor of *Harper's Weekly* for many years, where he penned an influential column about American politics. Even better known was the column that he wrote for *Harper's Monthly Magazine*, "The Easy Chair," a compendium of witty observations about social mores, literature and politics. This column impressed McCarthy, Yates and other London journalists because of its gossipy tenor, which seemed to unlock a dimension of human-interest previously hidden from the public.

Important press relationships were also nurtured in London. Smalley's influence in popularizing the telegraph there was profound, but as resident London correspondent of the *Tribune* for almost 30 years (the first American journalist to maintain such an extended posting abroad), he was influential in other ways. As a result of his friendships with British journalists, he was able to assuage some of the differences within transatlantic journalism. For example, his initiative led to the first successful cooperative agreement involving a British and an American newspaper: the reciprocal exchange of military news between the *Tribune* and the London *Daily News* during the Franco-Prussian War. John R. Robinson, the managing editor of the *Daily News*, initially resisted Smalley's proposal. But as it turned out his newspaper profited more from the arrangement than the *Tribune* because the latter's news department was better run. (On the other hand, the brilliant war dispatches of Forbes, also printed in the *Tribune*, proved to be an enormous boon to New York readers.)[7] Subsequently, another successful news sharing arrangement was commenced, this time between the *Herald* and the *Daily Telegraph*, involving the exploits of Stanley. The newspapers jointly sponsored the latter's famous expedition to locate Livingston, as well as his subsequent explorations in Africa. In all of these instances the *Herald* took the initiative and bore the brunt of the expenses.[8]

Smalley was an inveterate interviewer and a talented "descriptive writer." Both facets of journalism were incorporated into "Yesterday in London," his weekly report that appeared initially in the *Tribune* in 1879 and was one of the first columns to be cabled verbatim from London to New York. It intermixed political and literary news and, to some extent, gossip as well. Smalley's reputation as an unapologetic Anglophile assured the popularity of the column, and it was soon imitated by purveyors of political and social tittle-tattle on both sides of the Atlantic. The British trade journal, *Sell's*, commented in 1896: "No man who was ever connected with the Press has done more to inform Americans about English affairs than Mr. Smalley."[9]

Other American journalists working in London contributed to changes in the press during these years. Hurlburt spent most of his professional life in London from 1883 on; and Harold Frederic, the London correspondent of the *New York Times*, resided there from 1884 to 1898 and came to be referred to as the dean of American correspondents in Europe. Frederic exercised less direct influence than Smalley, with whom he was involved in a friendly press rivalry. But shortly after arriving in London he applied for membership in the Savage Club, so as to make himself acquainted with "newsy Bohemia." His application was accepted and he soon became friends with, among others, O'Connor and McCarthy. More of a collector of news (and a minor novelist) than its interpreter, in consonance with the emphasis on factual newsgathering on the *New York Times*, Frederic pushed hard for a cooperative arrangement between his paper and the *Manchester Guardian*. Little came of this idea, though it had the virtue of making clear to British journalists that "hard" news collecting of the kind favored by the *New York Times* was something to be emulated.[10] Shortly after the turn of the century, the *New York Times* signed an information-sharing agreement with the London *Times* that lasted for almost a decade.

Frederic's unheralded assistant on the *New York Times* from 1884 to 1886 was John H. Copleston, a little known British pressman who previously had edited the *Northern Echo* and worked as Night Editor in the London bureau of the New York *World*. Copleston did arduous "leg" work for Frederic, who ran the *New York Times* bureau without any other assistance. He covered for Frederic when he was away, wrote portions of his "London Letters" (which were criticized for their lack of bite), penned theatrical and musical reviews, and conducted interviews with politicians and visiting celebrities. After a heated quarrel concerning remuneration, Copleston left the newspaper but resurfaced shortly after in a more influential role. Espousing the virtues of "short, pithy, newsy and original" stories, he became editor of the halfpenny London *Evening Post*, a newspaper that under his management adopted American journalistic techniques, including an increased emphasis on crime stories. When the sensationalizing Scottish journalist Kennedy Jones and his financial patron, Alfred Harmsworth, purchased the *Evening Post* in 1894 (five years after it had been absorbed by the *Evening News*), a significant integration of "Americanized" press techniques occurred.[11]

There is a further dimension to transatlantic journalism that warrants consideration. Until the late 1870s, American newspapers hardly ever sent their own reporters to London. The explanation had primarily to do with expense, though it also reflected the strongly held conviction that in matters European the British were better able to disseminate and interpret news. Smalley and Frederic were among the first American journalists to be dispatched to London for extended periods of time and to do the bulk of their professional work there. The usual pattern was for British journalists to work as freelancers or stringers for American newspapers. This gave them an opportunity to supplement their incomes and, in some instances, to advance their literary aspirations. For example, Yates was hired as a London correspondent by the *Herald* in 1873 at the munificent sum of 1,200 pounds a year, which provoked his American friend, Sam Ward, to observe caustically: "My Edmund has an eye to the rainy day and makes a more systematic use of his pay than any Bohemian I ever knew."[12] In exchange for this ample remuneration, Yates penned a weekly "London Letter" for the *Herald* that competed with those written by Smalley and Frederic. He also acted as a "special correspondent" for Continental affairs, in which capacity he covered the Vienna International Exhibition of 1873 (together with Young, Taylor and other notable American journalists). On this occasion his dispatches were sent to New York by telegraph and cable and proved to be a minor sensation.

O'Connor and Sala were also briefly employed by the *Herald*, the latter as the result of a recommendation from Yates, while Whiteing acted as a resident correspondent for both the *Tribune* under Smalley and the *World* under Hurlbert. Joseph Hatton was another well-known London freelancer who wrote for a number of newspapers and for a time was the London correspondent of the *New York Times*, the Sydney *Morning Herald* and Melville Stone's *Chicago Daily News*. Hatton put to good use what he learned about American journalism in "Cigarette Papers," a popular gossip column that he later wrote for the *People*, a Conservative weekly newspaper. Hatton described this column as "a text for talk, a chapter of romance, a reminiscence of some famous man or woman, a wayside note of travel, (and) a peep behind the mimic scenes of life."[13] His scrappy observations – personal musings annexed to a thin commentary on passing events – were a quintessential embodiment of the American-inspired New Journalism. His book *Journalistic London*, which has come to be recognized as a minor classic of its kind, was originally published in parts, in *Harper's Magazine* in 1882. Yet another stringer who prospered during these years was J. Hall Richardson, who covered London and Continental affairs for the *Philadelphia Press* and several other American newspapers. Richardson later became the chief crime reporter for the *Daily Telegraph*, a newspaper that specialized in accounts of crime. His memoirs testify to the impact American journalism made on him as he undertook to apply speed and sensationalism to his work.[14]

There are also notable instances of American journalists who came to Britain to work and stayed behind permanently to convert. Two of the more important ones are Chester Ives and Ralph D. Blumenfeld. Relatively little is known about the early years of Ives, who worked for the *Tribune* and the *New York Times,* and for the *Herald* in Ireland, before coming to London in the early 1880s. An exuberant disciple of American popular journalism, he founded the *Morning* in 1892, a halfpenny daily paper with a down-market appearance and "un-English" features, including a front page filled with news. Heretofore no London morning newspaper had essayed this seminal American innovation. News on the *Morning*'s front page was mostly about crime, sports and natural disasters; it presented a "cheap look as well as a cheap price," which many critics believed to be an inevitable outcome of Americanization. In 1900, after several changes of title and proprietorship, the *Morning* resurfaced as the *Daily Express*, the great London newspaper founded by Charles Arthur Pearson that from the outset featured the American practice of filling the front page with news.[15]

Blumenfeld became editor of the *Daily Express* in 1902. Previously he had worked in New York for Albert Pulitzer's sensationalized *Morning Journal*, one of the earliest attempts at modern tabloid journalism, and had become an experienced space rate reporter assigned to cover fast-breaking news stories. When he arrived in London in 1890 to work for the *Herald*, he intuited that he had "to unlearn many things that I had considered to be essential for successful newspaper work." The atmosphere in Fleet Street newspaper offices was, he discovered, "sedentary" and "puddingy," with reporters proceeding to their assignments attired in frock coats and top hats. Blumenfeld set out to graft "my American branch on the British oak," and the results of this approach soon became

Figure 6.1 R. D. Blumenfeld; R. D. Blumenfeld: *In the Days of Bicycles and Bustles* (1930)

evident in the pages of the halfpenny *Daily Express*, which in addition to placing its news on the front page, engaged in hectic bouts of imperialistic flag-waving. Blumenfeld became a forceful proponent of American journalistic techniques, zestfully executing Pearson's instruction to his employees, to "never forget the cabman's wife." (The American equivalent of Pearson's observation is Bernarr Macfadden's admonition to his reporters on the madcap *New York Daily Graphic* in the 1920s, to "never print anything that a scrubwoman in a skyscraper cannot understand.")[16]

Blumenfeld introduced a policy of news condensation in the pages of the *Daily Express*, with Sidney Dark, who worked for him for many years, recalling his observation that anyone "who knew his business could write the history of the world in five hundred words."[17] He promoted American stylistic innovations on the paper: unembellished writing, the frequent use of verbs and interrogatives, as well as the cultivation of linguistic "human touches." Critics attacked the "massocratic journalism" of the *Daily Express*, and in later years Blumenfeld proffered a measured apologia for his part in bringing it to Britain. But there was little denying the impact of the front-page headlines (19 May 1900, "MAFEKING AND BADEN-POWELL'S GALLANT BAND SET FREE") and speedy news reporting that made the newspaper such an instant success. American journalism had come to London arrayed in all of its public finery.

An integral feature of this "massocratic" press was gossip, which subsequently was to become a central element of tabloid journalism. Together with sports and crime, it comprised a trinity of interests that attracted large numbers of readers and has continued to do so to the present day. Without gossip, in the words of Blumenfeld, "life would be dull and inexpressive." The voyeuristic urge to share intimate knowledge of other people's lives is as old as human history. But as nineteenth-century newspapers acquired immense readerships, such intimacies increasingly entered the public domain. Gossip was (and is) woven out of disaggregated materials. The very parceling out and reconfiguration of personal tidbits increases its titillation, which is not to suggest that it cannot possess legitimate appeal to the "broad and universal humanity" of its readers, as Blumenfeld vigorously maintained throughout his career.[18] The investigative potential of "gossip journalism," as in the inordinate success of the British humor magazine, *Private Eye*, is a testament to its possible value in the cause of reform. Still, as with other facets of modern journalism, entertainment is the primary justification of gossip, and this was self-evidently the case during the mid- to late-nineteenth century when it was in the process of locating a niche in the newly evolving mosaic of mass publishing.

As with the reporting of news, American journalism pioneered in gossip principally because, as has been suggested, the line between public and private life was much less sharply demarcated in the United States. The relatively supple nature of the American legal system also made it easier to publish frequently unverified, sometimes vicious, rumors with relatively little fear of retribution. Furthermore, American newspapers may have been unduly attracted to the assimilative properties of gossip because of the large numbers of immigrants who were becoming readers of its daily press.

Gossip columns in American newspapers date from the commencement of the penny press in the 1830s. In the absence of a traditional ruling class, the fascination with gossip was directed primarily at the newly rich and those who may loosely be characterized as having been granted ascribed, or celebrity, status. Not surprisingly, Bennett's *Herald* was the principal disseminator of gossip. Even before establishing the newspaper, Bennett had dispatched "personal" reports to the *Morning Courier* from Saratoga Springs, in which he retailed social and political gossip concerning some of the wealthy individuals who spent time in that fashionable spa town. Subsequently he made the *Herald* a fount of diverse information and unsubstantiated tittle-tattle. By the 1840s, prying reporters from the *Herald* seemed to be in every nook and corner in pursuit of the "floating gossip, scandal, and folly" of the day. Notwithstanding the grandiose title of that paper's gossip column, "Movement of Distinguished People," these reporters were sometimes barred from trespassing on social events because, in the words of an unsympathetic observer, "to submit to this kind of surveillance is getting to be intolerable, and nothing but the force of public opinion will correct the insolence."[19] More agreeably, the work of *Herald* reporters was sometimes facilitated by the objects of their attention, who enjoyed the attendant publicity and fed the voracious appetite of what in recent years has come to be referred to as the "search and destroy" media.

Greeley's *Tribune* and Dana's *Sun*, along with other papers, emulated the *Herald* in providing ample space for gossip. Personal spice became the rage in the American press, though in deference to the arbiters of taste most of the names (British style) were surreptitiously dashed to protect the "innocent." By mid-century, the popular press had gained a reputation for its tendency to fuse sensationalized tidbits of gossip with hard news. American newspapers ran columns with titles like "Gossip" or "Chit Chat," that were mostly published in weekend editions, while more specialized forms of gossip appeared irregularly, including gossip about the theater, politics and literature. Chicago newspapers rapidly caught up with their New York rivals in this area, taking special delight in abjuring all traces of "Gentlemanly Feeling," as an offended British commentator expressed it.[20] The *Chicago Tribune* gave a large amount of space to gossip, while the *Daily News* featured what was, perhaps, the most widely admired literary gossip column of the century, Eugene Field's "Sharps and Flats," a medley of impressionistic jottings that influenced Dreiser and other young writers. By the 1870s, gossip had become a permanent fixture of journalism, by which time it began to shift its attention to actors and other new-style celebrity entertainers. As George Flack, the gossip columnist in Henry James's, *The Reverberator*, commented: "Every one has something to tell, and I listen and watch and make my profit of it."[21]

Political gossip came to be increasingly disseminated, especially in the guise of "Washington Letters." The relative informality of political life in Washington made that city a focal point for ephemeral gossip, in contrast to the more "serious" analyses of parliamentary debates and political speeches that were the norm in London. As early as the 1830s and 1840s, gossipy reports from the nation's capital began to circulate in the American press, and once again it was Bennett who took the lead. When he began his career in journalism in the late 1820s, the custom was for Washington correspondents to ignore the "pleasant gossip of the day" and, in the view of one observer, to provide "no insight into what transpired behind the scenes at the national capital."[22] Bennett transformed this situation dramatically by apportioning significant space in the *Herald* to political "gossip and chat." He entertained his readers with dispatches from Washington that featured a frothy concoction of social and political information. Other journalists quickly followed suit, among them the acerbic Matthew L. Davis of the *Courier and Enquirer* ("Spy in Washington") and Nathan Sargent of the *Philadelphia Gazette* ("Oliver Oldschool"). Likewise Greeley's *Tribune* integrated political gossip into a popular column entitled "Rumors and Humors in Washington," written at the outset by William E. Robinson ("Persimmon"). The Irish-born Robinson employed mockery as a coruscating press tool and stirred a hornet's nest of controversy by giving publicity to closely guarded political and diplomatic secrets, which on one occasion led to *Tribune* reporters being banned from the House of Representatives. Greeley further compromised his reputation as a serious journalist when he instructed his Washington reporters to send him a daily letter, "on the doings of Congress or on anything spicy or interesting, letting the readers do their own thinking rather than see that you are doing it for them."[23]

Washington gossip gained additional traction during the Civil War. Both Whitelaw Reid of the *Cincinnati Gazette* ("Agate") and Henry Villard, whose syndicated "Washington Letter" appeared in the *Herald* and other newspapers and was one of the first widely circulated political gossip columns of its kind, were accused of sensation-mongering. They claimed to be making public "inside views" of what was transpiring in the capital, though Reid's information was generally thought to be more reliable since he simultaneously held an official position as clerk to a Congressional committee. (The practice of rewarding journalists with patronage appointments while they worked at their trade does not seem to have had a direct parallel in Britain.[24]) "Inside views" or not, the *Cincinnati Gazette* was not unusual among newspapers in trying to position itself in two directions. It pleaded guilty to the charge of disseminating political gossip, while at the same time deploring its potentially damaging effects: "(Journalists) hang about the Department offices; they button-hole the unhappy ushers; they besiege goers and comers; they read physiognomies; they absorb the contents of all leaky vessels like a sponge; they study hotel registers as faithfully as a monk his breviary."[25]

The consummate trafficker in Washington gossip was Benjamin Perley Poore ("Perley"), whose column, "Waifs from Washington," appeared in the *Boston Journal* starting in 1854. Poore seemed to know everybody and everything that was transpiring in the nation's capital. Several times a week he shared informal gossip and hard information with his readers based on extensive personal contacts and interviews. His evenings were spent in the vicinity of "Newspaper Row," on 14th Street, near the Willard and Ebbitt Hotels, where the offices of leading newspapers were located (including both the *Herald* and the *Tribune*), and where politicians and journalists mingled casually over drinks. Contacts of this type rarely occurred in Fleet Street or Westminster because social interaction between journalists and politicians in Britain was much more formal. One press novice exclaimed: "I used to open my eyes with wonder at the sight of so many distinguished statesmen visiting the office of Henry Boynton of the *Cincinnati Gazette*."[26] Boynton was a well-respected newspaperman, to be sure, but Poore entertained many more distinguished visitors, and although the latter privately contemned the excesses of gossip journalism, he added to the dubious reputation of the American press by filling his columns with mounds of political froth.

In Britain, newspaper gossip was more muted. It was principally limited to magazines, though court cases touching upon sexual transgressions and other delicate matters were often reported upon gleefully in the daily press. (American magazine gossip was also widespread, prominent examples being Curtis's "Easy Chair" column in *Harper's Monthly* and Richard Watson Gilder's "The Old Cabinet" in *Scribner's Monthly*.) On the whole British gossip was less acrid than its American equivalent, because the bulk of it was concentrated on traditional objects of displeasure: the aristocracy, the church, the royal family. It drew on longstanding conventions of satirical badinage and was featured in weekly society journals such as *Vanity Fair* ("Truthful Tommy"), Labouchere's *Truth* ("Entre Nous"), Henry Lucy's *Mayfair* ("The Chat of the Fair") and, above all, Edmund Yates's *World*. These periodicals aimed glancing weekly darts at individuals whose foibles were of interest to their predominantly middle-class readership. Only slowly did this type of gossip make its way into mainstream newspapers, where its circle of readers was broadened. Yates, who straddled the worlds of magazine and daily press journalism, was the chief intermediary in this process.

The earliest British newspaper gossip columns, often signified by the heading "Private and Confidential," date from the 1850s, where they appeared in the *Leader*, a weekly periodical, and several other short-lived journals associated with Yates and his bohemian colleagues. Yates was a quintessential Victorian gossip in his private as well as public life. He thrived on chitchat, spending almost every working night in a London theater or club, where he acquired teasing bits of information to share with his readers. He was the "Lounger at the Clubs" in the *Illustrated Times*, the "Flaneur" in McCarthy's *Morning Star* and a female impersonator in the "Five O'Clock Tea" column, which ran in the *Queen* during the 1860s. Above all, Yates was an irrepressible impresario who created two of the best-known gossip columns of the age, "What the World Says" and "Celebrities at Home," both of which were featured in his society weekly, the *World*, which began publication in 1874 and described itself as an "entirely novel experiment" in journalism. In initiating and authoring these columns, Yates drew upon the influence of Young and other American journalists. He linked gossip to interviewing, an American practice that until then had only been employed sparingly in Britain. Yates was a delineator of human interaction who combined an instinct for quasi-radical sensationalism with a compulsion to share personal secrets. His self-evaluation is incisive: "Light and flippant, wanting in indignity and tone, (my journalism) may have been; personal in the inoffensive sense of the word it undoubtedly was, but it was, I hope, neither vulgar, scurrilous, malignant, nor vindictive; above all, it was amusing."[27] The result of this was a critical role for Yates in the evolution of an American-inspired New Journalism in Britain.

By the 1880s gossip was making its presence felt in the mainstream British press. It became an integral part of the New Journalism, constructed as it was on an edifice of dispersed impressions and news presented in snippet form. It had the added virtue of being able to attract new categories of readers, including many women. Andrew Lang began to purvey gossip regularly in the pages of the *Daily News*, while admitting that most of it was "never meant for any ears except those in which it was uttered."[28] In the final two decades of the nineteenth century nearly all of the leading penny and halfpenny newspapers featured racy gossip columns, including T. P. O'Connor's *Star* ("Mainly About People") and Harmsworth's *Daily Mail* ("In Society"). "Mainly About People" was especially notable because it appeared on the front page. Although it was sometimes written by his wife, an American-born novelist, it was animated by O'Connor's firm belief that, with the exception of scurrilous material, "every thing that can be talked about can also be written about." In penning his column O'Connor maintained that, "No one's life is now private; the private dinner party, the intimate conversation, all are told." He publicized details of a hitherto private world ("a dash of personality," was how he characterized it), ranging from speculation about Gladstone's personal difficulties to the shape of the bunions on Lady Colin Campbell's feet.[29] To be sure, the great age of newspaper gossip on both sides of the Atlantic did not commence until the 1920s and 1930s, with the appearance of illustrious columnists such as Walter Winchell and "Cholly Knickerbocker" (a composite of writers) in the Hearst press, "Cassandra" (William Connor) in the *Daily Mirror* and "William Hickey" (Tom Driberg) in the *Daily Express*. But the origins of gossip journalism with its secure foundations in modern press history are to be found in the second half of the nineteenth century.

As early as the 1850s, "London Letters," similar to the Washington Letters, became a component of British journalism. These have links both to the rise of gossip as a genre of journalism and the emergence of the modern parliamentary lobby system. To understand their significance, it is necessary to take into account two aspects of British political culture: the persistent interest in parliamentary news and the centrality of London as the focal point of political activity. With the emergence of an energetic provincial press in the mid-1850s, the means for getting parliamentary news to local papers became of central importance. Many provincial newspapers arranged to have London dispatches sent to them by correspondents based in Fleet Street, whom they sometimes hired on a freelance basis. In the 1860s, salaried reporters such as Charles Cooper of the *Scotsman* began to replace these freelancers and to staff the London offices of provincial newspapers. The chatty, informational London Letters that Cooper and his associates wrote and forwarded to English and Scottish cities (mostly by wire) usually appeared on an inside page of their newspaper, next to fast-breaking foreign and domestic news provided by press agencies.

London Letters transmitted a large quantity of gossip, not all of it political in nature. Some letters closely resembled the gossip columns of society journals; in the words of a journalist, they chronicled everything of "real and genuine interest for all who are interested in the ordinary affairs of life."[30] Yates penned two early series of London Letters, in the guise of a "Looker-on in London" for the Belfast *Northern Whig* and as a "London Correspondent" for the *Inverness Courier*. He and his fellow newspapermen collected information by means of acquaintances and membership in clubs, or via backdoor political channels. Much of what they transmitted consisted of unfiltered leavings but some of it was well-informed, based as it was on American-style interviewing and personal contacts with politicians of influence. In a few instances, MPs wrote the London Letters, O'Connor being the best example. Several London Letters were transmitted by cable to the United States, including "Yesterday in London," written by Smalley for the *Tribune*, which appeared in the top left column of that newspaper's front page.

During the 1860s, the Central Press began to stereotype and distribute a London Letter, composed by Edward Spender, which became "indispensable to every provincial paper of any pretensions to lead public opinion."[31] It soon became the practice for London Letters to be written by teams of writers. Their literary quality seems to have improved as a result, as did the reliability of some of the information they imparted. Still, for the most part they consisted of gossip since their authors relied on rumors and private information. Before 1881, provincial newspapers were not permitted to seat reporters in the Press Gallery, and were therefore unable to print detailed accounts of speeches or comprehensive summaries of what transpired unless they could copy or purchase these from other sources. As a result, the London press began for a time to monopolize the "mechanical" side of political

Figure 6.2 Edmund Yates in 1865; Edmund Yates: *His Recollections and Experiences* (1885)

reporting, while provincial and Scottish newspapers tended to specialize in "descriptive" political gossip.

In addition to Yates, Thomas E. Kebbel, Joseph Cowen and Henry Lucy are among a notable group of journalists who wrote London Letters for provincial and Scottish newspapers. Kebbel, a leading correspondent for the *Yorkshire Post* beginning in 1866, privately distanced himself from the "social gossip, political rumours, literary intelligence, and anecdotes" that he circulated, and subsequently abandoned these letters for a more respectable position on the newspaper's leader page.[32] Cowen, a weightier analyst than Kebbel or Yates, penned a brilliant London Letter for the *Newcastle Daily Chronicle*, entitled "Politics and Parliament," which was a feature of that paper for many years. But of the many writers who worked in this sphere of journalism Lucy stands out because he nurtured and brought to maturity two key aspects of British political journalism in the late nineteenth century: parliamentary sketch writing and the creation of the parliamentary lobby.

Sketch writing, still an integral feature of British journalism today, has been described as "sensational," because of its focus on the "personal appearance and manner" of political figures rather than their substantive achievements.[33] It is an impressionistic form of political reporting that incorporates gossip, smart descriptive writing and, whenever possible, an entertaining narrative. By American standards there is little real sensationalism in it, though its emphasis on human-interest, in the words of the journalist Lincoln Springfield, signified a departure from the "dry-as-dust style of the old-fashioned news-chroniclers."[34] By the 1880s, almost every daily British newspaper of any consequence printed a parliamentary sketch, which was key to the success of its overall political coverage. London papers predominated in sketch writing since good quality work depended upon access to the Press Gallery, to be able to observe debates firsthand and distill their essence. There is no American equivalent of the political sketch. Nor can there be in a system that mostly bypasses spontaneous legislative debate and allows congressional speeches to be formally entered into the record without even being delivered.

The parliamentary sketch dates from the 1870s, shortly after London Letters began to circulate. And of the leading contributors to the genre, which included Edward M. Whitty of the *Leader*, Frank Hill of the *Daily News* ("Political Portraits"), David Anderson of the *Daily Telegraph*, O'Connor of the *Star* and Harold Spender of the *Westminster Gazette*, the most prolific by far was Lucy, a friend of Yates and Sala, and like them a pioneering figure in the New Journalism.[35] Although he was one of the best-known journalists of the late nineteenth century, Lucy is often assigned a small role in histories of journalism. Yet he moved gracefully between the worlds of light political gossip, London Letters (as the author of a syndicated daily report) and parliamentary reporting. Somewhere in the midst of this was to be located the political sketch, which he refined into a tool of information and amusement.

Lucy's sketches are discernible in almost every cranny of late Victorian journalism: in comic magazines like *Punch* ("Toby, M.P."); society journals such as the *World* and *Mayfair*, which he founded in 1877; and in the Sunday *Observer* ("Cross Bench") and *Daily News* ("Pictures in Parliament"), which he briefly edited in the 1880s. Lucy devised the format of the political sketch while performing regular turns in the Press Gallery and writing parliamentary summaries for the *Daily News*. Initially he resisted this form of journalism in the belief that "no well-regulated London morning paper would display in its windows small wares of that kind." By the 1880s, however, Lucy's "small wares" were being widely exhibited, sprinkled as they were with a touch of problematic gossip and a "dash of colour."[36]

The parliamentary lobby is the essential point of the triangle linking gossip to politics and it was Lucy ("the doyen of lobby men") who did more than anyone else to create it. It continues to exist today, though in attenuated form as a result of a series of changes instituted in the 1980s. The lobby is a physical space located just outside the House of Commons chamber and is the public site where journalists and politicians intermingle. It also refers to the institutional structure that facilitates (or restricts) such contacts. From the outset lobby rules were formalized, with accredited reporters gaining access to it under prescribed conditions. In the final decades of the nineteenth century the lobby generated an aura of mystery that, on the whole, compares unfavorably with the American practice of unstructured political informality. The observation of Leander Scroop, a lobby correspondent in David Hare's *Pravda*, provides a witty insight: "He told me everything, therefore he told me nothing. A perfect English arrangement. Everything that happened did not happen. I was present at a meeting at which no one met."[37] The lobby was formally instituted in 1885 when a list of accredited correspondents was drawn up. But in essence it came into existence a decade or so earlier, as the London Letters began to circulate and the American practice of interviewing political leaders slowly percolated into British journalism. Reporters sought news behind the scenes, which could best be gleaned from well-placed sources; for their part MPs often found it productive to curry favor with them. The ensuing mixture created, in the words of a journalist-MP, "the world's greatest gossiping ground."[38] More to the point, the evolving lobby was assessed by an observer as "one of the most remarkable and revolutionary of the developments which the press has undergone during the present reign," because it established a means for disseminating news that accelerated the sharing of information and increased the reporting capacity of newspapers.[39]

These developments in political and gossip journalism helped to foster a more Americanized version of the press in Britain. Even so, a measurable gap existed between the two types of journalism. The testimony of Cecil Thompson, a *Daily Express* correspondent based in the United States during the early years of the twentieth century, is relevant in this regard. Thompson recounts how he was expected to show deference to important politicians in London, "to look at a minister from the boots up." He observed that the Prime Minister was as "untouchable as an oriental joss." On one occasion it took Thompson an entire day to arrange a brief meeting with the press officer of a member of the Cabinet. He soon discovered that Washington journalism worked very differently. It was "as full of gossip as a ladies' cloakroom." A press conference conducted by President Theodore Roosevelt, recalled Thompson, was "almost indecent" in its informality and "infectious" in its "general good humor."[40]

To be sure, informality and infectious good humor do not necessarily yield greater enlightenment than a structured working environment. Obscurity and manipulation, as numerous reporters have discovered to their cost, is as integral to political life in Washington as at Westminster. Yet almost certainly the pulse of late nineteenth-century political journalism beat faster in America, as is made especially clear in the rapid spread of interviewing, the practice that most sharply distinguished the two versions of transatlantic popular journalism. Michael Schudson has observed that interviewing is "a vital, characteristic cultural invention and cultural force," and, in this sense, distinctively American since from the outset it epitomized aggressiveness, informality and, above all, an obsession with speed. By the 1880s and 1890s, acceleration clearly trumped privacy in America as "impertinent" reporters, asserting a form of press authority, made use of rapid-fire techniques of interrogation, including "door-step" interviews with celebrities and politicians. Accuracy was often sacrificed in such a situation, which provoked Raymond Blathwayt, a journeyman British interviewer, to denigrate American interviewing as a "trade" rather than a "profession."[41]

American reporters began to conduct interviews on a regular basis as early as the 1860s. Charles Mackay, a London *Times* correspondent during the Civil War, was quickly made aware of this to his irritation. He was ambushed by a *Tribune* reporter, who wanted to ascertain his views of the conflict and brazenly began to question him about them. The reporter stated forthrightly that he was "speaking for the great

American people." His manners, according to Mackay, were brutish. He "followed closely at the waiter's heels, and was already in the room when the words were uttered. He took a seat without invitation." Arnold Bennett was subjected to similar "improprieties" when he visited the United States for the first time four decades later. Although his most dire anxieties were unrealized, in that the "tepidly polite, conscientious, and rapid" group of reporters who interviewed him, "knew precisely what they wanted and how to get it," the "great national sport of interviewing" was on display in New York, as Bennett had anticipated. "Beneath a casual and jaunty exterior, I trembled. I wanted to sit, but dared not. (The interviewers) stood; I stood." The following morning's news stories (Bennett conceded that they were inoffensive enough) did nonetheless reveal to readers of the popular press that "the most salient part of me was my teeth" and that "I behaved like a school-boy."[42] If many Britons found such behavior to be vulgarly intrusive, the reasons were clearly enunciated by Harold Spender, who espoused a slower, more "gentlemanly" model of interrogation: "It is the high tradition of the British journalist to respect the position of the public man and scrupulously to avoid getting him into trouble."[43]

Interviewing entered into American journalism for the first time in the 1830s, during the coverage of the Robinson-Jewett murder case, when the *Herald* published its extensive "interrogation-interview" with the landlady of the house where the murdered prostitute resided. This was one of the earliest interviews to be printed in an American newspaper.[44] Other interviews followed, notably in the *Herald* and Greeley's *Tribune*, which soon took the lead in conducting political interviews. Almost from the outset it became evident that interviewing was a stream capable of flowing in different directions. An enterprising journalist might conceivably write a better story if based on an interview; at the same time, an interviewee would, perhaps, be able to make use of it to influence opinion, as Lincoln and other politicians did to their satisfaction during the Civil War.

By the final decades of the century, American reporters, it seemed, were chasing after people of almost every social level in pursuit of interviews. A prominent Chicago lawyer, for example, was compelled to answer questions by a determined reporter, while he was leaning out of his window in the middle of the night dressed in his pajamas.[45] Both of Pulitzer's newspapers, the *St. Louis Post-Dispatch* and the *World,* gave a stimulus to interviewing in the 1880s and propelled it in the direction of entertainment. Actresses and other newly minted celebrities began to be sought after for interviews in place of politicians and literary personalities. Pulitzer believed that celebrities were "public property" and that interviews should be accompanied by a "striking, vivid pen sketch," so as to bring the results "more clearly home to the average reader." In one instance he sent a team of reporters in pursuit of a wealthy young woman who had rebelled against her parents by marrying a man of inferior social background. The reporters were surreptitiously admitted to the woman's house by a maid and, upon exerting a little informal pressure, successfully interviewed the tearful mother. The next day's news accounts, preceded by titillating decks, created a minor sensation.[46]

At the outset American newspaper interviews were formal in structure. Questions and answers were printed in their entirety, in an effort to create a sense of immediacy and convey a respectable underpinning to the format. Shorthand was employed for accuracy, and the interviewee was allowed to amend the text prior to its appearance in print. By the 1860s, deferential interviewing of this type had largely disappeared in the United States, though it continued to be a common practice for several more decades in Britain.

Joseph McCullagh, the editor of the *St. Louis Globe-Democrat*, contributed to the development of a freer method of interviewing, which he integrated into American press methods. He maintained that interviewing was the core of effective journalism, because it lubricated the wheels of communication and gave the public access to information that would otherwise remain private and inaccessible. His most celebrated interviews were with President Andrew Johnson in the 1860s. Johnson trusted McCullagh and, in effect, presented his case against impeachment by means of a series of interviews printed in the *Globe-Democrat*. Although he was skilled at shorthand, McCullagh eschewed its use on this occasion since his intent was to distill the essence of what the president was attempting to communicate. He believed that impressionism was a more powerful tool than literalness in extrapolating truth. The subject of any interview needed to be encouraged to talk uninhibitedly while, at the same time, the questioner must be given the liberty to move beyond a controlled agenda. McCullagh was concerned with the effects a news story might have on its readers and insisted that writing with "dramatic power" be a part of the published version of the interview. He encouraged reporters to use "descriptive words," which were intended to delineate the personalities of those being interrogated (something akin to the British parliamentary sketch), because he assumed that these were "persons of strong individuality and well-recognized modes of thought and expression." Those excluded from this category, stated McCullagh, are not "really worth interviewing."[47]

British journalists, informed by different reader expectations, were slower to resort to interviewing and when they did it was carried out in a more respectful way. Richard Whiteing, for example, conceived of interviewing as an "abomination," even as he executed assignments for Pulitzer's *World*, including a well-publicized interaction with Gladstone at Hawarden in the 1870s.[48] An anecdote involving Fred Wile, a Chicago reporter, points up some of the difficulties in transferring the speedy, forceful style of American interviewing to a journalistic setting that continued to be distrustful of change. In 1906 Wile was temporarily hired to report on Berlin news for the *Daily Mail*, and as an "American-trained" journalist he attempted to get an impromptu interview with Viscount Haldane, the British Secretary of State for War. This breach of convention horrified the "smug, typically John Bullish correspondent" of the *Morning Post*, who was standing nearby, inasmuch as ministers of the Crown must never be "molested" by journalists, especially when they were abroad. Wile persisted nonetheless, got his interview and (as a successful ending to the tale) was hired on a full-time basis by Harmsworth.[49]

By the late 1870s interviewing began to take hold in portions of the British press, and once more it was Yates who played an important role. Two decades earlier he had published an interview series entitled "Men of Mark," in his monthly journal, the *Train*, in which literary personalities such as William H. Russell, Shirley Brooks and Wilkie Collins were sketched in a distinctive way. More ambitious were the "Celebrities at Home" profiles that he composed for the *World,* because these vivid "pen portraits" were elaborated in considerable detail, to the extent that prominent individuals vied with one another for a place in the column, despite the possibility of an unflattering outcome. (Anthony Trollope declined to be interviewed by the *World* because he claimed to disapprove of "society journalism.") Yates produced overall a unique series of Victorian interview sketches that included many of the leading political, social and literary personalities of the age.[50]

Although Yates was a pioneer interviewer, it was Stead, in the *Pall Mall Gazette*, who placed the practice at the core of British newspaper journalism. Stead was a wide-eyed enthusiast for American culture who believed that daily journalism mirrored popular behavior, warts and all. "We have democratized our institutions piecemeal," he affirmed, "but (unlike America) we are still far short of applying the principles thoroughly in such fashion as to make every man feel the stimulus of equality of responsibility (and) equality of opportunity." Interviewing was for Stead the foundation of democratic journalism because it was "the most interesting method for extracting the ideas of the few for the instruction and entertainment of the many which has yet been devised by man."[51] In 1884, the *Pall Mall Gazette* published 137 interviews, many of them little more than extended character sketches. Among the more significant interviews was one with General Charles Gordon, which acted as a trigger for the ensuing disastrous intervention in the Sudan. Interviews with several leading naval figures during the same year fueled an agitation for increased military expenditures. In later years Stead became a keen spiritualist and managed (without straining the credulity of all of his readers) to conduct a series of "posthumous" interviews, including one with Disraeli in 1909.

Like McCullagh, Stead's technique was to get at the crux of what was being stated. Not only did he abjure the use of shorthand while conducting interviews, he avoided the use of notes. This presupposed a level of trust between journalist and subject that, in his case, was well earned. For unlike the majority of American interviewers, Stead adhered to the British method in respecting the right to privacy. He did not ask questions that were "too personal or unduly intimate," and he allowed his subjects to examine and approve the text of an interview before he published it. In the opinion of a commentator, he acclimated the interview to British soil in a restrained way by exercising "good taste and good sense throughout a long career in journalism.[52] Such a judgment is culturally relative, because by derogating from the speed and informality of the interviewing process, he reinforced divisions within transatlantic journalism that in some areas were to persist until 1914 and even beyond.

Notes

1 Henry Lucy, *Lords and Commons* (London: T. Fisher Unwin, 1921), 195.

2 Escott, *Masters of English Journalism*, 343.

3 See Charles T. Congdon, *Reminiscences of a Journalist* (Boston: James R. Osgood and Company, 1880), 242.

4 Whiteing, *My Harvest*, 213–14.

5 Young, *Men and Memories*, 266. Young was dismissed by the *Tribune* for sharing New York AP dispatches with the *Philadelphia Press*, in contravention of regulations issued by the press agency. Kluger, *Paper*, 121–2.

6 Ward is the subject of several biographies including Lately Thomas, *Sam Ward: "King of the Lobby"* (Boston: Houghton Mifflin, 1965) and Kathryn Allamong Jacob, *King of the Lobby: The Life and Times of Sam Ward, Man-About Washington in the Gilded Age* (Baltimore: Johns Hopkins University Press, 2009).

7 For details about the sharing of news between the *Tribune* and the *Daily News*, see Smalley, *Anglo-American Memories*, 198–200.

8 Stanley's complicated relationship with the *Herald* is described in Tim Jeal, *Stanley: The Impossible Life of Africa's Greatest Explorer* (London: Faber and Faber, 2007), 62–72.

9 *Sell's* (1896), 55. A British journalist described Smalley's columns as "literature and not journalism," because of the brilliance with which they were written. Harry Theobald Cozens-Hardy, *The Glorious Years: Random Recollections of Prominent Persons in Parliament, in Literature, on and off the Platform, on the Playing Fields, and in the Pulpit, the Prize Ring and the Press* (London: Robert Hale, 1953), 212.

10 Henry Spenser Wilkinson, *Thirty-Five Years, 1874–1909* (London: Constable, 1933), 104.

11 There are scattered references to Copleston in George E. Fortenberry, Stanley Garner and Robert H. Woodward, *The Correspondence of Harold Frederic* (Fort Worth: Texas Christian University Press, 1977); Richardson, *From the City to Fleet Street*, 94–5, 103–6; Don C. Seitz, *Joseph Pulitzer: His Life and Letters* (New York: Simon & Schuster, 1924), 134.

12 Maud Howe Elliott, *Uncle Sam Ward and His Circle* (New York: Macmillan, 1938), 521.

13 *Cigarette Papers* (London: Anthony Traherne, 1902), 7. Hatton also worked as New York correspondent for the London *Standard* and in 1881 delivered a famous scoop on the assassination of President Garfield, "the longest message ever sent through the cable." Dennis Griffiths, *Plant Here "The Standard"* (Houndmills: Macmillan, 1996), 15.

14 Richardson, *From the City to Fleet Street*, chapter 14.

15 On Chester Ives, see *Sell's* (1893), 15. A typical issue of the *Morning* (23 May 1892) included front-page descriptions of a hanging in Australia and of several British children being starved by a stage manager. An inside story concerned a man who was "EATEN BY CANNIBALS." The jibe about the cheapness of the paper is by Kennedy Jones, *Fleet Street & Downing Street* (London: Hutchinson, 1919), 124.

16 Ralph D. Blumenfeld, *Home Town: Story of a Dream That Came True* (London: Hutchinson, 1944), 102–12. For a synopsis of Blumenfeld's philosophy of journalism, see *The Press in My Time* (London: Rich & Cowan, 1933).

17 Sidney Dark, *Not Such a Bad Life* (London: Eyre and Spottiswoode, 1941), 65.

18 For an interpretation of gossip, see Patricia Meyer Spacks, *Gossip* (Chicago: The University of Chicago Press, 1986), chapter 1. The reference to "broad and universal humanity" is in Blumenfeld, *Press in My Time*, 35.

19 The comments are by Philip Hone, as cited in Seitz, *James Gordon Bennetts*, 69.

20 See Charles Mackay, *Life and Liberty in America: or, Sketches of a Tour in the United States and Canada, in 1857–8* (London: Smith, Elder, 1859), II, 136.

21 James, *Reverberator*, 115. An excellent account of Eugene Field's career on the *Chicago Morning News* is by his colleague Slason Thompson, *Life of Eugene Field: The Poet of Childhood* (New York: D. Appleton, 1927).

22 Benjamin Perley Poore, *Perley's Reminiscences of Sixty Years in the National Metropolis* (Philadelphia: Hubberd Brothers, 1886), I, 105; Poore, "Washington News," *Harper's New Monthly Magazine*, XLVIII (1874), 228.

23 F. B. Marbut, *News from the Capital: The Story of Washington Reporting* (Carbondale: Southern Illinois University Press, 1971), 71–3; Stoddard, *Horace Greeley*, 144.

24 Horace White of the *Chicago Tribune* received an appointment as clerk of a Senate committee during the Civil War and in return gave favorable press coverage to his sponsor. Joseph Logsdon, *Horace White, Nineteenth Century Liberal* (Westport: Greenwood, 1971), 79. There is considerable information about "corruption" of this type in Donald A. Ritchie, *Press Gallery: Congress and the Washington Correspondents* (Cambridge: Harvard University Press, 1991).

25 Andrews, *North Reports the Civil War*, 642.

26 O. O. Stealey, *Twenty Years in the Press Gallery* (New York: Published by the Author, 1906), 2.

27 Edmund Yates, *His Recollections and Experiences* (London: Richard Bentley and Son, 1884), II, 307. See Joel H. Wiener, "Edmund Yates: The Gossip as Editor," in Wiener, *Innovators and Preachers*, 259–74; Laura Smith, "Society Journalism: Its Rise and Development," *Mitchell's* (1898), 80–1; Edwards, *Dickens's Young Men*, 136–42.

28 Andrew Lang, "Letter to a Young Journalist," in Lang, *Essays in Little* (New York: Charles Scribner's Sons, 1907), 191–7.

29 O'Connor, "The New Journalism," *The New Review*, I (1889), 430; *Memoirs of an Old Parliamentarian* (London: Ernest Benn, 1929), II, 259. In the view of George Bernard Shaw, O'Connor understood that "washerwomen are as keen on society gossip as duchesses." Quoted in Roger Wilkes, *Scandal: A Scurrilous History of Gossip* (London: Atlantic Books, 2002), 8.

30 T. Wemyss Reid, "Our London Correspondent," *Macmillan's Magazine*, XXXXII (1880), 20. See also Michael MacDonagh, "The London Letter," *Mitchell's* (1899), 12–14.

31 Hunt, *Then and Now*, 67.

32 T. E. Kebbel, *Lord Beaconsfield and other Tory Memories* (London: Cassell, 1907), 227.

33 In the words of Colin Seymour-Ure, the sketch writer "paints a lively pen portrait of debates, sensing the tone of them, picking out the highlights and so on." *Press, Politics and the Public: An Essay on the Role of the National Press in the British Political Tradition* (London: Methuen, 1968), 243.

34 Lincoln Springfield, *Some Piquant People* (London: T. Fisher Unwin, 1924), 25.

35 Whitty's "descriptive and critical essays" in the *Leader* were an early version of parliamentary sketch writing that, in the words of Justin McCarthy, represented a new "style of newspaper correspondence." Edward Michael Whitty, *St. Stephen's in the Fifties: The Session, 1852–3: A Parliamentary Retrospect* (London: T. Fisher Unwin, 1906), xxxv. Frank Hill's *Political Portraits*, intended "to note and illustrate certain leading features of character," appeared for many years in the *Daily News*. Frank Harrison Hill, *Political Portraits: Characters of Some of Our Public Men* (London: Strahan, 1873), vi. Anderson's sketches were published in the *Daily Telegraph* between 1879 and 1887. David Anderson, *"Scenes" in the Commons* (London: Kegan Paul, Trench, 1884).

36 Lucy, "Early Days in the Press Gallery," *Daily News Jubilee*, 106. In an otherwise fine book, Andrew Sparrow unfairly describes Lucy as "a dapper, ultra-prolific smoothie who became the most prominent political hack of his generation."

Obscure Scribblers: A History of Parliamentary Journalism (London: Politico's, 2003), 54.

37 David Hare, *Pravda* (London: Methuen, 1986), 75. An excellent summary of the lobby system is in Seymour-Ure, *Press, Politics and the Public*, chapter 6. See also Stephen Koss, *The Rise and Fall of the Political Press in Britain: The Nineteenth Century* (Chapel Hill: The University of North Carolina Press, 1981), 238.

38 Sir Harry Brittain, *Happy Pilgrimage* (London: Hutchinson, 1946), 167.

39 Reid, "Some Reminiscences of English Journalism," 64.

40 C. V. R. Thompson, *I Lost My English Accent* (New York: G. P. Putnam's Sons, 1939), 38–40. In the 1890s a formal request for an interview with a British politician was usually sent about ten days in advance. In the United States, this was frequently accomplished on the spot. Richard Kenin, *Return to Albion: Americans in England, 1760–1940* (New York: Holt, Rinehart and Winston, 1979), 223.

41 Michael Schudson, *The Power of News* (Cambridge: Harvard University Press, 1995), 48; Raymond Blathwayt, *Interviews* (London: A. W. Hall, 1893), 352.

42 Mackay, *Forty Years' Recollections*, 418–19; Bennett, *Those United States*, 19–23. Justin McCarthy described his "martyrdom" while lecturing in the United States in 1886–7: "The interviewers...appeared everywhere, and they would take no denial, and the life of a lecturing tourist on the American continent owns no soft hours of selfish privacy." Justin McCarthy, *Reminiscences* (London: Chatto & Windus, 1889), II, 4.

43 Harold Spender, *The Fire of Life: A Book of Memories* (London: Hodder and Stoughton, 1926), 32.

44 Carlson, *Man Who Made News*, 159–61; Kenton Bird, "Who Conducted the First Interview?," *Journalism Studies Review*, no. 4 (1979), 8–14.

45 Frederic William Wile, *News is Where You Find It: Forty Years' Reporting at Home and Abroad* (Indianapolis: Bobbs-Merrill, 1939), 57–8.

46 Joseph Rammelkamp, *Pulitzer's Post-Dispatch, 1878–1883* (Princeton: Princeton University Press, 1967), 70; Seitz, *Pulitzer*, 422.

47 Quoted in Clayton, *Little Mack*, 51. Frank A. Burr, a well-known American interviewer, expressed views similar to those of McCullagh in "The Art of Interviewing," *Lippincott's Monthly Magazine*, XLVI (1890), 391–402.

48 Whiteing, *My Harvest*, 98–107.

49 Wile, *News*, 152.

50 Wiener, "Edmund Yates," 269–70; Edmund Yates, *Celebrities at Home* (London: Office of the World, 1877–9), 3 volumes.

51 W. T. Stead, *The Americanization of the World, or the Trend of the Twentieth Century* (New York: Horace Maikley, 1901), 290, 395; John Stokes, *In the Nineties* (New York: Harvester Wheatsheaf, 1989), 20.

52 Raymond Blathwayt, *Through Life and Round the World: Being the Story of My Life* (London: George Allen & Unwin, 1917), 156; Michael MacDonagh, "The Newspaper Interview," *Mitchell's* (1900), 12.

7
The New Journalism: Pulitzer and Stead

In the 1880s the specter of popular journalism finally became a reality, as the full impact of transatlantic influence began to be felt and absorbed in Britain. As Matthew Arnold was to accurately declaim (though without some of the dire consequences he hinted at), a cheap press was rapidly making its way across the Atlantic seeking a home amidst the relatively unruffled groves of Fleet Street and other centers of newspaper activity in Britain. At the outset of the decade, Britain continued to produce papers that were midway in appearance between the densely concentrated broadsheets of the 1820s and the mass circulation press of 1914. A conventional format of six columns predominated. Crossheads were used only in exceptional circumstances and illustrations appeared relatively infrequently. Both typography and pictures were a means of diversifying what has been described as a "traditionalist, pack-it-in, single-column" text.[1] The use of headlines was also limited. Multiple decks had been introduced into American journalism, and were a consistent feature of that nation's press by the 1880s. Occasionally, ten or more decks preceded a story. (The *Herald* used 17 decks when reporting on the assassination of Lincoln.) The purpose of decks was to label the news and summarize it, though most "banks" (another term for decks) continued to be little more than generic mantras such as "A Terrible Tragedy" or "Yesterday in Washington."[2] Typefaces and cases were varied slightly to lighten a monotonous vertical sequence. Even in the American press, however, the single column rule prevailed into the 1880s, which made it difficult to use headlines and pictures effectively. Technical obstacles remained the chief barrier because the type used in rotary presses would frequently scatter as it was spun rapidly about, although in Britain an additional psychological block to visual excess existed. Harmsworth believed, for example, that "changing the type is a most serious thing," and that "the effect on ... readers may be disastrous." It is instructive to note that the *Times*, in its effort to perpetuate an image of "dignity, respectability, tradition, and cultivation," did not publish any double column headlines before 1932.[3]

In cultural terms this adherence to conventional forms helps to explain the tempered reaction in Britain to mass journalism. As John Carey has observed, British intellectuals of the late nineteenth century feared that popular journalism would make a "traditional cultural elite" redundant and that the "alternative culture" replacing it would underwrite the wants of semiliterate groups of readers.[4] As if to document these anxieties the journalist Edward Raymond Thompson deplored the "complete standardisation of things of the spirit" that would inevitably transpire when and if a journalism of amusement – typified by visual libertinism – replaced one of restraint. Thompson affirmed that serious teaching was required in journalism as in every walk of life; unless an agreed upon standard was adhered to, a deep "spiritual gulf" would inevitably widen between the classes and the masses.[5] Even James Gordon Bennett, Jr. had doubts. He told a *Herald* reporter in 1888: "With money, any d—fool can get the news; but it takes a man of brains to know how to display and treat it after it arrives in the office."[6]

The key developments in British and American print journalism in the 1880s took place against a background of deep social change. In America, a surge of immigration began at about this time that greatly increased the size of the potential newspaper reading public. Until then educational and charity institutions had facilitated the integration of waves of newcomers into daily life; these institutions now found it a formidable task to cope with the millions of non-English speaking peoples who were arriving from central and southern Europe, as well as from Asia. Reflecting this trend, a foreign language press came into existence – German, Polish, Yiddish, Russian, Italian, Chinese – that "Americanized" many of these immigrants, who in disproportionate numbers settled in New York, Chicago and St. Louis, three cities where powerful traditions of urban journalism had already taken firm root. One of these immigrants was Joseph Pulitzer, who was to become the foremost innovator of New Journalism in America during the late nineteenth century. The Hungarian-born Pulitzer arrived in St. Louis in 1865 at the close of the Civil War and initially found a job as a reporter on the *Westliche Post*, a German-language newspaper. He learned the craft of journalism, which he put to work in the service of other immigrants when he subsequently acquired ownership of two of the foremost newspapers in the Anglo-American world: the *St. Louis Post-Dispatch* (1878) and the New

York *World* (1883). The "culture of pastiche" that Pulitzer and other pioneering newspapermen developed in response to the diverse needs of these newcomers did much to revolutionize the American press.[7]

Comparable patterns of immigration occurred in Britain, which also gave an indirect jumpstart to the establishment of a mass circulation press. But the number of immigrants was smaller in size, and on the whole British culture was less responsive to the rapid assimilation of these new groups. As a result, in Britain the cheap press of the final decades of the century took aim instead at native-born clerks and workingmen, many of them beneficiaries of the newly created system of state education. During the 1880s and 1890s, a resurgent labor movement attracted support among the working classes, though the great majority of penny and halfpenny daily newspapers that sprang into existence to provide them with entertaining and readable content abjured serious political content. In both Britain and America therefore a path was cleared for key transformations in journalism, what one former newspaperman has described as a deathblow to its "mandarin style."[8]

The vogue phrase that, more than any other, signified a break with the old journalism during the 1880s was "human interest," an American term first used in the pressroom of Dana's *Sun* in the middle years of the century.[9] In the journalistic sense "human interest" was permeable enough to absorb a multiplicity of textual and visual meanings. It allowed for the kind of diluted sensationalism that found a footing amidst the raucous journalism of Pulitzer and Stead. It also encouraged a "tabloid" style of discourse reflecting both the increased demands of speed and the need to reach out to less literate readers. Some British pressmen (along with a growing number of women) aped the zippy, news-oriented form of reporting that had become characteristic of urban journalism in America, what at the time was described as a "brief, breezy and briggity" form of composition. Others adopted the Americanized news language of the wire agencies, which, at its best, was redolent of an objective kind of factuality and, at its worst, was "unimaginative, flat (and) dependable rather than daring."[10]

Irrespective of the form it took this concision of prose represented a repudiation of the "descriptive style" of writing popularized by the *Daily Telegraph* and other London newspapers. In the hands of Sala and a number of his contemporaries, "journalese" had become allusive and meandering. It connected only tangentially with less sophisticated readers and, in some ways, embodied an element of condescension in addressing working-class consumers in the process of self-education. A more demotic means of discourse was required, of the kind to be found (in one form or another) in the American press. In the soothing words of Frederick Greenwood, the editor of the *Pall Mall Gazette*, a hackneyed style of journalism had to give way to a "good English of common life." Among other things, this emergent journalism featured speed, increased objectivity, short paragraphs ("paras") in place of extended leading articles, the crossheading of columns and the dissemination of news by means of "ordinary" speech patterns, "a splashy, jolly, colloquial style," in the words of Robert Blatchford, the Manchester socialist and journalist. Dullness needed to be eschewed at all costs, and a measure of visual fluency generated without sacrificing too much in the way of substance.[11]

Among those journalists in Britain most adroit at making the initial transition to this American-inspired New Journalism were W. T. Stead, in the *Pall Mall Gazette,* and T. P. O'Connor, in the *Star*, the *Sun* and several other newspapers. O'Connor's advocacy of a discourse of condensation in journalism is especially worthy of notice. In a widely quoted passage from an essay that he published in 1889, he compared modern journalism to a street piano that yielded music, neither "classical, nor very melodious, and (with) a certain absence of soul," but with notes that were "clear, crisp, (and) sharp." O'Connor affirmed that the obligation of the journalist was to "tell the story of each day in the briefest, the most picturesque, the most graphic fashion."[12] He and Stead set out to fulfill this obligation during the 1880s, a development that critics of the New Journalism (still very much in the majority) condemned for its vulgarity and lowering of standards.

As Roger Rosenblatt has observed, presentation is an important facet of human-interest journalism. (Rosenblatt wittily quipped that "if a journalist could get his message across with fish, the world would stink with misinformation.")[13] Yet content is also critical, and this embodies strands of journalism such as color and presentation, news provided on a culturally democratic basis and, most disturbing of all to opponents of mass circulation journalism, anything that smacks even peripherally of sensationalism. The lines demarcating these several areas are blurred. Yet irrespective of emphasis, the shift from an older to a more innovative form of press discourse became pronounced in the 1880s, as did the undisputed phenomenon of American influence.

To understand the idea of color or presentation in journalism, one can do worse than turn to the writings of Ralph Blumenfeld. In the *Press in My Time* (1933), a penetrating analysis of modern journalism, Blumenfeld summarized human-interest journalism in the following way: "It recognises that all the episodes of life worthy of being reported in print are stories about human beings, dramas or comedies, the pathos or humour of which is intensified by the fact of their being true."[14] The crucial phrase here is "stories about human beings," as it had been for Bennett in the 1830s and 1840s, and was to be for Harmsworth and Hearst in the 1890s. The idea of news as a story embodying a continuing narrative thread is American in origin. Bennett was the first important journalist to make this explicit by engendering a state of expectancy in his readers, as he wove episodes of crime news into the pages of the *Herald*. His aim was to present news in a sequentially comprehensible and exciting way, as if it were a literary plot line. And when "real" news proved deficient in its possibilities, a good journalist, he believed, should make the atmosphere vibrate with "feature stories, color, (and) romance," a point made by Theodore Dreiser while working in a newsroom in St. Louis much later in the century.[15] Bennett, Dana, Pulitzer, Raymond and other American pressmen came to believe that if a story was told well and the lines between fiction and reality conjoined by means of familiar narrative devices, readers would invariably return the following day to find out what happened. Before the 1890s relatively little in the way of a "good story" framework of this kind existed in British journalism, other than, perhaps, in parliamentary sketch writing, which offered a kind of personalized vision of politics set within a conventional framework.[16]

Human-interest journalism was also integrally linked to a version of the news that was egalitarian in scope. It applied a democratic formula to the tastes of its readers, who by the 1880s were assumed to represent nearly every point in the social spectrum. "Everything that happens in the world is news which interests somebody," wrote James Annand in the *Newcastle Daily Leader*, a penny paper that he founded in 1885. "We are not in our news columns the censors, but the historians of public morals."[17] Annand banned racing tips from his paper as if in contradiction to this assertion (as did a number of other British journalists including Stead), but a puritan inconsistency of this kind was relatively minor when set within a larger context. More significant was the belief that undifferentiated news coverage represented an exciting point of embarkation, which took hold in American pressrooms and an increasing number of British pressrooms by the mid-1880s. Journalism, affirmed the New York *Tribune* in support of this conviction, "busies itself with everything that affects the public welfare."

Lord Salisbury sneeringly categorized this conception of news as one in which papers were "written by office boys for office boys" (he was alluding to the *Daily Mail*). But it became a central component of the New Journalism and was taken up with enthusiasm by numerous journalists. "It would be worth my while, sir, to give a million dollars," commented Raymond of the *New York Times*, "if the Devil would come and tell me every evening, as he does Bennett, what the people of New York would like to read about next morning."[18] More than any other British newspaperman of the day, Alfred Harmsworth possessed the editorial instincts necessary for this type of journalism. He believed that newspapers were fundamentally "news recording machines," whose chief rationale was "the quick, accurate presentation of the world's news in the form of a careful digest." Energized with this conviction, he helped to execute a press revolution in Britain that appropriated the American definition of news, which was conceived as socially and politically neutral, and more important, as shaped by the needs of a general interest audience.

A further variant of human-interest journalism was sensationalism, a broad term that, in Harmsworth's view, signified "anything out of the ordinary." (The press historian Mitchell Stephens uses the phrase "peculiar subset of life" to define sensationalism, which is redolent of something slightly more off kilter.) Morrill Goddard, a journalist who worked at sensational journalism effectively for both Pulitzer and Hearst, was deeply cynical, if insightful, about this phenomenon. He believed that "sensations, emotions or instincts" are "normal, natural impelling forces born into us." Intelligence is a less elemental force than "natural predatory instincts"; it is therefore best to attire the news in garish colors since this represents a practical obeisance to the unpleasant vagaries of human behavior.[19]

For much of the century, American editors gave scope to a mild version of sensationalism appropriate to the mid- to late-nineteenth century, that is, one featuring the atypical, while continuing to set aside a proper amount of space for public advocacy. Pulitzer fits this paradigm well. He believed that he could crusade against corruption in public life more successfully if he held the attention of his readers. "I want to talk to a nation, not to a select committee," he commented. To maintain the interests of these readers, he believed it necessary (as did O'Connor and Harmsworth) to give them what he thought they wanted, which meant random peeps into that level of life (admittedly unsavory) where a man is said to bite a dog, rather than the opposite.[20] Stead resembled Pulitzer in this way, though he was a little more finicky about playing to the crowd. Both men have been accused of engaging in self-justifying commercial behavior, which is true to a degree. Yet each of them imbibed the democratic notion that the press must reflect the predilections of its readers at all times, even if, as Evelyn Waugh's fictional journalist, Corker, candidly observed: "News is what a chap who doesn't care much about anything (else) wants to read."[21]

More than anything else speed emerged as the transformative element in transatlantic journalism during the 1880s and played a decisive role in the Americanization of the British press. By the second half of the century, it had begun to penetrate nearly all aspects of journalism. It was a palpable phenomenon to visitors to America, who depicted the "rush" and seeming frenzy of life in that country. Since the days of Bennett American reporters appeared to be moving about restlessly in search of "beats" and "scoops." (Both of these key press terms are of American derivation.) They used the telegraph wires whenever they could and were occasionally described as "legmen." Their editors instructed them to "rush it lively," so as to prevent news from turning stale. A statement attributed to Frederic Hudson, the well regarded managing editor of the *Herald*, illustrates this: "Bear in mind that the Herald must never be beaten."[22] Chicago appears to have been driven by speed even more than New York. The ineffable Ben Hecht-Charles MacArthur saga of modern journalism, *The Front Page*, with its ceaseless chatter and frantic obsession to find and disseminate news, was set in that city in the 1920s, and has served ever since as a paradigm for American big city journalism. Martin Mayer, who has written about the media in late twentieth-century America, contends that "the tradition of the scoop has been cultivated more jealously and singlemindedly in Chicago" than anywhere else in the world."[23]

Speed is not invariably synonymous with unreliability. Some of the best news stories have been composed under accelerating pressure; some of the worst have been written amidst conditions of relative calm. Still, there is a rough correlation between the need to get a story into print as quickly as possible and the likelihood of that story containing inaccuracies. In the late nineteenth century, American reporters were known to turn up suddenly – at a police station, a city morgue, a public meeting – and demand information. If they did not get what they wanted, they sometimes wrote the story rapidly anyway, with or without factual validation. This was especially true on evening newspapers, which were published under conditions of intense activity and, on the whole, had a larger readership base in America than in Britain. The key requirements for an evening newspaper, according to Kennedy Jones, were "exceptional quickness, quickness of perception, quickness of decision, quickness of execution." He asserted that the commuters who read these papers, which featured brief news summaries, serialized fiction, and shortened leaders and parliamentary reports, were "desirous of amusement and relaxation but bored if special mental effort be demanded." In a rush to get a scoop into print, editors sometimes winked and nodded at inaccuracies and sometimes paid special bonuses for speedy news stories. That such machinations created difficulties for at least some journalists is evident from the comment of a New York reporter: "I find I am falling into the habit of tinging things and of trusting to my imagination. I am frequently forced to do this because I have no time and because it is often impossible to make personal investigation."[24]

By the 1880s, speed was coming to be an integral part of British as well as American journalism. On both sides of the Atlantic newspapers made extensive use of the telegraph and promoted the virtues of speed in their news columns. The *Times,* tied to conventional journalism in so many areas, made nearly as much of a fetish out of collecting and distributing news rapidly as did Bennett's *Herald.* Even the reporting of parliamentary debates in Britain was based increasingly upon speed. Newspapers published detailed reports of the evening's debates in the following morning's editions, an outcome achieved by groups of short-hand reporters who took "turns" in the gallery that sometimes lasted less than three minutes each. In his book, *English Journalism,* published in 1882, Charles Pebody captured the essence of this highly specialized world of speed, characterized by "the constant patter of telegraph boys all through the night, with their showers of pink envelopes ... the rattle of machinery ... the glare of gas ... the busy scenes in the printing office." Writers of leading articles worked under conditions of intense speed, "at the point of the pen," to use the words of a literary primer of the period. Henry Wilkinson recollects writing editorials for the *Morning Post* in the early hours of the morning while debates in parliament were still taking place. His paragraphs were transmitted to the compositor's room slip by slip as he composed them while the lawmakers were still delivering their speeches.[25]

Notwithstanding this shift towards "American-style" speed in the British press, there continued to be important differences between the two countries. Bernard Weisberger has defined the two prevailing approaches to journalism: "racy, aggressive, and independent" in America; "solid, careful, and slightly bent under a sense of official responsibility" in Britain.[26] By the 1890s, the Park Row neighborhood of lower Manhattan, where New York's leading newspapers were published, could validly be described as "seething and bubbling," while in journalistic terms at least no similar words might be applied with any degree of accuracy to Fleet Street. American city reporters were given regular beats to cover by the 1880s, which increased the likelihood that they would be able to acquire steady sources of information, whereas the practice in London was for reporters to be given assignments in a more leisurely fashion as they arrived for work or in advance by post. When John Augustus O'Shea was employed by the *Standard* in the late 1870s, he spent most of his days (as he shamefacedly confessed) "killing time." He complained about this to his editor and was reprimanded: "Upon my word, you are a most unreasonable fellow. Don't you get paid regularly? We cannot invent work for you." This relaxed attitude sometimes produced impressive results, as at the time of the "Jack the Ripper" murders in 1888, when reporters for the *Star* and other London papers diligently scoured the East End in pursuit of "picturesque and lurid" details of the crimes. Too often, though, in the words of the press historian Harold Herd, it made for a diminished "news sense."[27]

On the morning of October 22, 1881, a group of young boys were seen to be parading snappily down Market Street in Manchester. They wore "Tit-Bits" bands in their green caps to herald the arrival of a new type of periodical, one that was to play a major role in the New Journalism. *Tit-Bits (From the Most Interesting Books, Periodicals and Newspapers in the World)* was launched amidst a flurry of enthusiasm and it continued to circulate until 1984. During its 103 years of existence, it spawned numerous imitators on both sides of the Atlantic, including the phenomenally successful *Reader's Digest*, founded in Connecticut in 1922. For decades *Tit-Bits* sustained a large circulation. It left behind a significant, if controversial, legacy to mass circulation journalism.

What was the appeal of this penny weekly magazine, which one historian has deftly characterized as "prototypical junk food," and others have referred to as "boiled" or "snippets" journalism?[28] How did it fit into the pattern of experimentation and innovation in the popular press? *Tit-Bits* mostly consisted of excerpts from other publications and was intended to meet the ephemeral requirements of busy readers. Its early numbers featured anecdotes, tales, historical ruminations and miscellaneous "tit-bits" of information. Subsequent issues were more varied in content and included a series of competitions. For example, prizes were awarded to the reader who submitted the best Christmas story (a "Tit-Bits Villa" worth 600 pounds), or to those correctly answering a question such as: "Why does anxiety turn the hair grey?"[29] George Newnes, who created *Tit-Bits,* as well as the enormously successful *Strand Magazine* (1891) and the *Westminster Gazette* (1893), was a Lancashire businessman who understood that the "crowds of hardworking people" nurtured in state primary schools hungered after non-demanding reading matter. One writer has characterized Newnes as "a veritable literary physician" who took the "public's pulse" and knew "exactly what it wanted," while a recent biographer has described him more sympathetically as a man who created "a kind of synergy between business and benevolence, popular and quality literature, old and new journalism, and ultimately, culture and profit."[30] *Tit-Bits* possessed just enough gruel to satisfy those craving a thin literary diet; at the same time, it fulfilled the modest expectations of readers who were seeking little more than amusement.

Several things need to be said about "T-B" and its immediate successor journals, Harmsworth's *Answers to Correspondents* (1888) and *Pearson's Weekly,* launched by Cyril Arthur Pearson in 1890, whose logo read: "To Interest, To Elevate, To Amuse." The negative side of such journalism is patent, namely, its extreme disconnectedness. Textual fragmentation of this kind risked becoming at worst a near-parody of the intense compression of print already under way. Digests and summaries, or so it seemed, were becoming available everywhere. And while the contents of such periodicals exemplified a developing ideal of cultural democracy, in the sense that something was there for everybody to read, they produced little more than a distilled reworking of what had already appeared in print. Stead was not far off the mark when he referred to these journals as constituting a "gramophone press."[31]

Viewed in a larger framework, though, *Tit-Bits* and its competitors served up a version of "junk food" that was not wholly insalubrious. Typical issues included articles about legal and historical subjects, as well as abridged translations from European literature. *Answers* (formerly *Answers to Correspondents*) published quips, riddles and inspirational essays in an interactive format, with titles such as "1000 Ways to Earn a Living" and "How to Make Money at Home." (It also featured a sensationalized section called "Strange Experiences," which resembled American popular journalism at its most extreme.)[32] None of this was likely to significantly elevate the minds of readers, especially because most of the articles rarely exceeded two or three sentences or a brief paragraph. Yet even that feature of *Tit-Bits* or *Answers* most deprecated by contemporaries – the numerous contests intended solely to boost circulation – occasionally raised it to a modestly higher level. For example, competitions were held periodically to determine the best work of fiction submitted, and on one occasion, Grant Allen, later to be a much-admired novelist, won the contest.

In both Britain and the United States, popular culture was steeped in elements of self-help, which contributed to the success of this "junk food" journalism. The ambitious clerks and skilled workingmen and women of the late Victorian and Edwardian period who read *Tit-Bits* and aspired to upward mobility were recognizable figures of the social landscape. Even allowing for a degree of literary hyperbole, such cultural strivers represent a solid modicum of reality. To be sure, this variant of educational self-help with its "trivial pursuit" kind of useful knowledge, was pallid when set against a hard-grained journal, such as the *Penny Magazine* of the 1830s. And as critics have rightly pointed out, it bore the imprint of unalloyed commercial endeavor by publishers who were quick to intuit the possibilities of amassing large profits. Yet it also underscored the widespread existence of a genuine urge to improvement among the less affluent classes and, to a degree, satisfied this democratic aspiration.[33]

The relationship of *Tit-Bits* to daily newspaper journalism is important. By the 1880s the content of magazines and newspapers had begun to intersect, particularly in America. Cheap newspapers there were beginning to incorporate magazine features (of the *Tit-Bits* style), thus obscuring the differences between these two forms of journalism. This was especially true of the American Sunday press, which oriented its contents towards feature stories and entertainment ("gossip and small talk and fashion and society news"), a departure from the daily focus on news coverage. Unlike Britain's Sunday papers, which were largely stratified by readership (as they still are today), the American "Sundays" were essentially classless. At the same time, *Tit-Bits* type magazine elements were beginning to be absorbed into some daily newspapers in Britain, such as the *Daily Telegraph*.

Tit-Bits and its competitors also had personal links to the New Journalism. Pearson and Harmsworth subsequently moved on to found two of the seminal products of mass circulation journalism: the *Daily Express* and the *Daily Mail*. Pearson, who was described caustically by Stead as a "champion hustler" because of his proclivity to lift ideas from others, managed *Tit-Bits* for seven years before launching *Pearson's Weekly*. He gained for the latter journal the largest of the "junk food" circulations by promoting "pleasant and profitable" stunts and, in the words of a historian, anticipating "just what the average person wants to read." The *Daily Express*, which he established in 1900, became an enormous commercial success, in part because it applied the *Tit-Bits* formula of condensation and brevity to its news coverage.[34]

Harmsworth was even more directly influenced by *Tit-Bits*. His career as a newspaper proprietor, the most important in Britain's history prior to 1914, derived from the nature of his initial interaction with *Tit-Bits*. As a freelance journalist in Fleet Street in the 1880s, he was inspired by the "crazy nature" of the magazine and the compelling personality of Newnes. He later told Max Pemberton that Newnes was "only at the beginning of a development which is going to change the whole face of journalism." Harmsworth contributed regularly to *Tit-Bits* before founding *Answers to Correspondents*, which proffered the spurious claim to be an "absolutely new kind" of paper, when it was in fact an imitation of *Tit-Bits*. The subsequent contributions to popular journalism of Harmsworth, this "completely convinced democrat," were derived to a considerable extent from the *Tit-Bits* philosophy of discovering exactly what it is that ordinary people wanted and giving it to them.[35]

Tit-Bits and its rivals comprised a major form of the New Journalism. But more serious by far was the kind of daily newspaper journalism personified by Pulitzer and Stead, which has understandably enjoyed a healthier reputation among historians. The critical contributions made by both men to press history can best be assessed within a transatlantic setting. It is inadequate, for example, to attempt to make sense of the work of Stead (or even Harmsworth) without taking into account Pulitzer, whose most important innovations preceded theirs by several years and had a decisive influence on them. Nor is it sufficient for American press historians to frame Pulitzer's innovations exclusively in a national setting. During these decades a rich transatlantic tapestry was created by the work of numerous American and British journalists. If *Tit-Bits* stood for a degree of literary slumming, Pulitzer and Stead presented a contrasting combination of highmindedness and sensationalism. Both men nurtured a public service model of journalism in which the interests of the community, however broadly defined, were rigorously upheld. At the same time, they used whatever press techniques they had acquired to gain their immediate objectives and, notwithstanding their persistent denials, enjoyed the public success that accrued to them.

Joseph Pulitzer spent his early years in St. Louis and, like Stead, was a working journalist before becoming an editor-proprietor of newspapers. His perspective was that of a hands-on pressman who understood exactly how a newspaper was put together and what motivated its employees to do their best. His experiences on the *St. Louis Post-Dispatch* (1878–83) and the *World*, which he owned and managed from 1883 until his death in 1911, are among the most impressive in transatlantic press history because in both St. Louis and New York he converted newspapers of moderate influence and attainments into enormously successful popular journals. He did this by introducing a potpourri of imaginative typography, daring illustrations, stunts, interviews ("exclusives"), demotic content, imperialistic rhetoric, women's features and investigative work on behalf of reform. He also drew upon the resources of a brilliant staff, including John A. Cockerill, his managing editor, who followed him from St. Louis to New York, and Charles Chapin, the celebrated city editor of the *World,* who, in the words of Irvin Cobb, worshipped the "inky-nosed, nine-eyed, clay-footed god called News." Both men helped to bring about a revolution in journalism that was based to a considerable extent on speed.[36]

Pulitzer's motto for the *World* was "Forever Unsatisfied," which reflected his questing approach to journalism. Everything was grist for his mill, including crime, politics, baseball and madcap stunts like the "Around the World" extravaganza undertaken by "Nellie Bly" (Elizabeth Cochran) for the newspaper in 1889–90, as well as her spectacular debut articles in 1887, which involved getting herself incarcerated in the Women's Lunatic Asylum on Blackwell's Island in Manhattan, in order to report on the abusive treatment of its unfortunate inmates. The detective writer, James M. Cain, got it about right when he described Pulitzer as having "an editorial page addressed to intellectuals, a sporting section addressed to the fancy, a Sunday magazine addressed to morons, and twenty other things that don't seem to be addressed to anybody."[37] Pulitzer possessed the unbridled enthusiasm of the self-made immigrant who believes in the limitless potential of his adopted country. And he created press bombshells in both St. Louis and New York, with the two-cent *World* (reduced to a penny in 1896) attaining for a time a circulation of 250,000, the largest of any daily newspaper in America. Pulitzer was a democrat in the cultural meaning of the word (as was Stead) because he understood – drawing upon the work of journalists on both sides of the Atlantic who had trod a populist path before him – that in a mass circulation press, coverage of the news needed to intersect with ordinary interests. Most revealing were his instructions to his editors: to go after news that was "original, distinctive, dramatic, romantic, thrilling, unique, curious, quaint, humorous, odd, (and) apt to be talked about." Equally illuminating were the words that adorned the placards hanging on the walls of his office: "Accuracy, Terseness, Accuracy!"[38]

Pulitzer believed strongly in visual journalism, though he tended to shun some of its more elaborate techniques. He aimed to entrap the eye by making pictures a complement to text, especially in the pages of the *Post-Dispatch,* an evening newspaper. Evening papers rely heavily upon visibility since they are dependent upon chance buying. Commuters returning home after a day's work are more likely to make a purchase if their eyes are drawn to a striking headline or picture, and

Figure 7.1   Joseph Pulitzer: Don C. Seitz, *Joseph Pulitzer* (1924)

in the 1880s such commuters existed in far greater numbers than previously. According to a journalist who knew Pulitzer well, he aimed to make his newspapers "typographically handsome," so that they would not be ignored by "the toiling masses who rush downtown on the East Side elevated railways or surge across the bridges."[39] During the 1860s, evening newspapers gained support in America because they published fast-breaking news in successive editions, including late sports results or stock prices. Pulitzer was one of the first journalists in the transatlantic world to comprehend the potential of evening papers as mass circulation organs and integrate their features fully into his journalism. (In 1887, the *World* began to publish an evening edition as a complement to its morning edition.) By 1890, two thirds of the newspapers published in the United States appeared either in the late afternoon or early evening.

Improved typography was a key to Pulitzer's journalism. He published illustrations (line drawings and half tones), together with political caricatures and cartoons on the front page of the *World*, many of them executed by Walt McDougall, who achieved considerable renown during these years. With the encouragement of Cockerill, an avid proponent of visual print, he reduced the number of decks for purposes of clarity, and substituted assorted typefaces and ink shadings to highlight news stories. At the same time, the remaining decks were more sensationalized ("A Bullet-Proof Skull," "Beaten with Blazing Brands").[40] Pulitzer also introduced indented sub-heads (or crossheads) to draw attention to news stories, a device subsequently adopted by Stead in his *Pall Mall Gazette*. He was also the first important journalist to run his leading news story in the right hand column of the front page, a practice still largely followed in the United States, though not in Britain. This tactical placement had a dual purpose: it made it easier to continue to read a lengthy news story, which could then be carried over into the left hand column of the second page, and it increased the likelihood that the story would visually attract passersby.

In addition, Pulitzer used inverted pyramids, or summary leads, in the *World*, though not with any consistency until the early 1890s, when they began to come into general use in Britain as well. The summary lead is a key innovation of modern journalism, because it signified a further shift away from traditional narrative reporting to a form of journalism emphasizing speed. The nearly universal use of the telegraph, together with the tendency to condense news, made it incumbent to squeeze the essence of a news story into the first paragraph. The employment of the summary lead meant that even if an item of interest subsequently emerged (necessitating a radical shortening of the original story), the gist of the account would have been conveyed to readers. The days of Russell's serendipitous literary narrations were nearing an end.

Although Pulitzer transformed journalism visually, his primary contribution to transatlantic journalism (like that of Stead) had to do with content. His chief aim was to make human-interest news available, and the best examples of this are to be found in his crime and sports reporting, and in his investigative work. Intensive front-page coverage was given to crime in both the *Post-Dispatch* and the *World*. Pulitzer elaborated upon Bennett's conception of the "crime story" as a developing narrative and brought news accounts of crimes to the attention of his readers by means of striking headlines. He did not regard this as "mere sensationalism"; instead he viewed it both functionally and from a "moral point of view," even while engaging in intense competition with less scrupulous proprietors like Hearst.[41]

Another central component of the New Journalism was sports reporting, which in America meant primarily the coverage of boxing and baseball. In 1884–5, reporters from the *World* closely tracked the exploits of John L. Sullivan, the heavyweight champion, helping to stoke interest in boxing and, as a byproduct, assisting in the creation of one of the country's first celebrities. "Prize fighting is coarse and demoralizing and … vulgar," declaimed Pulitzer with a touch of sanctimony, but "people like to read about (it), and we endeavor to supply the demand as best we can."[42] Baseball was even more pivotal. By the late 1880s, American newspapers were starting to give intensive coverage to this national sport, and Pulitzer's *World* was one of the first to do so, notably in its evening edition, which provided the latest scores and results. Pulitzer was the first newspaper proprietor on either side of the Atlantic to hire journalists with expertise in a particular sport and the first to create a regular sports department. When the *World* began to publish turf news and racing results it generated opposition from religious groups (as was the case in Britain) because it was alleged, no doubt correctly, that such a practice was likely to stimulate an appetite for gambling. Yet in a more positive way the dissemination of racing news by means of telegraph wires further demonstrated how speed (when tied to the interests of ordinary readers) was becoming a critical element of an emerging mass press.

Investigative crusades are among the best-known feature of Pulitzer's journalism, an area that links him closely to Stead. Unlike Stead, Pulitzer had important precedents to draw upon. Beginning with the penny press of the 1830s, reporters in the United States had become accustomed to ferreting out information from clandestine byways, and Pulitzer found it comparatively easy to tap into this practice. While other journalists, including some in Britain, had undertaken investigative campaigns with the object of gaining narrowly defined ends, he launched continuing crusades against corrupt local interests, placing both the news and editorial columns of his newspaper at the service of these causes for extended periods of time. He genuinely believed that news was an appendage of views. "My heart was, still is, and in spirit always will be in the editorial page," Pulitzer declaimed. Accordingly, he issued the following instructions to his editors: "Never drop a big thing until you have gone to the bottom of it. Continuity! Continuity! Continuity! until the subject is really finished."[43]

Pulitzer concentrated his energies on those corrupting social evils he believed to be most in need of radical change. The Standard Oil and Bell Telephone companies, tax evaders, corrupt policemen, white slavers, proprietors of sweatshops: all of these and more were targets of unceasing attacks in the *World*. By indirection at least this confirmed a growing conviction (based in part on the experience of the Sunday press in Britain) that an overlay of popular radicalism helped to sell newspapers. Yet if Pulitzer's crusades were craftily interfused with dollops of modulated sensationalism, they had a deeper public purpose, just as did those of Stead. "Above knowledge, above news, above intelligence," observed Pulitzer, "the heart and soul of a paper lies in its moral sense, in its courage, its integrity, its humanity, its sympathy for the oppressed, its independence, its devotion to the public welfare, its anxiety to render public service."[44] He and Stead were both widely distrusted as enthusiasts. Yet, at the same time, they were persuasive enough to make hundreds of thousands of readers in both America and Britain believe in their passion and integrity. For the most part these readers were probably right to do so.

Pulitzer acted as an inspiration to Stead, though the latter acknowledged his debt only sparingly. Both men championed an "Americanized" democratic press. Pulitzer's feelings were harvested as an immigrant from Europe in the densely populated streets of St. Louis; Stead gazed with rapture at America, the idealized nation of his dreams. Twice he visited the United States, in 1893–4 and again in 1897: the first time to attend the World's Fair in Chicago, on the second occasion to investigate social conditions in New York. A planned third visit to his "adopted homeland" was unexpectedly aborted, in April 1912, when he drowned as a passenger on the Titanic. According to a popular account that was most likely apocryphal, he helped women and children descend into life-boats and, as the luxury liner sank, directed the ship's orchestra to play "Nearer My God to Thee."[45]

Stead was an irrepressible enthusiast for American culture. Unlike many of his colleagues, he does not appear to have cultivated a wide range of personal contacts among American journalists. But he identified intimately with what he perceived to be the fluid, egalitarian nature of life in the United States. His book, *The Americanization of the World, or the Trend of the Twentieth Century,* published in 1901, exudes these sentiments in an impassioned way. Americanization, according to Stead, represented a culmination of Britain's destiny; a common citizenship of the two peoples would represent a valid acknowledgement that "the hegemony of the race has passed from Westminster to Washington." He kept a large "Anglo-American" flag in his office, which merged the colors of both countries and which he described as "the flag of the future." Stead believed that America excelled in three areas: popular education, efficient productivity and, most striking of all, democracy. He wanted Britain to ingest the best qualities of each area, and he maintained that journalism offered the means for doing this since it articulated "the aspirations, the ideas, and the prejudices of the masses of the people." "The English newspaper press twenty years hence will be Americanised," Stead wrote. "It will be more intelligent, better printed, more copiously illustrated, less stodgy, more enterprising."[46]

Stead was a great reforming pressman who demonstrated spasmodic touches of originality and brilliance. He did much to create the New Journalism in Britain in its "worthiest form," as a contemporary observed, because he approached his task with sincerity and fixity of purpose. He believed that a journalist must be animated by an "inspiring ideal," so as to become "the uncrowned king of an educated democracy." Perhaps Kennedy Jones came closest to the mark when he observed that Stead "flung wide open every window in his newspaper office."[47] The son of a Congregationalist minister, he began his career as a novice on the halfpenny Darlington *Northern Echo* in the early 1870s, and after securing a reputation for his editing skills, moved to the *Pall Mall Gazette*, a respected London evening newspaper with a small circulation. His innovatory work on this paper was considerable, but as with the contributions of others it must be viewed in context. Just as Pulitzer's ventures involved incursions into territory partly plowed elsewhere, the same was true for Stead. Under the guidance of Frederick Greenwood, its first editor, the *Pall Mall Gazette* had a palpable impact on the press. Greenwood encouraged investigative work by journalists, including his brother James, and among other things introduced an "Occasional Notes" section into the *Pall Mall Gazette,* which Stead appropriated effectively after he became editor.

When Stead became John Morley's assistant editor in 1880 and three years later was appointed sole editor, he was ready to undertake a wholesale transformation of the newspaper. "I will revolutionise everything and sink or swim," he wrote.[48] His changes fit broadly into three categories: sensationalism; typography and interviewing; and news condensation. It is the first of these that links him most closely to Pulitzer. His series of investigatory articles entitled "The Maiden Tribute of Modern Babylon," which exposed child prostitution in London, made him a household name. Even earlier he had popularized the genre of personal journalism by waging an aggressive campaign to improve housing conditions for the poor, based on an influential pamphlet by the Reverend Andrew Mearns titled *The Bitter Outcry of Outcast London* (1883). Stead also pursued other "sensational" agitations, including one on behalf of General Gordon, whose martyrdom with his soldiers inside the walls of Khartoum in 1885, at the hands of a native force, led to a prolonged political crisis in Britain.

In each instance (though especially during the "Maiden Tribute" campaign), Stead invigorated his news coverage with striking decks such as "Strapping Girls Down" and "You Want a Maid, Do You?" These "Americanisms" made him even more controversial (and distrusted) than Pulitzer, whose reforming predilections were less attuned to issues of personal morality. In 1894, Stead published an electrifying volume, *If Christ Came to Chicago,* which attacked with unexampled fury the power of the trusts and monopolies he had discovered in that city after two extended visits. Stead proffered Jesus as an "accepted standard of ideal character," and denounced the plutocracy in Chicago for establishing a tyranny that was "being installed behind the convenient mask of republican form." To be sure, he and Pulitzer sold many more newspapers and made far more profit than they would have done without this kind of sensationalism. Yet they claimed with justification that their fiery campaigns against injustice caused readers to sit up and take notice. Stead convincingly told the young journalist, Wickham Steed: "To be a journalist, not a mere cumberer of the ground, you must have something to say." Both he and Pulitzer may have been what Alfred Milner shrewdly opined of the former alone: a combination of Don Quixote and P. T. Barnum. Yet whatever their motives (which undoubtedly fluctuated from time to time), they imparted a serious tone to the development of mass circulation journalism in the 1880s.[49]

Typography and interviewing may helpfully be viewed as a common strand because they exemplify Stead's continuing efforts to adapt American ideas to Britain. As with pictorial journalism in general, typography derives from the conviction (in Stead's words) that "good journalism consists much more of the proper labelling and displaying of your goods than in the writing of leading articles." He began to use American-style crossheads ("sub-heads") and multiple decks, which until then had appeared only intermittently in Britain.[50] Sometimes these decks verged on the lurid (as in the "Maiden Tribute" series); on other occasions he merely attempted to highlight a story by providing it with an equivalent to chapter titles or epigraphs. During his editorship Greenwood had taken a hesitant step in this direction by subdividing the *Pall Mall Gazette*'s leaders into short paragraphs. Stead effectively made the newspaper accessible to a wide spectrum of readers, though its average circulation never exceeded more than about 12,000 daily, a miniscule figure by transatlantic standards.

Interviewing was as prominent a feature of Stead's journalism as typography. He arranged conversations with miscellaneous subjects, ranging from ambitious politicians to socially conscious churchmen to evanescent "spirits." His interview with General Gordon in January 1884 helped to spark the crisis over Britain's imperial role in Africa. Also well publicized were the telepathic "mental exchanges" that he printed in the *Pall Mall Gazette*, including a particularly controversial interaction with Gladstone's deceased wife. Stead's uncritical belief in the reality of psychic phenomena is incidental to his role in the New Journalism. But it gave an edge to his critics, who repeatedly mocked him and his "journalistic enterprise," in part at least as a way of intensifying their campaign against American-inspired journalism.[51]

News condensation reflects still another aspect of Stead's journalism that links him to the phenomenon of Americanization. By the 1880s, American newspapers had begun to print capsule indexes of their contents on the front page, to break down news stories into easily digestible segments and significantly reduce the size of editorials. Pulitzer believed strongly in condensing news, and among British pressmen, Stead articulated the case for brevity and sought to incorporate it into every facet of his journalism. He printed American-style indexes in the *Pall Mall Gazette*, adjacent to "penny Steadfuls" (as they were jocularly referred to), which were digests of literary works. And in two of his subsequent periodicals – the *Review of Reviews*, a monthly that commenced publication in 1890, and the short-lived *Daily Paper* (1904) – he brought this summarizing tendency to an astonishing denouement. In the former journal, which he established with the help of Newnes and Pearson, he sought to "enlighten the busiest and poorest in the community," by providing them with a "readable compendium of all the best articles in the magazines and reviews." He had it in mind to promote an active engagement between reader and read, or consumer and product. "I need the eyes, the ears, and the brains of all my readers to help me in my task," he affirmed. Every issue of the *Review of Reviews* included a shortened news survey, condensed fiction and extracts from magazine articles. In essence, this was *Tit-Bits* with a defined moral purpose, and its success was based on its ability to entice readers who had little time for anything else.[52]

Stead's *Daily Paper* was an even more ambitious undertaking, though it only survived for 32 numbers. Characterized by him as "the dream of my life," it sought to attract "busy men in the rush hours of the day." Everything of importance was to be sketched in its pages: a diary of events, an abstract of the previous day's news ("a Great Historical Romance"), financial information, political crusades, interviews, serialized fiction and, from time to time, "Yesterday's Long Ago Historical Events." As with the *Review of Reviews*, Stead's intention in publishing the *Daily Paper* was to demolish the wall between journalist and reader and to establish a focal point for moral pressure. He contemplated a "Messenger Brigade" to facilitate communication among bodies of subscribers. The press might then be "wired" into every home and become a "new social nerve-centre that would make its influence felt throughout the whole English-speaking world."[53] This glimpse into the future possibilities of media communications represents an extraordinary "psychic" prefiguring of today's information highway and testifies to Stead's powerful intellect.

T. P. O'Connor lacked the genius of Stead but he also fused a compelling vision of press development with an uninhibited affinity for American ways. "The American paper will be my model," he unhesitatingly affirmed.[54] As with Stead and Pulitzer, O'Connor commenced his working life in journalism as a reporter. He covered stories for newspapers in Dublin and London, including the *Daily Telegraph* and the *Echo,* and was a London stringer for the New York *Herald* for 18 months. (It has been claimed that in this capacity he handled Stanley's reports that he had found Livingston.) He learned how to write about every conceivable type of news in conditions of speed, from the latest murder to grand opera to women's fashion. Then, in 1880, he was elected to Parliament as an Irish Home Ruler, and for the remainder of his life attempted to forge a union out of the twin vocations of politics and journalism, assigning to each an interactive public role. As with Pulitzer and Stead, O'Connor brewed medium with message. Presentation was all-important to him, and he rejected the "high and dry school" of journalism, opting instead for "vitality, picturesqueness, and humanity." Good writing must strike the eye at once," he stated, with "broad effects" being necessary to achieve this. He attempted to create "the intimacy and friendliness of a personal tie" with each of his readers and to elucidate the "human, personal and social" element of the news.[55] Not surprisingly, he introduced bright typography into both of the halfpenny evening newspapers he was associated with: the *Star* and the *Sun*. In each instance, he made liberal use of multiple decks and crossheads. Drawing upon the earlier work of Pulitzer and Stead, he also resorted to pictorial innovations, including the dissemination of political cartoons, illustrated weather reports and courtroom sketches.

Human-interest news was central to O'Connor's journalism. His "Mainly About People" column in the *Star* was one of the foremost gossip columns of the age, and his extensive coverage of crime and sports resembled the best (and worst) aspects of American journalism. In September 1888, the *Star* made a breakthrough into mass circulation journalism when it publicized in sensational terms the killings in the East End of London. The exploits of Jack the Ripper, the first mass murderer to gain celebrity status in the daily press in Britain, were reported on in crisply personal terms and topped with suggestive banks such as "THE RIPPER SURPASSES HIMSELF IN FIENDISH MUTILATION" and "THE LEGS CUT OFF AND CARRIED AWAY." Even Hearst would have found it difficult to surpass this, though in fairness to O'Connor (who seemed figuratively at least to cringe with embarrassment at some of these escapades), his able sub-editor, Ernest Parke, who expressed the hope of attaining "gigantic circulations hitherto unparalleled in evening journalism," was primarily responsible for them.[56]

Sports news translated less easily into outright sensationalism. But it was as integral to O'Connor's "personal journalism" as crime, and he gave his readers substantial helpings of it, including a popular column in the *Star* entitled "Sporting Chat" and another in the *Sun* called "Sporting Gossip." O'Connor's newspapers provided intensive coverage of cricket and football, and also late racing results in successive "Stop Press" editions. "Captain Coe" (Edward C. Mitchell) became an interpreter of cricket for hundreds of thousands of readers of the *Star* and the *Sun*. His popularity helps to explain in part the enormous success of O'Connor's newspapers.[57]

O'Connor had a more focused political objective than either Pulitzer or Stead: to disseminate pro-Irish as well as pro-reform views. In the first

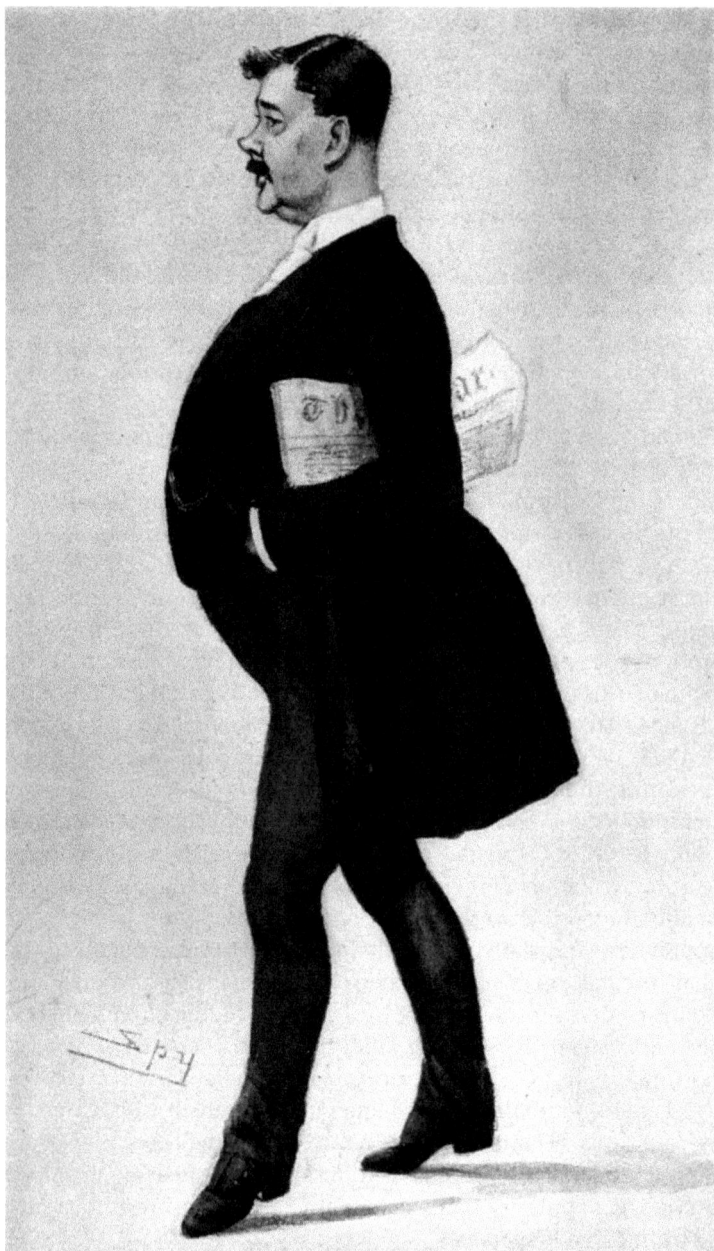

Figure 7.2   Caricature of T. P. O'Connor in 1888; O'Connor, *Memoirs of an Old Parliamentarian* (1929)

issue of the *Star* (17 January 1888), he issued a "Confession of Faith," in which he affirmed his intention to oppose all forms of privilege. He advocated Home Rule, a struggle against "market monopolists" and the imposition of a tax on ground rents that was intended to alleviate the plight of the Irish peasantry. Subsequently he propounded other socially advanced positions, including support for the rights of labor and a more equal distribution of wealth. O'Connor's vision of human betterment was unswerving, and it probably helps to explain his inability after two extended visits to the United States to warm to that country's enthusiasm for capitalism, which seemed to him to exacerbate differences between rich and poor. Nonetheless he expressed his admiration for the democratic culture of America, as exemplified by its press, which encapsulated the heterogeneity of its readers and was committed to excluding "nothing worth recording." Newspapers, O'Connor stated, must be a "weapon in the conflict of ideas." But in addition they needed to give publicity to everyday activity, what he called "unpolitical literature," which in his view was as inherently valuable as political pleading in winning the battle for reform. Stead paid a generous, well-deserved, tribute to his comrade-in-arms when he wrote: "We broke the old tradition, and made journalism a living thing, palpitating with actuality, in touch with life at all points."[58]

O'Connor's *Star*, which he left in 1890 after a rift with the paper's directors, was among the best effusions of the New Journalism because it captured a mood of transient excitement and popularization. O'Connor accepted that Britain still lagged behind the United States in press experimentation. Yet he believed that the gap was narrowing, especially in reference to the evening press, with its protean appeal to commuters. The *Star* ("half a joke and half a crusade") was the most popular British evening newspaper of the late nineteenth century with an estimated circulation of 120,000 readers. It featured a daily package of condensed news stories, large dollops of human-interest news, a popular women's section, visual flair, a zest for reform and a reputation for rapid interviewing. Its impressive staff included Bernard Shaw as leader writer and music critic; Clement Shorter, the respected drama critic; three future editors of considerable renown (Henry Massingham, Robert Donald and Thomas Marlowe); and Ernest Parke, described by several contemporaries as the best sub-editor working on either side of the Atlantic.[59]

Like Stead and O'Connor (and Pulitzer and Cockerill), Parke possessed a shrewd mixture of crassness and idealism. And if successful popular journalism reflects the efforts of men and women working unobtrusively (under the radar, so to speak), he was among the ablest of them. On both the *Star* and its stable mate, the *Morning Leader*, which he helped to found in 1892 and to which the quickening process of Americanization was extended, he "inspired everything that was written," according to a close friend. Sports news, crime, gossip, pictures, a weather column: all of this and more made both newspapers a "perfect kaleidoscope of all that (was) going on," as well as a bellwether for what was to follow during the coming decades.[60]

Notes

1   Hutt, *Changing Newspaper*, 48.
2   For a discussion of the use of multiple decks and typography generally, see Helen Ogden Mahin, *The Development and Significance of the Newspaper Headline* (Ann Arbor: George Wahr, 1924).
3   The Harmsworth quote is in Hutt, *Changing Newspaper*, 71. The reference to the *Times* is to be found in D. L. LeMahieu, *A Culture for Democracy: Mass Communication and the Cultivated Mind in Britain Between the Wars* (Oxford: Clarendon Press, 1989), 68–9. In 1916, Harmsworth (now Lord Northcliffe) was criticized by an American editor for continuing to run advertisements on the front page of the *Times*. He replied: "Advertisements! They are the most important news. And where would you have it if not on the front page."
4   Carey, *Intellectuals and the Masses*, 6–7.
5   Raymond, *Portraits of the Nineties*, 304.
6   Quoted in Chambers, *News Hunting on Three Continents*, 287.
7   I have borrowed the phrase "culture of pastiche" from Taylor, *In Pursuit of Gotham*, 82.
8   Ray Boston, "Fleet Street 100 Years Ago," *Journalism Studies Review*, I (1977), 16–17.
9   Helen MacGill Hughes, *News and the Human Interest Story* (Chicago: University of Chicago Press, 1940), 46.
10 Richard A. Schwarzlose, *The Nation's Newsbreakers, Volume II: The Rush to Institution, from 1865 to 1920* (Evanston: Northwestern University Press, 1989), 64.
11 Scott, *Story of the Pall Mall Gazette*, 129; Robert Blatchford, *My Eighty Years* (London: Cassell, 1931), 184. Donald Matheson maintains that a shift in writing style was the key event in creating a modern news form. ("The Birth of News Discourse: Changes of News Language in British Newspapers, 1880–1930," in *Media, Culture and Society*, XXII (2000), 557–73.
12 O'Connor, "New Journalism," 434.
13 *New Republic*, 6 November 1989.
14 Blumenfeld, *Press in My Time*, 91. See also Philip Gibbs, *Adventures in Journalism* (London: William Heinemann, 1923), 8.
15 Dreiser, *Book About Myself*, 65.
16 A recent study deftly analyzes the ways in which nineteenth-century British newspapers incorporated narrative conventions of this type into their news reporting. Matthew Rubery, *The Novelty of Newspapers: Victorian Fiction and the Invention of the News* (Oxford: Oxford University Press, 2009).

17 George B. Hodgson, *From Smithy to Senate: The Life Story of James Annand, Journalist and Politician* (London: Cassell, 1908), 102, 239.

18 Quoted in Fermer, *Bennett and the New York Herald*, 23. Whitelaw Reid, whose news sense was less well honed than that of Bennett, agreed with Raymond. He stated: "The essence, the life-blood of the daily paper of to-day, is the news." Quoted in Lee, *Daily Newspaper*, 629.

19 Stephens, *History of News*, 136; Morrill Goddard, *What Interests People and Why* (New York: Privately Printed, 1935), especially 10–19. "Putting life in a story" is how one historian sympathetically characterizes sensationalism. Warren Francke, "An Argument in Defense of Sensationalism: Probing the Popular and Historiographical Concept," *Journalism History*, V (1978), 72.

20 Pulitzer's statement is in Rammelkamp, *Pulitzer's Post-Dispatch*, 163. Charles Tatum, the scheming tabloid reporter in Billy Wilder's film, "Ace in the Hole," gave the man/dog comparison more point: "If there's no news, I'll go out and bite a dog."

21 Evelyn Waugh, *Scoop* (Boston: Little, Brown and Company, 1966; first published in 1937), 91. Interestingly, Rupert Murdoch has defended the *Sun* in the following terms: "A press that fails to interest the whole community is one that will ultimately become a house organ of the elite engaged in an increasingly private conversation with a dwindling circle." Quoted in Charles Wintour, *The Rise and Fall of Fleet Street* (London: Hutchinson, 1989), 235.

22 Starr, *Bohemian Brigade*, 12.

23 Martin Mayer, *Making News* (Garden City: Doubleday, 1987), 46.

24 Jones, *Fleet Street*, 132. The reporter's quote is in Baldasty, *Commercialization of News*, 90.

25 The description by Charles Pebody is in *English Journalism and the Men Who Have Made It* (London: Cassell, Petter, Galpin, 1882), 24. The literary primer cited is A. Arthur Reade, *Literary Success: Being a Guide to Practical Journalism* (London: Wyman & Sons, 1885), 133.

26 Weisberger, *American Newspaperman*, 3.

27 O'Shea, *Leaves from the Life*, II, 310; L. Perry Curtis, Jr., *Jack the Ripper and the London Press* (New Haven: Yale University Press, 2001); Harold Herd, *The Making of Modern Journalism* (London: George Allen & Unwin, 1927), 55.

28 The "junk food" statement is by Christopher Kent in his Introduction to Alvin Sullivan (ed.), *British Literary Magazines: The Victorian and Edwardian Age, 1837–1913* (Westport: Greenwood Press, 1984), xx. For "boiled" and "snippets" references, see "The Lament of a Leader Writer," *Westminster Review*, CLVII (1899), 662; Hulda Friedrichs, *The Life of Sir George Newnes, Bart.* (London: Hodder and Stoughton, 1911), 56.

29 For example, see *Tit-Bits*, 22 October 1881 and 17 March 1888.

30 Quoted in D. G. Boyce, "Crusaders Without Chains: Power and the Press Barons, 1896–1951," in James Curran, *Impacts and Influences*, 98; Kate Jackson, *George Newnes and the New Journalism in Britain, 1880–1910* (Aldershot: Ashgate, 2001), 274. A journalist who knew Newnes wrote that he "staked the course" for Harmsworth and others who followed. H. G. Hibbert, *Fifty Years of a Londoner's Life* (London: Grant Richards, 1916), 276.

31 *Review of Reviews*, XXX (1904), 577.

32 For example, see *Answers to Correspondents*, 23 November 1888. Readers submitted questions such as the following: "Was Dumas a Negro?" and "How

Often Does a Watch Tick in a Year?" Another journal of this type was *The Success (The Most Readable and Cheerful Paper in the World)*, published from 1895 to 1900, which emphasized sports, tidbits and gossip.

33   Although he is correct in general terms, John Carey overstates the case when he writes: "As a means of awakening interest in books, arousing curiosity and introducing its readers to new ideas, *Tit-Bits* must compare very favorably with more acclaimed organs such as T.S. Eliot's *Criterion* and F. R. Leavis's *Scrutiny*, and its effects were infinitely more widespread." *Intellectuals and the Masses*, 109.

34   Stead's unfavorable view of Pearson is offered in *Review of Reviews*, XXX (1904), 595. Joseph Chamberlain voiced an identical sentiment when he described Pearson as "the greatest hustler I have ever known," Quoted in Harold Herd, *The March of Journalism: The Story of the Present Press from 1622 to the Present Day* (London: George Allen & Unwin, 1952), 259. On the promotion of stunts, see *Pearson's Weekly*, 26 July 1890. The historian quoted is Dilwyn Porter, in *Dictionary of Business Biography*, IV, 575.

35   Reginald Pound and Geoffrey Harmsworth, *Northcliffe* (London: Cassell, 1959), 54; Max Pemberton, *Lord Northcliffe: A Memoir* (London: Hodder and Stoughton, 1922), 30; *Answers to Correspondents*, 2 June 1888.

36   Among the many fine studies of Pulitzer are Rammelkamp, *Pulitzer's Post-Dispatch* and George Juergens, *Joseph Pulitzer and "The New York World"* (Princeton: Princeton University Press, 1966). A fine recent biography is James McGrath Morris, *Pulitzer: A Life in Politics, Print, and Power* (New York: HarperCollins Publishers, 2010). Cockerill's biographer states: "Pulitzer, contrary to a commonly accepted image of the publisher, often had to be persuaded to try fresh ideas. (Cockerill) was often the persuader." Homer W. King, *Pulitzer's Prize Editor: A Biography of John A. Cockerill, 1845–1896* (Durham: Duke University Press, 1965), xvii. An interesting study of Chapin (who shot and killed his wife) is James McGrath Morris, *The Rose Man of Sing Sing: True Tale of Life, Murder, and Redemption in the Age of Yellow Journalism* (New York: Fordham University Press, 2003). Irvin Cobb's comment about Chapin is in *Exit Laughing* (Indianapolis: Bobbs-Merrill, 1941), 119.

37   See Brooke Kroeger, *Nellie Bly: Daredevil, Reporter, Feminist* (New York: Random House, 1994). Cain is cited in Brendon, *Life and Death of the Press Barons*, 107.

38   Quoted in Seitz, *Pulitzer*, 416. The reference to the placards is in Alleyne Ireland, *An Adventure with a Genius: Recollections of Joseph Pulitzer* (London: Lovat Dickson, 1938), xi.

39   Villard, *Some Newspapers and Newspaper-Men*, 47.

40   For the headlines cited, see *World*, 1 September 1883, 5 October 1883.

41   The Pulitzer quotes are in a letter to Charles M. Lincoln in 1911, cited in Seitz, *Joseph Pulitzer*, 424.

42   *St. Louis Post-Dispatch*, 8 February 1882, as quoted in Rammelkamp, *Pulitzer's Post-Dispatch*, 180.

43   Stoddard, *Horace Greeley*, 91; James K. Markham, *Bovard of the Post-Dispatch* (Baton Rouge: Louisiana State University Press, 1954), 22.

44   Joseph Pulitzer, "The College of Journalism," *North American Review*, CLXXVIII (1904), 607. According to one of his biographers, "no journalist ever used

(crusades) with such persistence, skill and effect as Pulitzer." W. A. Swanberg, *Pulitzer* (New York: Charles Scribner's Sons, 1967), 57.

45 See the dramatic account of Stead and the Titanic in Victor Pierce Jones, *Saint or Sensationalist?: The Story of W. T. Stead, 1849–1912* (East Wittering: Gooday Publishers, 1988), 78–83.

46 Stead, *Americanization of the World*, 15, 290; Henry Leach, *Fleet Street from Within: The Romance and Mystery of the Daily Paper* (Bristol: J. W. Arrowsmith, 1905), 191. The reference to the "Anglo-American" flag is in W. B. Northrop, *With Pen and Camera: Interviews with Celebrities* (London: R. A. Everett, 1904), 157.

47 Stead, "Government by Journalism," 664; Jones, *Fleet Street & Downing Street*, 114.

48 Quoted in J. W. Robertson Scott, *The Life and Death of a Newspaper: An Account of the Temperaments, Perturbations and Achievements of John Morley, W. T. Stead, E. T. Cook, Harry Cust, J. L. Garvin and three Other Editors of the "Pall Mall Gazette"* (London: Methuen, 1952), 120.

49 W. T. Stead, *If Christ Came to Chicago! A Plea for the Union of All Who Love in the Service of All Who Suffer* (London: Office of the *Review of Reviews*, 1895; first published in Chicago in 1894), x, 349; Henry Wickham Steed, *Through Thirty Years, 1892–1922: A Personal Narrative* (Garden City: Doubleday, Page & Company, 1923), 6. The Milner characterization of Stead is in Frederic Whyte, *The Life of W. T. Stead* (New York: Houghton Mifflin, 1925), I, 104. Laurel Brake maintains persuasively that Stead was both critical of, and favorable to, American journalism. "Who is 'We'?: The Daily Paper Projects and the Journalism Manifestos of W.T. Stead," in Marysa Demoor (ed.), *Marketing the Author: Authorial Personae, Narrative Selves and Self-Fashioning 1880–1930* (Houndmills: Palgrave Macmillan, 2004), 54–72.

50 Stead, *Americanization of the World*, 292. According to Stanley Morison, Stead's typographical innovations represented "the first notable breakaway from mid-Victorian journalism." (*The English Newspaper: Some Account of the Physical Development of Journals Printed in London between 1622 and the Present Day* (Cambridge: Cambridge University Press, 1932), 281.)

51 An example of a well-publicized interview by Stead was one with the Vicar of Pemberton, who favored prohibiting the employment of women at the pit-brow. It was captioned "The victory of the Pit-wives." *Pall Mall Gazette*, 18 May 1888.

52 *Review of Reviews*, I, 14, 54. On the "penny Steadfuls," see Nigel Cross, *The Common Writer: Life in Nineteenth-Century Grub Street* (Cambridge: Cambridge University Press, 1985), 209.

53 *Review of Reviews*, XXVIII (1903), 571–83, and XXIX (1904), 11–13; W. T. Stead, "The London Morning Dailies that Are and Are to Be," *Sell's* (1892), 113. See also J. O. Baylen, "W.T. Stead as Publisher and Editor of the Review of Reviews," *Victorian Periodicals Review*, XII (Summer 1979), 70–84.

54 *Pall Mall Gazette*, 16 January 1888.

55 T. P. O'Connor, "Journalism as a Career," *Sell's* (1894), 23–4; *Weekly Sun*, 8 January 1893. See also O'Connor, "New Journalism," 434. The claim regarding Stanley is in *Sell's* (1893), 29. O'Connor maintained that it was the duty of a journalist to depict "the environment and the nether world

which lie around and below the public event, to describe the green-room as well as the play on the stage." *Sun*, 27 June 1893.

56 O'Connor, *Memoirs*, II, 257. Parke admitted that concerning circulation, "a big sporting affair makes a tremendous difference, (as) does a showy murder." *Sketch*, 25 April 1894, 686.

57 On the relationship between sport and mass journalism, see Matt McIntire's fine article, "Embracing Sporting News in England and America: Nineteenth-Century Cricket and Baseball News," in Wiener and Hampton, *Anglo-American Media Interactions*, 32–47.

58 *Star*, 17 January 1888; O'Connor, "New Journalism," 434; W. T. Stead, "Mr. T.P. O'Connor, M. P.," *Review of Reviews*, XXVI (1902), 479. The best biography of O'Connor is Hamilton Fyfe, *T.P. O'Connor* (London: George Allen & Unwin, 1934), although a more detailed study of his politics is in L. W. Brady, *T.P. O'Connor and the Liverpool Irish* (London: Royal Historical Society, 1983).

59 On the *Star*, see W. Pope, *The Story of the "Star", 1888–1938: Fifty Years of Progress and Achievement* (London: "The Star" Publications Department, 1938) and John Goodbody, "The 'Star': Its Role in the Rise of the New Journalism," in Wiener, *Papers for the Millions*, 143–64.

60 Sir Linton Andrews, *Problems of an Editor: A Study in Newspaper Trends* (London: Oxford University Press, 1962), 142; Spencer Leigh Hughes, *Press, Platform and Parliament* (London: Nisbet, 1918), 25; *Morning Leader*, 2 January 1893. For the underestimated Ernest Parke, see J. W. Robertson Scott, *'We' and Me: Memories of Four Eminent Authors I Worked with, a Discussion by Editors of the Future of Editing, and a Candid Account of the Founding and Editing, for Twenty-One Years, of my Own Magazine* (London: W. H. Allen, 1956), 166–84.

8
A Mass Press: Hearst and Harmsworth

During the final decade of the nineteenth century Anglo-American popular journalism acquired the form that was to characterize it for much of the succeeding hundred years. A crescendo of press activity marked this decade, a sense of unprecedented journalistic excitement, with words like "novelty" and "sensation," and phrases such as "Yellow Journalism," being freely bandied about. Technology and commerce merged fortunes in a drive for increased productivity and profits, while large-scale advertisements jostled for space with fast-paced news stories. Newspaper staffs proliferated in size. Pictures and text increasingly complemented each other. Banner headlines appeared on the front pages of penny and halfpenny newspapers. Crime, sports and gossip became integral facets of news coverage, while defined reading markets (women, children, consumers of fiction) were catered to within a general interest format. Cartoons and comic strips became syndicated and, as personal by-lines gradually replaced anonymous authorship, a handful of journalists emerged as celebrities in their own right. It was in many ways journalism run slightly amok, though responsive to multiple groups of readers in ways that would have been unimaginable 70 years earlier.

Technological innovation developed rapidly and had a decisive impact on the ability to publish newspapers at "lightning speed" and (so it seemed) in unlimited quantities. By 1900, almost every phase of press production was becoming mechanized. Of chief importance was the invention of the Linotype machine, which cast lines of type, or "slugs," mechanically, thereby increasing the rate of productivity of skilled compositors from 2,000 to about 6,000 letters an hour. The Linotype machine was invented by Ottmar Mergenthaler, a German immigrant to the United States, and was used for the first time on the *Tribune* in 1886. Within a few years it made its way to Britain, where it was at first employed on two leading provincial papers: the *Newcastle Weekly Chronicle* and the *Leeds Mercury*. By the late 1890s, it was in extensive use on both sides of the Atlantic. Initially Harmsworth resisted this American import, as he did with several other improvements in technology. He subsequently admitted, however, that the *Daily Mail* employed it on "a scale unprecedented in any English newspaper office," which allowed for a "saving of from 30 to 50 per cent and (for the newspaper) to be sold for half the price of its contemporaries."[1] It is instructive to note two other instances of "Americanization" in connection with "line casting" technology. While in transit between the *Herald* and the *Daily Express*, Blumenfeld helped to organize the Empire Typesetting Machine Company, which tried unsuccessfully to acquire the British rights to this invention. Several years later Oliver Borthwick, the managing editor of the *Morning Post* and a leading personality in London journalism, visited the United States to study the application of the Linotype. His objective was to make his newspaper – conservative in politics, receptive to new ideas in other ways – one of the most mechanically advanced in the transatlantic world.[2]

Proprietors and editors constantly traveled back and forth across the Atlantic, seeking to improve their technological infrastructure. For example, firsthand observation of New York printing machinery by John Walter III, who owned the *Times,* led to the improvement of the web perfecting press (Walter Press) in Britain. This was subsequently re-adapted to meet American needs and patented in a more sophisticated form by the Hoe Company, including the manufacture of color perfecting presses used extensively in the 1890s by Pulitzer and Hearst.[3] A dramatic fall in the price of paper resulted from the replacement of expensive cotton rag paper by newsprint made from wood pulp (esparto grass was used briefly in the 1860s and 1870s). The timing of these and other innovations was partly fortuitous, but in general falling costs aligned with an increased emphasis on speedier product-ivity helped to create a mass circulation newspaper industry. By 1913, a single web perfecting advanced press could print several hundred thousand copies of a 12-sheet newspaper within an hour. A historian of journalism has observed: "The newspaper tiger was out of the cage. The price of a newspaper came within the reach of almost everyone."[4]

Two additional inventions of the period – the typewriter and the telephone – had an enormous impact on transatlantic journalism, although the differing responses to them signify the persistence of a cultural divide between Britain and America. Neither invention was fully established in newspaper offices until after 1900. However, both were fulsomely welcomed by Pulitzer and Hearst and rapidly became central elements of American journalism. Initially some pressmen in America resisted the use of typewriters, believing that their function was purely "mechanical" and that they were bound to stifle creativity, an argument advanced against speed generally. But they soon became popular in America (where they were first brought into commercial use in the 1870s by the Remington company) and were taken up by wire agencies and "rewrite men" on evening newspapers who typed reporters' stories into copy before sending it to the compositors. Typewriting bureaus sprang up near Park Row in the 1890s, where the *Sun*, the *Herald*, Hearst's *Evening Journal* and other newspapers were based. By 1907, type-writers had become essential newspaper equipment in America.[5] On the other hand, in Britain, resistance to their use was intermittently pronounced. A notable dissident to this view was T. P. O'Connor, who welcomed typewriters because they promised a dramatic increase in speed. He typed his "Mainly About People" column and his political sketches, the latter right in the gallery of the House of Commons. An authoritative textbook on British journalism avers that by 1931 the typewriter had become "indispensable." even though "up to a few years ago, there was a considerable prejudice against it in reporters' rooms."[6]

The telephone also found a warmer welcome in American newsrooms. In 1880, the *Sun* became the first newspaper to acquire a telephone for its reporters' use, notwithstanding Dana's frequently expressed skepticism about modern technology. By the turn of the century it was in general employment, notably (as with the typewriter) by "rewrite men" on evening papers, who provided a critical intermediate function by culling information from reporters on beats, sending it to compositors and then putting the newspaper to bed. As with the telegraph and the typewriter, the chief selling point of the telephone was the enormous compression of time and distance it brought about. Early telephones tended to be noisy, as people shouted into receivers and frequently had to redial several times before establishing a firm connection. Such a frustrating process (reminiscent in some ways to our own initial experiences with mobile phones) was more easily integrated into American culture, where "intrusiveness" and subversion of privacy were more readily tolerated. Not surprisingly, a historian of the telephone has described the United States as the "natural home" of this invention.[7]

There was sporadic resistance to the use of the telephone in Britain. In the 1880s the *Times* briefly set up a telephone line inside the Commons for its parliamentary reporters but by 1894 it had abandoned the practice. At the turn of the century most British newsrooms still relied on "flimsies," or carbons, for the dissemination of local news and on the telegraph for long distance reporting. As with the typewriter, O'Connor emerged as a firm advocate of the telephone, though in this instance he was joined by Harmsworth, who required his staff to use telephones and became so personally obsessed with this magical instrument that he kept one adjacent to his bedside until the day he died. By 1910 or so, about a decade later than in the United States, telephones had become an integral part of British journalism.

The application of improved technology to journalism, in effect its modernization, generated renewed anxiety about the spread of commercial values. For one thing, heavy capitalization was now indispensable to the newspaper industry. Staffs were much larger, as were the salaries of reporters and editors. The cost of producing pictures had also dramatically increased, as the halftone process started to replace wood engraving in the 1890s and it became possible to replicate photographs with a grainy "reality" that had not previously existed. For better or worse, newspapers were becoming a "paradigm of Victorian enterprise," no longer a "cottage industry" but rather "a major industrial undertaking."[8] As early as 1851 joint stock companies started to replace family firms, when the Tribune Association with a capital of 100,000 dollars took control of Greeley's newspaper.[9] Printer-publishers such as Day of the *Sun* were by then gone from the scene. Day had launched his paper for 300 dollars in 1833; two years later Bennett commenced the *Herald* with an investment of 500 dollars. By the 1870s, the staff of the *Herald* exceeded 500 employees and the newspaper was beginning to purchase expensive printing machinery. It has been estimated that in 1913 a minimum of three million dollars would have been needed to launch the *Herald*.[10] Another perspective from which to view these commercial upheavals in the newspaper world is as follows: In 1870, American newspapers and magazines were capitalized at an estimated total sum of 115 million dollars; by the end of the century, this notional figure had increased by at least nine times.

The emergence of press proprietors ("press lords") with grandiose reputations to uphold and boundless sums of money to spend, such as Hearst, Harmsworth, Pearson, Pulitzer and Bennett, Jr., made for a greatly increased concentration of resources. In 1890, not a single newspaper was listed on the London Stock Exchange. Twenty years later, in an extraordinary reversal, more than 90 per cent of all London and provincial newspapers were listed.[11] Similarly, corporate management of the press in the United States hovered at about 15 per cent near the beginning of the 1890s and exceeded 80 per cent by 1914. By then, Hearst and Harmsworth had created press empires of formidable size and scope.[12] Hearst founded or bought a large number of news-papers sited in major American cities, together with numerous maga-zines, and established wire and feature services to compete with press agencies such as the Associated Press and the United Press. He sub-sequently acquired additional newspapers and journals, along with radio stations and a movie studio. By the 1930s, this interlocking network of properties comprised the largest communications empire in the world.

Harmsworth did not lag far behind Hearst. Although he launched the *Daily Mail* in 1896 with an initial capital of only 15,000 pounds (in part by using the machinery and business infrastructure of the *Evening News*), his profits and investments rapidly soared in value. In 1905, his company, now named Associated Newspapers, Ltd, had a working capital of 1.6 million pounds. Subsequently he bought the *Observer* (1905), the *Times* (1908) and a number of magazines including the profitable *World*, originally founded by Edmund Yates. Unlike Hearst, who inherited enormous family wealth, Harmsworth possessed no appreciable resources of his own at the outset, being the son of a legal practitioner of modest means. Yet this archetypal self-made man, referred to as "Napoleon" by his associates, became one of the leading press lords of all time with spectacular holdings in book publishing as well as journalism. His brother Harold Harmsworth, subsequently Viscount Rothermere, paralleled his financial and personal ascent, as did several other British newspaper proprietors, such as George Cadbury, the cocoa manufacturer who owned the *Daily News* and several Mid-lands papers. By 1914 the commercial structure of the press in both America and Britain had been reconfigured beyond all recognition, a development that was to influence the history of journalism in incalculable ways throughout much of the succeeding century.

Surprisingly, notwithstanding the formidable nature of the Hearst organization, British press concentration for a time surpassed that in America. By 1910, Harmsworth (who became Baron Northcliffe in 1905), Cadbury and Pearson controlled about two thirds of the total national daily circulation of newspapers.[13] This prefigured a situation in which the provincial press was made subordinate once more to its London rivals, a predictable outcome given the relatively small size of the country and the vastly increased speed of communications. A further development gave an even greater stimulus towards concen-tration. This was the practice dating from 1900 of London newspapers launching northern editions, in effect satellite hookups, by wiring their contents ahead to offices in Manchester and other cities, where they were printed after being modified to suit local conditions. The *Daily Mail* was the first paper to do this (initially as a way of rapidly disseminating Boer War news), and in the words of Harmsworth's biographer, this made it "in the true sense Britain's first national newspaper." Other newspapers, such as the *Daily Express* and the *Daily News*, copied this example so that within a short time the words "Fleet Street" and "British press" had became nearly synonymous to millions of newspaper readers.[14]

American journalism exhibited fewer consolidating tendencies initially, not because its proprietors were reluctant to try to maximize their profits, but due to the existence of numerous competing urban centers. Even the Hearst publishing empire, with its far-reaching tentacles, was thwarted in its efforts to construct a consolidated national power. Harold Spender noted at the time that "nothing at all corresponding to our (national) London press" existed in America.[15] On the contrary, Spender observed, a diffuse form of commercialism was snaking its way across the United States, one that was quite different from the British experience, though not necessarily less effective. What Spender had in mind was the practice of American newspapers selling and distributing large quantities of syndicated printed matter to other newspapers. British publishing companies like Tillotsen's had been pioneers in disseminating stereotyped material but the practice soon became more widespread in the United States. By 1912, nearly 16,000 American newspapers received syndicated materials on a regular basis, a situation that enormously accelerated the process of standardization.[16] Hearst was notably active in this area. His International News Service and International Feature Service, both established before 1914, sold popular features from his newspapers. These included segments of *American Mercury*, his celebrated Sunday magazine, as well as the columns written by Dorothy Dix, the best known and most highly paid "agony aunt" in the country.

However, it was another American pressman, Edward W. Scripps, the founder of the Scripps chain of newspapers, who first parlayed the commercial syndication of news into an effective centralizing process. The approach used by Scripps diverged from that of Hearst, who sought to accumulate as many large metropolitan newspapers as he could. The Scripps strategy was to establish a chain of profitable newspapers across the country by purchasing papers with small circulations at knockdown prices (or taking majority control of their equities) and synchronizing the contents. Beginning in the 1880s, he and several partners organized the first informal chain of newspapers in the United States, the Scripps-Macrae League of Newspapers (subsequently Scripps-

Howard), which was principally situated in the rapidly expanding midwestern cities of Cleveland, Cincinnati, St. Louis and Detroit. By 1908, the Scripps syndicate had effective majority control of 47 newspapers, the bulk of them aimed at a working-class readership. Unlike Hearst's press empire, which operated loosely, it appointed most of the editors and coordinated their news coverage though frequently not their editorials. In 1907, it established a news agency, the United Press Association ("United Press"), together with several smaller feature agencies. This prefiguring of the big business side of modern press ownership was mitigated to an extent by Scripps's liberal political views and his disinclination to exercise power crassly, as Hearst, and even Pulitzer, sometimes did.[17] But his objective was broadly similar to theirs: to construct a unified cultural and media organization. The credo expounded by Scripps was luminous: "Humanity was vulgar, so we must be vulgar. It was coarse; so we must not be refined. It was passionate; therefore, the blood that ran in our veins and in our newspapers must be warm."[18]

In Britain, comparable efforts at syndication and standardization of this kind, such as those undertaken by Samuel Storey, who was a Sunderland newspaper proprietor, and Andrew Carnegie, the American steel magnate, were less successful. In the 1880s, the Storey-Carnegie Newspaper Syndicate and the Midlands News Association, which was associated with it, purchased 14 newspapers, principally in the Northeast and the Midlands, and for a brief period held a majority interest in the London *Echo*. Unlike Scripps, though, the efforts of Carnegie, Storey, Hugh Gilzean Reid and other newspapermen who established syndicates in Britain were intended primarily to curb the power of the London-based "national press" and strengthen the position of provincial newspapers. Most of these syndicates were dissolved before 1914.[19]

In both the United States and Britain corporate control of the press and increased syndication quickened an impassioned debate over literary and press standards. To a greater extent than earlier, the perils of cultural uniformity were underlined. Edward Lawson of the *Daily Telegraph* observed wittily that newspapers "resemble fashionable ladies of the West End in that they are more concerned with their *figures* than with their *morals*."[20] Other commentators set out the case against commercialism in stark terms. An American observer maintained that with "stock companies now controlling our large morning dailies, the effacement of the individual has been complete." In Britain, *Sell's*, the media journal, sponsored a symposium in 1914 entitled "Are Papers Too Cheap?" The response among journalists was almost uniformly affirmative. One editor (Hall Caine) asserted that "commercialisation of the newspaper interests can bring nothing but evil in its train"; another maintained that acceptable press standards faced obliteration in the same way that the rush of modern industry was inevitably undermining the sanctity of craftsmanship.[21] It was emphasized repeatedly that advertising had become an indispensable ingredient in the financial success of newspapers, and that it posed a severe challenge to the continued independence of the press. Many proprietors, it was suggested, were rushing headlong to capture a general interest audience whose numbers and "classlessness" made it difficult, if not impossible, to contemplate a positive outcome. As James Creelman, the Hearst newspaperman, observed sardonically: newspapers were a "wonderful rainbow, with uncounted gold at the other end of it."[22]

The rise of what is commonly referred to as Yellow Journalism in America exacerbated premonitions of cultural doom. Ervin Wardman first used this phrase in 1897, at a time when Pulitzer and Hearst were competing vigorously for dominance of the New York newspaper market. A core feature of their confrontation, involving the *World* and Hearst's raucous *Evening Journal*, was "Hogan's Alley," a popular cartoon series colored yellow that Richard F. Outcault originally devised for Pulitzer in 1895, but which Hearst appropriated in the following year when he hired Outcault. Pulitzer quickly responded with a second "yellow kid" series, this one drawn by George Luks; a vicious comic strip war then ensued between the two leading American newspaper proprietors, which became so intense and far-reaching in its reverberations that Wardman's term for it stuck.[23]

It is not entirely fortuitous that a comic strip was at the center of this newspaper war. Strip cartooning had originated in Britain in the 1860s, when the inimitable cartoon figure of "Ally Sloper" appeared for the first time (initially as a bulbous-nosed confidence man, in later years as a mischievous dandy). By the 1880s, "Ally Sloper" and other comic characters were wildly popular in magazines and weekly comic journals, some of them aimed primarily at a children's market, including *Comic Cuts*, commenced by Harmsworth in 1890. However, American comic strips ("funnies") were the first to be printed on color presses (by Pulitzer in 1894) and, more important, the first to be fully integrated into mass circulation journalism. It has been suggested that these comic strips represented "an indigenous American art form" and were, in their own way, "as significant as the cinema in creating a national market for visual images."[24] Like other aspects of modern popular journalism influenced by American usage comic strips lent themselves to rapid scanning and the fragmentation of reality. It was also easy to exploit their commercial potential in the advertisement of goods and services. Likewise they gave decisive shape and form to the American Sunday newspaper, where they mostly appeared in the form of colored supplements. After 1900, comic strips were widely syndicated, especially by Hearst, who distributed "Katzenjammer Kids," the most popular comic strip of the pre-1914 period and the first to narrate a continuing story in a succession of weekly panels. In Britain the first comic Sunday supplement specifically created for a newspaper did not appear until 1921, and only in the 1930s did comic strips gain widespread popularity in the press.

The cognomen Yellow Journalism has come to be generically employed to refer to any no-holds-barred version of American journalism that focuses exclusively on the search for a mass readership. It has not been as frequently used as a descriptive epithet in Britain, where the mantra "tabloid journalism" remains more popular. Nonetheless, Yellow Journalism should be interpreted as a transatlantic phenomenon rather than one inscribed with national labeling. For although the British equivalent of Yellow Journalism in the pre-1914 period (referred to by a handful of historians as the "Newer Journalism") is more sober and less "sensational" in tone, it elicited similarly intense anxieties about the pervasive effects of American-inspired popular journalism in the years before 1914.

What were the defining elements of Yellow, or Newer, Journalism? How much of it persists today, exacerbating the public's obsessive distrust of the tabloids and of a cheap press in general? Kelvin Mackenzie, a former editor of Rupert Murdoch's *Sun*, offers an answer to these questions with his breezy dictum: "Every page must amaze." Just as today's British "redtops" provide a ceaseless diet of semi-clothed young women and embellished narratives of marital infidelity, their American equivalents often feature crime stories, especially murder and rape, and headlines of inimitable boldness like the one that graced the front page of the *New York Post* in April 1983: "HEADLESS BODY IN TOPLESS BAR." Speed and novelty are common denominators of the Yellow Press phenomenon on both sides of the Atlantic, what one of Hearst's editors characterized as the "Gee-wiz" emotion. Arthur McEwen, the journalist in question, came directly to the point: "We run our paper (the *San Francisco Examiner*) so that when the reader opens it he says 'Gee-wiz'."[25]

The key to the success of Yellow Journalism in the 1890s derived from its ability to sustain a feverish, rapidly accelerating, pitch of excitement, and to work news into a story with "a rush and a dash," so as to attract and sustain the reader's interest.[26] A drive to increase circulation became the professional bottom line; anything that helped to achieve this tended to be viewed positively. "Make the news exciting, even when it (is) dull ... Make the unreadable readable," exclaimed Arthur Christiansen, the legendary editor of the *Daily Express* in the 1930s. "A machine of perpetual motion" is how Horace White, an inveterate critic of popular journalism at the turn of the century, characterized the Yellow Press.[27] Among the surefire ingredients of such a press were murder and sex (the colorful phrase employed by Hearst was "crime and underwear," and by another journalist, "blood, money and broads"), pictures, titillating headlines, bellicose imperialist rhetoric, non-stop crusades against corruption, exaggerated news accounts and personalized features by by-lined columnists like "Dorothy Dix" (Elizabeth M. Gilmer), whose "Advice to the Lovelorn" catered to millions of women readers. A sympathetic observer commented: "It gives the people what they want – sensation, crime and vulgar sports, – thus inducing them to read." Arthur Brisbane, one of its more successful protagonists, described the Yellow Press as "the power of public opinion, the mental force of thousands or millions of readers utilized with more or less intelligence in the interests of those readers."[28]

Every one of the fundaments of sensational journalism were prefigured by earlier changes on both sides of the Atlantic, and among these were the contributions – too often overlooked – of the Irish-American writer, Frank Harris. Harris is best remembered for the self-promoting exuberance with which he publicized his abilities as a sexual athlete. But between 1883 and 1887 he edited the London *Evening News*, which he transformed into a halfpenny newspaper whose journalistic focus on "kissing and fighting" nearly rose to the level of his own alleged exploits. Harris maintained that these intertwined subjects were "the only things I cared for at thirteen or fourteen, and those are the themes the English public desires and enjoys today." Racing results, interviews and crime news were also heavily featured in the *Evening News*. After being circumvented in his efforts to fill its pages with "astonishing stories of London life," Harris left the paper to become editor of the *Fortnightly Review*.[29] In 1894 Kennedy Jones, a journalist with a resume of Scottish work experience and a passion for American press ideas, linked arms with Harmsworth to buy the refashioned *Evening News* and propel it even more decisively in the direction of sensational journalism.

Irrespective of the label applied, Hearst and Harmsworth were the most successful practitioners of mass circulation journalism. And of the two, Hearst remains the more intriguing personality, perhaps because he cultivated a larger than life image. In Orson Welles' screen portrayal of "Citizen Kane," he is transformed into a caricature of expressionism whose feats appear to be formidably outsized, though they do not depart too radically from those of the real Hearst. The latter carved an empire out of two glittering newspapers: the *San Francisco Examiner*, which his father gave to him as a gift in 1887 when he was 22, and the *New York Journal*, which he founded in 1895 and which produced in the following year its memorable offshoot, the *New York Evening Journal*, effectively his major newspaper. (In 1901 the morning edition of the *New York Journal* was renamed the *New York American*.)

William Randolph Hearst's career has been fully documented. At its peak, his publications were avidly consumed by nearly a quarter of the reading population of the United States. He was several times a candidate for public office, served a single term in Congress, made a stark ideological shift from liberal crusader to political conservative late in life, hired and amply remunerated some of the best male and female journalists in the United States, and almost certainly attracted the most stinging criticism that any press proprietor has ever drawn. Relatively few kind words have been written about Hearst, though two of his recent biographers, David Nasaw and Kenneth Whyte, provide more nuanced portraits of a complicated man. Here is a sampling of the more extreme negatives: a "ruthless Fascist capitalist" for whom "such concepts as truth and sincerity came to have literally no meaning" (Oliver Carlson); a "petulant, selfish, arrogant and occasionally callous" figure who exercised influence through "loud-mouthed" newspapers (Hugh Cudlipp); a "colossal failure" who will "depart loved by few and respected by none whose respect is worthy of respect" (Charles Beard); "an eccentric, a supreme screwball, a serio-comic vaudevillian who took the whole world as his stage and enacted there an endless series of fantastic charades for more than a half-century" (W. A. Swanberg). Even Stead, who had ambiguous feelings about Hearst, ultimately came down against him: "He is self-assertive, pushing, defiant, and determined at whatever cost to 'get there' every time."[30]

Yet despite all of his well-documented excesses, there is something about the early Hearst at least that commands respect. For one thing, whatever he set out to accomplish in the sphere of journalism, he did with undiminished energy and enthusiasm. "We cannot wait for things to happen; on the *Journal* we make things happen," Hearst proclaimed loudly.[31] To be sure, he lacked ideological consistency, and other than in his later years, when his newspapers adopted a position on the far right of the political spectrum, it was never clear exactly why and to what extent his newspapers advocated the political line that they did. Yet profit was never Hearst's primary motive, as it was for many of his contemporaries. On the contrary, he lost huge sums of money on many of his newspapers and did not even begin to earn a positive balance until well after 1914, when the profits from his diversified media holdings began to converge in his favor. He paid high wages to get the best journalists he could, women as well as men (thereby subverting the prevailing labor market in gender exploitation), invested heavily in advanced printing machinery and attempted (in a mysterious psychological way, it would seem) to become a tribune for the people. "If newspapers are to be successful," Hearst affirmed, "they must express the opinion of the public."[32] In this limited sense, it can be claimed that Hearst played a critical role in the shift to a democratic culture signified by the creation of a mass circulation press.

From his university days at Harvard, when he was expelled for academic deficiencies, Hearst admired Pulitzer, and it was as a cub reporter for the *World* that he first gained an understanding of the workings of popular journalism. During his early years as a press proprietor, Hearst was an inveterate opponent of what he described as the "monied interests." He fought even harder than Pulitzer or Stead to combat economic and social injustices. The Southern Pacific Railroad, led by Collis P. Huntington, bore the brunt of his antagonism for many years, as did private companies that controlled the water supply, venial owners of saloons, monopolistic utilities and businesses that exploited their employees. In 1887, within months of taking charge of the *San Francisco Examiner*, Hearst launched more than a dozen public crusades. He continued this practice for many years, tapping into a vein of popular disenchantment that newspapers on both sides of the Atlantic had mined successfully from the middle decades of the century. It is significant that Stead praised Hearst for coming down with "spiked boots upon so many dishonest people's toes."[33]

A number of Hearst's press innovations strongly influenced the transformation of Anglo-American journalism. He broke the single column rule more frequently and spectacularly than any other press proprietor, including Pulitzer, and was the first newspaperman to make effective use of banner headlines. He sought to win the loyalty of millions of readers, many of them lacking adequate literacy skills, by means of instant visual appeal, which meant bold headlines alongside pictures. "If the headline is big enough, it makes the news big enough," Orson Welles affirms (in a paraphrase of Hearst) during a key scene in "Citizen Kane." The most serious charge against Hearst is that he tried to appropriate news events for private purposes without, seemingly, being constrained by any ethical considerations. He used headlines to sensationalize news, whether involving street crimes ("STABBED WITH SCISSORS") or, as in 1898, belligerent calls to military action against Spain. Under pressure from Hearst, Pulitzer responded by engaging in a war of scare-heads, streamers and undocumented news stories that lasted almost six years. By the time he conceded defeat to Hearst in 1901 (and retired to quieter precincts in Paris) the entire public face of journalism had been permanently changed in New York and across much of the transatlantic world.

Hearst was an invigorating proprietor to work for, sometimes too much so since he was prepared to dismiss employees instantaneously. He sent teams of reporters digging after scoops, forming them into "Wrecking Crews" or "Murder Squads," that blanketed city morgues and police offices. He instructed his staff: "Get the news. Get it first. Spare no expense."[34] It was when Hearst crossed an as yet poorly defined professional line and blatantly "manufactured" news that he opened himself to harsh criticism. If authentic news did not transpire, he was prepared to fill the daily press vessel anyway. As one of his reporters commented, "When nobody was being robbed or murdered ... (Hearst) would come down to the office with despondency written on his face." From his days as a neophyte proprietor of the *San Francisco Examiner*, he was fascinated with the idea of creating news. He would parlay small stories into big ones and, like Bennett and Pulitzer, extend them artificially for days or weeks to provide a non-stop source of entertainment for his readers. At other times he and his reporters literally became the news as they shimmied off in hot pursuit of alleged malefactors. (To be sure, Wilbur Storey had done this successfully more than once on the *Chicago Times*.) Hearst might direct his employees to rescue a damsel in distress or apply their forensic abilities to solving a murder. The most sensational incident of this kind occurred in 1897, when one of his reporters, Karl Decker, freed a Cuban woman from a Havana prison. Amidst an unprecedented outpouring of public excitement, the *Journal* printed accounts of the brutality accompanying her incarceration, together with detailed reports of her "rescue." The banner headlines accompanying these stories served the dual purpose of arousing jingoistic feeling and significantly increasing circulation. The veteran reporter, James Creelman, concluded that on this occasion Yellow Journalism had "broken the bars of the Spanish prison." Interestingly, Stead also gave a full-throated endorsement to Decker's exploit because, he maintained, "it boldly asserts (Hearst's) determination to supersede the journalism that chronicles by the journalism that acts."[35]

Hearst initiated numerous publicity stunts. Nellie Bly had parti- cipated in fearless extravaganzas on Pulitzer's behalf. In imitation Hearst led "Annie Laurie" (Winifred Black) and a group of equally emboldened journalists (male and female) on a series of similar escapades that gen- erated even more publicity. From time to time he also unabashedly fabricated news reports and interviews, usually complementing these with faked pictures. Many of the "firsthand exclusives" he published that detailed Spanish atrocities in Cuba were actually written covertly by his New York staff in the vicinity of the *Journal*'s office in lower Manhattan. By 1900, the combined editions of the *Journal,* including its enormously successful Sunday paper, edited by Morrill Goddard, attained a daily circulation of almost one million readers, the largest for any set of newspapers in the United States.

In many ways, Hearst was a greatly magnified version of Pulitzer, especially in regard to his contribution to the creation of the Sunday press in America. British Sunday papers are fundamentally of two kinds: those like the *News of the World* that have appealed to a working-class readership and are deeply rooted in elements of popular culture; and those such as the *Observer* that feature an analytical approach to the events of the week. American Sunday newspapers, on the other hand, as defined by Pulitzer and Hearst, offer a general interest format topped with a profusion of popular trimmings. In the words of a critic, they are a "melange of suggestive misinformation and half truth ... plenty of paper but little news."[36] These Sunday newspapers, which included magazine inserts, colored pictures, comic strips and celebrity features (they still do today) were the virtual creations of two great working journalists of the 1890s, Arthur Brisbane and Morrill Goddard, both employed by Pulitzer before defecting to Hearst. In succession they sensationalized the *Sunday World* and, more strikingly, the *Sunday Journal* (later the *Sunday American*).

Brisbane was a quintessential tabloid journalist, who achieved fame with his tersely written essays on a wide range of subjects, which were syndicated to millions of readers throughout North America. He claimed to have composed each of them in about 15 minutes, while focusing his mind on the imagined mental tergiversations of his elderly German housekeeper. "If I think she'd miss the point of a sentence, I write it over again in a clear form with fewer big words," he stated. His aim was to hit a newspaper reader "between the eyes with the first sentence; all else would follow naturally." In an egregious moment of self-revelation, Brisbane (the best paid journalist in the world under Hearst) declared: "I am the yellowist journalist in the world. If I am not, I want to be."[37]

Yet despite Brisbane's spectacular career in journalism, Goddard, an unrivalled dispenser of sensationalism, who has been described as the "greatest circulation go-getter on earth," was, in some ways, the more interesting and important of the two men. He created many of Hearst's famous banner headlines, as well as the concept of the modern "supermarket tabloid" non-story ("MARS PEOPLED BY ONE VAST THINKING VEGETABLE"). He made extensive use of color printing, specialized in cutaway drawings of human innards and conceived of the original "yellow kid" comic strip even before Outcault, the cartoonist, did. It is interesting to note that both Harmsworth and the Lawson family, who owned the *Daily Telegraph*, tried to ape the Sunday newspaper success of Pulitzer and Hearst. They carried out a joint experiment in 1899, by publishing Sunday editions of the *Daily Mail* and the *Daily Telegraph*, a new venture in British journalism that represented an "American style" extension of the daily newspaper to seven days. Both efforts failed within weeks in the face of intense opposition from Sabbath-minded churchmen and newsagents. Further efforts in this area were not resumed until after 1918, another indicator of persistent cultural differences between the two countries.

Hearst has been condemned for the strident imperialism of his papers, particularly during the two years leading up to war with Spain in 1898. He did just about everything he could to facilitate this conflict, making use of brightly colored streamers, provocative pictures and news stories of dubious provenance. His motives had little to do with policy considerations, though he appears to have felt a genuine sympathy for those Cubans who rose in rebellion against Spain. Rather, his no-holds-barred support for war was primarily intended to generate increased publicity and circulation, as it did. Battlefield deaths almost always play well at the journalistic box office, as Bennett, Harmsworth, Pulitzer, Hearst and others in the trade during the nineteenth century independently concluded. In one instance, a five-column Hearst headline ("DOES OUR FLAG PROTECT WOMEN?") cascaded forth to the accompaniment of a half-page drawing of a naked Cuban girl. If readers of the *Journal* had been polled they would, undoubtedly, have responded to the question with a heartfelt negative. In a much-publicized incident (the veracity of which has been questioned by Hearst's recent biographers), he reportedly sent a telegram to Frederick Remington, his chief illustrator in Havana, stating: "You furnish the pictures, and I'll furnish the war."[38] During the conflict, Hearst received notable assistance from James Creelman, who had been employed previously by the *Herald* and the *World*, where he gained plaudits for his coverage of the Sino-Japanese

War. Creelman has been characterized as "the sort (of reporter) who believed in making news when there is none." Like other war reporters of the period he seems to have adjusted reality to the excessive demands of Hearst.[39]

Pulitzer was also drawn into a campaign of jingoism in 1898. And during the Boer War Harmsworth pursued a similarly fervent imperialistic line in the *Daily Mail,* which has been summarized as "aggressive, boastful, and euphoric." Reportedly, he concluded that his readers enjoyed "a good hero and a good hate," and, to the surprise of few of his contemporaries, he sought to provide them with either one or both. Kennedy Jones, who collaborated with Harmsworth in founding the *Daily Mail,* was a bellicose imperialist who devised the enduring press slogan, "One Flag, One Empire, One Home." Jones concluded that news of overseas conflicts was attractive to the new breed of late nineteenth-century readers whose lesser social status made it more likely that they would be receptive to nationalistic appeals. Somewhat less stridently than Hearst and Pulitzer, he sought to make Harmsworth's newspapers the "voice of Empire in London journalism."[40]

The flag-waving and xenophobia that coursed through the transatlantic world at the turn of the century gave a distinctive shape to its popular journalism. Several hundred American reporters, including more than 20 from Hearst's *Journal,* and including a handful of female journalists, covered that nation's war with Spain. A reporter testified to the excitement in Manila in 1898, when the city was under blockade: "(The journalists) came tramping in, some of them veterans of the Greek and Balkan conflicts, others tasting for the first time the delectable fruit of war."[41] Large numbers of British correspondents rushed to the South African heartland during the Boer War (1899–1902), inducing the *Daily Mail* (which hired many of them) to create a "war train" that "nightly shrieked at maddening speed through the country."[42] The Spanish-American War and the Boer War, along with Britain's campaign of revenge in the Sudan in 1898, led by Kitchener, and the Boxer Rebellion in China in 1900, yielded some of the defining stories of the age. Speed in reporting, a strident tone and the presence of celebrity authors like Richard Harding Davis, made for continuous excitement. The accompanying pictures, including the contributions of sketch artists and photographers, helped to stoke sentiments of gratitude and anger, as in May 1900, when the uproariously welcome news of the relief of Mafeking was broadcast. It would be naive to deny that these feelings were manipulated for commercial purposes by proprietors of newspapers intent on building circulations. But it is important to note that they also reflected genuine sentiments that coursed across the Atlantic in both directions.

During these years reporters in Britain and America began to compete relentlessly for scoops. American-style reporting with its overriding emphasis on speed continued to transform journalism. Bennett Burleigh, who reported on the Boer War and other overseas conflicts for the *Daily Telegraph*, took note of this change, as did his colleague, Aubrey Stanhope, an American correspondent who worked for the *Herald*. Stanhope moved about widely during these years, among other things managing the Paris edition of the *Herald* and residing in London for several years where he worked as an overseas correspondent. He was a throwback to the days of Yates and Sala, in combining a predilection for rapid reporting with a bohemian lifestyle. Like Burleigh, Stanhope encapsulated the essence of late nineteenth-century American-driven transatlantic journalism. The most important quality of a reporter, he wrote, was his "instinctive intuition as to find out where news is, and a quick and ready initiative, so as to know what to do at once, whatever turns up."[43] George W. Steevens ("G. A. S.") of the *Daily Mail* was another thoroughly "Americanized" war reporter. He was reminiscent of Januarius MacGahan in the brevity of his career (he died in South Africa at the age of 30), the prolificacy of his writings and the condensed, rushed style of journalism that he embodied. Winston Churchill, who cut his journalistic teeth in South Africa during these years of imperial freebooting, described Steevens as "the most brilliant man in journalism I have ever met."[44]

Overall, Alfred Harmsworth was a less flamboyant participant in mass circulation journalism than Hearst, or even Pulitzer, though he had much in common with both men.[45] He was a fervent admirer of the American press and was profoundly influenced by American ideas. He had considerable respect for Pulitzer and got on well with him. In 1894, two years before launching the *Daily Mail*, Harmsworth traveled to New York to observe Pulitzer's *World* in action. "Every young man ought to go to the United States," he wrote. During this visit he was impressed by the absence of "wearisome prolixity" in the *World* and the *Sun*, which was still managed by Dana, as well as the advanced machinery used by both papers. Subsequently Harmsworth traveled to the United States a number of times and sent members of his staff to New York to observe American press methods up close, including Pulitzer's innovative use of the summary lead, which he then incorporated into the *Daily Mail*.[46]

At the outset of 1901, Pulitzer and Harmsworth collaborated in a singular venture. Harmsworth traveled to New York for the sole purpose of bringing out a special New Year's Day edition of the *World* for Pulitzer. (It was on this visit that he met Hearst and Arthur Brisbane for the first time.) He published this sample newspaper in tabloid format, making it one of the first daily newspapers of this size to appear in either Britain or the United States since Day's *Sun* in the 1830s. Harmsworth believed that the tabloid – "small, portable (and) neatly indexed" – was destined to become the "newspaper of the 20th century."[47] Three years later, he brought out his own tabloid-sized *Daily Mirror*, initially as a paper for women and then much more successfully as a pictorial newspaper.

Harmsworth's feelings about Hearst were less enthusiastic than about Pulitzer, primarily because he distrusted the uninhibited techniques of the former as well as his gargantuan journalistic appetite. Furthermore, Hearst's increasing outbursts of Anglophobia alienated Harmsworth, as they did many of his contemporaries. Hearst's attitudes towards Britain were complex, though generally negative. As a young newspaper proprietor, he trumpeted himself loudly as "American," by dressing in checked jackets and brightly colored hats. And in his fulsome advocacy of a classless consumer-led democracy, he leveled indirect criticism at the weakness of Britain and that country's debilitating social hierarchy. During the First World War, his newspapers espoused opinions that were uninhibitedly anti-British, culminating in a breakdown of personal relations with Harmsworth, who commanded a mission to the United States and was in charge of his country's propaganda during the war.

Yet despite his coolness towards Hearst, Harmsworth's journalism was an integral segment of a converging web of transatlantic relationships, and it drew heavily upon the innovative ideas of Bennett, Pulitzer, Dana, Hearst and other American newspapermen. Harmsworth hired many American journalists to work for him, among them Pomeroy Burton, formerly of the *World* and the *Evening Journal*, who became the general manager of his newspapers. As the owner of the *Evening News*, the *Daily Mail* and the *Daily Mirror*, Harmsworth was a publisher of international reputation who was at the forefront of those cultural and economic forces reshaping the Anglo-American press during these years. Like Hearst, he erected a vast media empire, though he never realized his ambition to print a "simultaneous newspaper" of coordinated news stories based on a centralized press. By 1913, his publishing company had become the largest public business in Britain. It controlled 29 newspapers and magazines, including several issuing from provincial cities.

The similarities between Harmsworth and Hearst are striking. Both men appreciated the limitless potential of modern journalism and tried to exercise power in an uncompromising fashion. They relied on a small number of trusted employees to carry out their objectives: Hearst on Brisbane and Goddard, Harmsworth on Kennedy Jones, his chief counselor, and Thomas Marlowe, who edited the *Daily Mail* with enormous aplomb for 27 years. Both Hearst and Harmsworth required a mass readership for the success of their enterprises and attempted comparably to understand and give expression to the interests of their readers. Harmsworth believed that the phrase "Government by the People" (in reference to journalism) should replace "Government by Newspaper," and stated that, "We don't direct the ordinary man's opinion. We reflect it." John A. Spender, the editor of the *Westminster Gazette*, who did not ordinarily engage in verbal excess, described him as "the only completely convinced democrat I ever knew."

Yet one must be cautious in ascribing the word "democrat" to Harmsworth and to Hearst, even in a general cultural sense. Jones, after all, never ceased to remind journalists working on Harmsworth's newspapers that they were "writing for the meanest intelligence." And Philip Gibbs, who worked for Harmsworth on the *Times* and knew him well, was, perhaps, not totally wide of the mark when he described him as "typical to a supreme degree of the average man, as produced by the triviality, the restlessness, the craving for sensation, the desire to escape from boredom, the impatience with the length and dullness and difficulty of life and learning."[48] Both Harmsworth and Hearst reveled in the power of print and, with linguistic irony, were referred to by the same cognomen, "The Chief." (So, for that matter, was Stead.) "The Chief remains for me an almost sacred personage," commented Edgar Wallace, the celebrated fiction writer, who worked as a correspondent for Harmsworth for many years."[49]

Both Hearst and Harmsworth are also similar in that neither man wrote particularly well or espoused coherent political views, unlike Stead and Pulitzer. They enlisted their newspapers in what may perhaps be described as a non-ideological game of power. Marlowe made the following observation: "I once asked (Harmsworth) ... what he was after. He replied, like a schoolboy, 'Power', but could not give any indication of the sort of power he wanted or what he would do with it."[50] In a sense, Hearst and Harmsworth were "neutral" observers of passing events, even while advocating for strong public positions, in the same way that they comprised part of a new breed of "classless" press lords who lacked binding social allegiances. Where they differed was in Hearst's obsession with activism and Harmsworth's more temperate adherence to the concept of the media as entertainment. Hearst promoted himself and his newspapers as doers ("While Others Talk the Journal Acts"); Harmsworth's success in journalism derived from his ability to provide print at a level that combined value and affordability. There is an important cultural signifier at work here since Americans tend to equate success with quantity and verbal overkill. For Britons on the other hand, a quieter adherence to prevailing conventions is more frequently proffered as a virtue.

To understand with any precision how Americanization worked under Harmsworth, it is best to focus upon his three leading newspapers: the *Evening News*, which he purchased in 1894, the *Daily Mail* (1896) and the *Daily Mirror* (1903). (The *Times*, which he bought in 1908, responded somewhat languidly to innovations in popular journalism, though in the years before 1914 it began to brighten its typography and publish more pictures.) Frank Harris had partially transformed the *Evening News* into an American-style newspaper during the 1880s. However, Kennedy Jones, its editor after 1894, introduced large-scale changes with the assistance of Walter Evans, who had previously worked on the *Star*. Liberal doses of crime, sex and imperialism were sprinkled throughout the pages of the *Evening News*, as were attention-catching decks and a column entitled "Woman's World," dedicated to subjects deemed of special interest to female readers. The newspaper also notably expanded its sports coverage, including a Saturday edition devoted to football results that was one of the first of its kind to be printed in Britain. Jones was imbued with the American emphasis on speedy news coverage, "told in a natural way and presented in a manner agreeable to the eye and intelligible to the mind." Consequently he transformed the paper into a "typical" evening product, which reported on the day's events rapidly and dynamically, as these unfolded in "real time." For a time the *Evening News* gained the largest circulation of any evening paper in Britain; in a moment of braggadocio, Jones, consumed by its success, exaggeratedly described it as ushering in the birth of the "modern newspaper."[51]

The halfpenny *Daily Mail* was more comprehensive in scope, and though a morning paper it incorporated techniques of evening journalism into its pages. Whereas Jones aimed at news across the entire spectrum of reader interest, Harmsworth opted for packets of amusement, including serialized fiction, stunts and stories about "Food, Money and Women," which, he believed, were likely to attract large numbers of readers.[52] This coalescence between an Americanized emphasis on news and a focus on "trivial" magazine-style features created a key new entrant in the morning field, which swamped its competitors within a short

Figure 8.1   Alfred Harmsworth; William E. Carson, *Northcliffe* (1918)

period of time. The *Daily Mail* employed a talented staff that hunted energetically after "American-style" scoops, making extensive use of the typewriter (notwithstanding Harmsworth's initial reservations) and the telephone. Like Pulitzer's *World*, it mostly substituted pleasure for pedagogy. Harmsworth provided the news in capsule form so that the *Daily Mail* would be "lighter than the ordinary morning paper." According to Tom Clarke, one of his editors, he claimed to imbibe ideas for the day's news stories by riding on an omnibus across central London and listening to the conversations of passengers.[53] Not surprisingly, parliamentary coverage was vastly curtailed in the pages of the *Daily Mail*. Sketch writing ("Parliamentary News") and a daily feature called "Political Gossip," in which news and scuttlebutt were interfused, largely replaced it. To his discredit, a slightly nonplussed Harmsworth asked his editor on one occasion why a "very strange piece of news" about a girl killed in a whirlwind was buried on an inside page behind several political news stories.[54]

Notably striking – though Pulitzer prefigured it with his "For and About Women" column in the *World* and the introduction of a woman's page in the *Sunday World* in 1891 – was the emphasis of the *Daily Mail* on "women's news." Harmsworth was one of the first press proprietors in the transatlantic world to recognize the enormous potential of a women's market. He told Marlowe that the features section of the paper "ought to be almost entirely feminine. It ought, I think, (to) be a woman's page, without saying so." On another occasion he instructed him as follows: "Don't forget the women. Always have one women's story at the top of all the main news pages of your paper."[55] While presenting the *Daily Mail* as a general interest newspaper weighted primarily towards a middle-class suburban readership, therefore, Harmsworth presented some of the news in a way that he assumed would be of particular interest to women. Several female journalists were hired to write for the paper, including Lady Sarah Wilson, who covered the Boer War, and to edit its "Daily Magazine," which was transformed into a women's page with features on cooking, domestic management, health and fashion.

The *Daily Mail* was a great success, though in some ways it was less innovative than its successor, the *Daily Mirror*, which became the first successful pictorial tabloid newspaper in the world. The *Daily Mirror* was preceded by two illustrated daily journals: the *Daily Graphic* (1872–9), published in New York, and the London *Daily Graphic*, commenced in January 1890 and extant until 1926, when it was merged with the *Daily Sketch*. The New York "picture-sheet" was a five-cent tabloid-sized evening paper that was more "sensational" than its London successor because its primary objective was to disseminate fast-breaking urban news. It broke new ground in the history of pictorial journalism by publishing copies of photographs, though in order to do this it made use of an expensive "chalk-plate" process that at its best produced crude results. In its seven-year existence, the New York *Daily Graphic* rarely achieved a circulation of more than 10,000.

More successful by far was the London *Daily Graphic*. From the outset this paper, an offshoot of the *Weekly Graphic*, disseminated less hard news than its New York predecessor. It focused on non-topical, magazine-style features and gossip, often leading to an unsatisfactory integration of pictures and text. The difficulty in reproducing sketches and photos rapidly enough to complement the increased speed of news collection made for a disjunction between print and pictures that was not to be satisfactorily resolved until after 1900. Even so, the early numbers of the *Daily Graphic* possessed visual immediacy, as in its front-page woodcut of a colliery disaster in Wales (3 March 1890). By the mid-1890s, the newspaper started to break new ground in the history of photojournalism. It was the first transatlantic newspaper to make use of the halftone process block on a regular basis, thus launching the age of the cheap "picture paper." The halftone process eliminated the need for line drawings in transcribing photos into woodcuts. It was invented at Cornell University in the 1880s, though employed initially in the British press, a reversal of the usual nineteenth-century pattern. Up to about 1897 the halftone process was primarily used to reproduce portraits; then it began to be applied effectively in daily journalism, as in the *Daily Graphic*'s coverage of the Boer War. The age of the staff engraver was effectively nearing its end, though not yet of the peripatetic sketch artist.

At first Harmsworth's *Daily Mirror* was intended to focus solely on the concerns of "gentlewomen": to be "a daily reflector of women's interests, women's thought, women's work."[56] This concept proved unworkable and, to be sure, unprofitable. In January 1904 the newspaper was radically transformed into the *Daily Illustrated Mirror* (subsequently it reverted to its original name, the *Daily Mirror*), a picture daily with an all-photographic front page, in which news and illustrations were blended into an integrated entity. At the outset it announced its revolutionary intent: "The old tradition that pictures were only a makeweight, and a sop to the less serious kind of reader, has altogether passed away. Our pictures do not merely accompany the printed news. They are a valuable understanding of it."[57] It continued to give some emphasis to "women's news," but its success derived principally from its ability to reproduce photographs by means of the halftone process, which could now be used on high-speed rotary presses. It set aside a segment of each daily issue for the publication of pictures: some were sensationalized ("WHITE MEN AND WOMEN SLAIN IN SAVAGE AFRICA"); others were posed photographs of well-known people; still other pictures popularized the indiscretions of celebrities in a titillating way. Harmsworth gave speed primary consideration, sending his cameramen out with hand cameras in place of those that were previously mounted on tripods.[58] The *Daily Mirror* gave a premium to crime stories, among them the sensational pictorial coverage of the capture of Dr. Hawley Crippen in Canada in 1910 by means of wire telegraphy. Crippen was subsequently convicted of murdering his wife and executed, a series of events covered by the paper with pictorial panache. Not surprisingly, a critic described the *Daily Mirror* as being fit for "those who could see but could not read."[59]

Between 1907 and 1915 the editor of the *Daily Mirror* was Alexander ("Alec") Kenealy, a Briton who had worked for both Pulitzer and Hearst in New York for several years, and was steeped in speed-driven American city journalism. Kenealy played a decisive role in transforming the newspaper into a successful pictorial tabloid. He emphasized "talking points" and stunts, as well as a heavy dose of photographs. His dictum, according to Beverley Baxter, a future editor of the *Daily Express,* was as follows: "If you have anything to say, say it brightly. If not, don't say it. When you have a story that matters throw everything else away. Give it hot, give it strong, and give a lot of it."[60]

By 1914, the *Daily Mirror* had begun to purchase photos from picture agencies, and its sales exceeded one million daily, the largest certified circulation of any single newspaper in the Anglo-American world. During the 1920s and 1930s it became a brash working-class tabloid, which despite its shortcomings made a seminal contribution to the history of the popular press. Not until the commencement of the *Illustrated Daily News* in New York in 1919 (subsequently renamed the *Daily News)* and of Hearst's New York *Daily Mirror,* in 1924, was there a successful American tabloid equivalent. (The *New York Star*, a tabloid-sized newspaper published by Frank Munsey, had circulated briefly in 1896.) In some ways, the *Daily Mirror* represented Harmsworth's most significant long-term achievement as a press proprietor. Pictorial journalism (with the exception of comic strips) was, perhaps, the one major area in which the British press largely transcended its American competition in the age of New and Yellow Journalism, a development that intensified the bitterness of its critics, who attacked it as vulgar, cheap and, most wounding of all, "an essentially low American colonial intrusion into British life."[61]

Notes

1 Pound, *Northcliffe*, 205. The Linotype machine has been described as "the most significant printing development since the introduction of moveable type in the middle of the fifteenth century." (Gramling, *AP*, 102.)
2 Wilfred Hindle, *The Morning Post, 1772–1937: Portrait of a Newspaper* (London: Routledge, 1937), 216.
3 On the early impact of web feeding machines see Reid, "Modern Newspaper Enterprise," 712–14. For the Walter Press, see *History of the Times, 1841–1884*, 348–9.
4 Pauline Wingate, "Newsprint: From Rags to Riches – And Back Again?," in Anthony Smith (ed.), *Newspapers and Democracy: International Essays in a Changing Medium* (Cambridge: The MIT Press, 1980), 68.
5 Given, *Making a Newspaper*, 204.
6 Charles Perry, "The British Experience 1876–1912: The Impact of the Telephone During the Years of Delay," in Ithiel de Sola Pool (ed.), *The Social Impact of the Telephone* (Cambridge: The MIT Press, 1977), 69–96; John Brooks, *Telephone: The First Hundred Years* (New York: Harper & Row, 1975), 118.
7 Peter Young, *Person to Person: The International Aspect of the Telephone* (Cambridge: Granta Editions, 1991), 111. Arnold Bennett wrote: "The European telephone is a toy, and a somewhat clumsy one compared with the inexorable seriousness of the American telephone." (*Those United States*, 91.)
8 Donaldson, *Popular Literature*, ix.
9 Tribune Association stock was initially held by a small group of investors, including Greeley. Seitz, *Horace Greeley*, 108–9.
10 For the *Herald* of 1870–1, see McCabe, *Lights and Shadows*, 247. The 1913 estimate is in Given, *Making a Newspaper*, 306–7.
11 James D. Startt, *Journalists for Empire: The Imperial Debate in the Edwardian Stately Press, 1903–1913* (New York: Greenwood Press, 1991), 8.
12 Lee, *Daily Newspaper*, 197.
13 James Curran and Jean Seaton, *Power Without Responsibility: The Press and Broadcasting in Britain* (London: Routledge, fourth edition, 1991), 52.
14 Pound, *Northcliffe*, 260. See Jeremy Tunstall, *The Media are American: Anglo-American Media in the World* (London: Constable, 1977) and Robert Whitehouse, *The Other Fleet Street* (Altrincham: First Edition, 2004). Maurice Milne states that this was "the real beginning of the metropolitan invasion into the world of the provincial press." (Milne, *Newspapers*, 193.)
15 Spender, *Briton in America*, 54.
16 The figure is in Lucy Maynard Salmon, *The Newspaper and the Historian* (New York: Oxford University Press, 1923), 134.
17 E. W. Scripps, *I Protest: Selected Disquisitions*, ed. Oliver Knight (Madison: The University of Wisconsin Press, 1966), 78–83; Gerald W. Baldasty, *E.W. Scripps and the Business of Newspapers* (Urbana: University of Illinois Press, 1999).
18 Charles R. McCabe, *Damned Old Crank: A Self Portrait of E.W. Scripps: Drawn from his Unpublished Writings* (New York: Harper & Brothers, 1951), 212.
19 "Samuel Storey," in Dennis Griffiths (ed.), *The Encyclopedia of the British Press, 1422–1992* (London: Macmillan Press, 1992), 539–40. On Carnegie, see Hodgson, *From Smithy to Senate*, 83, and Viscount Northcliffe, *Newspapers and Their Millionaires: With Some Further Meditations About Us* (London, 1922), 6.

208 *The Americanization of the British Press, 1830s–1914*

20 Henry Wickham Steed, *The Press* (London: Penguin Books, 1938), 162.
21 Rogers, *American Newspaper*, 93. The quote by Hall Caine is to be found in *Sell's* (1914), 21. For a critical assessment of the impact of commercialism on journalism, see Oswald Garrison Villard, *The Disappearing Daily: Chapters in American Newspaper Evolution* (New York: Alfred A. Knopf, 1944).
22 The Creelman quote is in Brendon, *Life and Death of the Press Barons*, 132.
23 For a perceptive study of Yellow Journalism, see W. Joseph Campbell, *Yellow Journalism: Puncturing the Myths, Defining the Legacies* (Westport: Praeger, 2001).
24 John A. Lent, *Comic Books and Comic Strips in the United States: An International Biography* (Westport: Greenwood, 1994), xxi; Ian Gordon, *Comic Strips and Consumer Culture, 1890–1945* (Washington, D.C.: Smithsonian Institution Press, 1998), 7. Peter Bailey has written a fine article entitled "Ally Sloper's Half-Holiday: Comic Art in the 1880s," in Bailey, *Popular Culture and Performance in the Victorian City* (Cambridge: Cambridge University Press, 1998), 47–79. See also David Kunzle, *The History of the Comic Strip: The Nineteenth Century* (Berkeley: University of California Press, 1990).
25 Emery, *Press and America*, 353.
26 Rogers, *American Newspaper*, 55.
27 Arthur Christiansen, *Headlines All My Life* (London: Heinemann, 1961), 144; Horace White, "The School of Journalism," *North American Review*, CLXXVIII, 31. H. L. Mencken has observed caustically: "No one ever lost money by underestimating the intelligence of the American public."
28 Commander, "Significance of Yellow Journalism," 155; Oliver Carlson, *Brisbane: A Candid Biography* (New York: Stackpole Sons, 1937), 154. Brisbane wrote (p. 154): "People are dull, life is dull, crime, races, politics, divorces – all these are dull when seen by dull brains."
29 The quotes by Harris are in *My Life and Loves* (ed.) John F. Gallagher (New York: Grove Press, 1963, originally published in 1925), 630, 636.
30 Oliver Carlson and Ernest Sutherland Bates, *Hearst: Lord of San Simeon* (New York: The Viking Press, 1936), xiv; Hugh Cudlipp, *The Prerogative of the Harlot: Press Barons & Power* (London: The Bodley Head, 1980), 15, 24; Charles A. Beard, preface to Ferdinand Lundberg, *Imperial Hearst: A Social Biography* (New York: The Modern Library, 1937), vii; W. A. Swanberg, *Citizen Hearst: A Biography of William Randolph Hearst* (New York: Bantam Books, 1961), 625. Stead's comment is in *Americanization of the World*, 296–7. The best recent studies of Hearst are David Nasaw, *The Chief: The Life of William Randolph Hearst* (Boston: Houghton Mifflin, 2000) and Kenneth Whyte, *The Uncrowned King: The Sensational Rise of William Randolph Hearst* (Berkeley: Counterpoint, 2009).
31 Hughes, *News and the Human Interest Story*, 204.
32 Lee, *Daily Newspaper*, 195.
33 Stead, *Americanization of the World*, 299.
34 Lee, *Daily Newspaper*, 217.
35 *Review of Reviews*, XVI (1897), 457. For an account of the incident, see James Creelman, *On the Great Highway: The Wanderings and Adventures of a Special Correspondent* (London: Charles H. Kelly, 1901), 178–86.
36 Simon Michael Bessie, *Jazz Journalism: The Story of the Tabloid Newspapers* (New York: E. P. Dutton, 1938), 56.

37 Carlson, *Brisbane*, 115; Lee, *Daily Newspaper*, 638. The *New Republic* observed that Brisbane "spoke the simple language of millions of American people – especially those millions who read as they run."

38 The telegram is quoted in Creelman, *On the Great Highway*, 178, though Nasaw states that the incident was most likely apocryphal (*Chief*, 127).

39 Willis J. Abbot, *Watching the World Go By* (London: John Lane The Bodley Head, 1933), 220.

40 Jones, *Fleet Street*, 144–51. For a racial dimension to this imperialism, see Catherine Hughes, "Imperialism, Illustration, and the Daily Mail, 1896–1904," in Michael Harris and Alan Lee (eds), *The Press in English Society from the Seventeenth to Nineteenth Centuries* (Rutherford: Fairleigh Dickinson University Press, 1986), 188.

41 John T. McCutcheon, *Drawn from Memory* (Indianapolis: The Bobbs-Merrill Company, 1950), 116. See Joyce Milton, *The Yellow Kids: Foreign Correspondents in the Heyday of Yellow Journalism* (New York: Harper & Row Publishers, 1989) and Charles H. Brown, *The Correspondents' War: Journalists in the Spanish-American War* (New York: Scribner, 1967).

42 *Sell's* (1903), 157.

43 Aubrey Stanhope, *On the Trail of the Great: Recollections of a "Special Correspondent"* (London: Eveleigh Nash, 1914), 282–3.

44 Quoted in David Linton and Ray Boston, *The Newspaper Press in Britain: An Annotated Bibliography* (London: Mansell Publishing, 1987), 263.

45 Ralph Blumenfeld described Harmsworth exaggeratedly as "the inevitable originator of all things in modern journalism." Blumenfeld, *Press in My Time*, 105. Bernard Falk, who worked for Harmsworth, claimed that he "revolutionized modern journalism and made newspaper life a thrilling experience." *He Laughed in Fleet Street* (London: Hutchinson, 1933), 216.

46 Richard Heathcote Heindel, *The American Impact on Great Britain, 1898–1914: A Study of the United States in World History* (Philadelphia: University of Pennsylvania Press, 1940), 19.

47 Alfred Harmsworth, "The Newspapers of the Twentieth Century," *North American Review*, CLII (1901), 75; Pierce, "How the Tabloid was Born," 28; Ray Boston, "The First of the Tabloids," *British Journalism Review*, X (1999), 63–8.

48 Jones, *Fleet Street & Downing Street*, 166; Gibbs, *Adventures in Journalism*, 84. Sydney Dark describes Harmsworth even less favorably as an "Aston Villa tough." *Not Such a Bad Life*, 52.

49 Edgar Wallace, *People: A Short Autobiography* (London: Hodder and Stoughton, 1926), 164.

50 Marlowe to Blumenfeld, 12 September 1893, Blumenfeld Papers, House of Lords Library.

51 Jones, *Fleet Street & Downing Street*, 120. A sampling of editions of the *Evening News* in 1881, 1888 and 1894 provide evidence for key changes in this newspaper, including a regular use of decked headlines, increased emphasis on crime and sport, and (predictably) enhanced triviality.

52 William Beach Thomas, *A Traveller in News* (London: Chapman and Hall, 1925), 65. Harmsworth told Tom Clarke that good stories should focus on "crime, love, money and food." Fyfe, *Sixty Years of Fleet Street*, 65.

53 Tom Clarke, *Journalism* (London: Robert Ross, 1945), 48.

54 Northcliffe to Tom Marlowe, AM 62, 198, 24 February 1911, Northcliffe Papers, British Library.
55 Northcliffe to Marlowe, AM 62, 198, 10 March 1909, Northcliffe Papers. On Pulitzer's contribution to this area, see Jan Whitt, *Women in American Journalism: A New History* (Urbana: University of Illinois Press, 2008), 39, and Adrian Bingham, *Gender, Modernity, and the Popular Press in Interwar Britain* (Oxford: Clarendon Press, 2004), 28–9.
56 *Daily Mirror*, 2 November 1903.
57 *Daily Illustrated Mirror*, 28 January 1904.
58 The picture captioned "White Men and Women Slain in Savage Africa" is in the *Daily Illustrated Mirror*, 26 January 1904. See Bernard Grant, *To the Four Corners: The Memoirs of a News Photographer* (London: Hutchinson, 1933).
59 Lord Salisbury's contemptuous comment is to be found in J. Lee Thompson, *Northcliffe: Press Baron in Politics, 1865–1922* (London: John Murray, 2000), 113.
60 Beverley Baxter, *Strange Street* (London: Hutchinson, 1935), 281.
61 Chris Horrie, *Tabloid Nation: The Birth of the Daily Mirror to the Death of the Tabloid* (London: Andre Deutsch, 2003), 30.

9
The Modernization of Journalism

Four months after the new century began, the halfpenny *Daily Express*, the most Americanized newspaper to appear in Britain up to that time, commenced publication. Founded by Charles Arthur Pearson, its most illustrious days lay ahead of it after Beaverbrook gained financial control during the First World War and Arthur Christiansen became editor in 1933. Yet from the outset, it plowed new ground with a front page given over to news ("nothing like having your best goods in the shop-front window," observed Stead[1]), and it rapidly amassed a readership of several hundred thousand. Its selling points were derived almost entirely from transatlantic models. Pearson was an enthusiast for all things American and he visited the United States several times before launching his newspaper. As early as 1895 he had conceived of publishing a daily paper in London that was to be aimed primarily at American readers. Nothing resulted from this project, but from the very outset the *Daily Express* was an "American-style" product transplanted to British shores, as became evident in 1902 when Blumenfeld was appointed editor.

Blumenfeld was steeped in American popular journalism before coming to London, and during his lengthy stewardship of the paper, he institutionalized front-page news (although his competitors in the morning field, including the *Daily Mail*, did not do the same) and created the first banner headlines and streamers to be seen in the British press. He also insisted that his staff write in a concise "American" style. For these reasons Beverley Baxter, who succeeded him as editor, credited Blumenfeld with playing a role in journalism analogous to that of Queen Victoria, who had witnessed "the whole change from an absolute monarchy to the monarchy in chains to democracy."[2] During his years as editor, Blumenfeld hired a number of American-trained journalists to assist him, including Perceval Phillips, who had previously covered the Spanish-American War for Pulitzer's *World*, and Alexander Kenealy, subsequently to become editor of the *Daily Mirror*.

Pearson's objective in establishing the *Daily Express* was to make it "the most readable newspaper in the world." Yet he unhesitatingly rejected the "yellow journalism" tag that doggedly stuck to him and his paper for many years. "We have no scent for blood, no appetite for horrible detail," he averred.[3] Unlike Britain's penny evening press (and the bulk of American city newspapers), the *Daily Express* assigned a relatively tempered role to crime, sports and gossip. But it imprinted a new style of journalism in its pages. Its leading articles were sub-divided into "Matters of Moment," coverage of the news was distinctly "humanized" (meaning, according to its critics, that it was sensational-ized), a woman's page magazine format was introduced in emulation of the *Daily Mail*, interviews became a regular feature of the paper and pictorial supplements, often intended to be titillating, adorned its news columns. It also introduced a front-page index to the news, which was an American innovation. As with Pulitzer, Harmsworth and Hearst, imperialistic rhetoric was given a wide berth in the *Daily Express*, though, in the words of Stead, who admired Pearson, it was a "non-partisan patriotic imperialism."[4] During the Boer War the newspaper featured banner headlines such as "THE BOERS' LAST GRIP LOOSENED: MAFEKING AND BADEN-POWELL'S GALLANT BAND SET FREE" (19 May 1900), that became totems around which millions of modestly literate readers coalesced in peals of sentiment and enthusiasm. Not surprisingly, the paper gave a critical impetus to the development of mass circulation journalism in Britain.

In the years prior to 1914 hundreds of newspapers were launched in Britain. None of them possessed the immediate impact of the *Daily Express* but nearly all were shaped to some degree by the changes ushered in during the previous decades. Many new entrants were evening papers, where speed was by now an indispensable ingredient for success. Kennedy Jones stated: "The very first essential for an evening journalist is exceptional quickness – quickness of perception, quickness of decision, quickness of execution."[5] For the most part press circulations tended to soar. An estimate based upon certified auditing procedures reveals that six London newspapers published in 1910 had a daily circulation of 300,000 or more.[6] Consolidation of ownership was likewise strengthened and business models of proprietorship set firmly into place. Charles Russell, who edited the *Glasgow Herald*, commented in 1912: "We are slow to Americanise our papers."[7] However, Russell partly missed the point, because although British journalism absorbed structural changes from America in unpredictable and, in the view of some observers, insufficient ways, it had begun an irreversible transformative process. A mass circulation press was coming into existence, even though (by comparison with America) it represented a kind of "middle-of-the road" journalism that tempered the more extreme elements of sensationalism and news competition.

When Blumenfeld first entered the pressroom of the *Daily Express* he was made immediately aware that the organizational structure of the paper badly needed change. One of his first steps was to instruct a sub-editor, "an old man with a long white beard who sat on a high stool," to correct a proof as speedily as possible. The elderly gentleman accepted the challenge halfheartedly at best, informing his new editor that he would take it home with him in the usual fashion and return it the next morning.[8] To be sure, this was not the pattern followed in most American newspaper offices (nor to be fair in the majority of Fleet Street offices), where the innovations of preceding decades had brought into being elaborate staff structures intended to print and distribute hundreds of thousands of copies of a paper as rapidly as possible. For the most part this involved a complicated web of specialized reporting and editorial functions whose emphasis was primarily on news collection. A News Editor (or "Night Editor" on evening papers) was responsible for selecting the next day's news stories, writing the headlines and doing a "make-up" of the paper before putting it to bed. (A person with the title Chief Sub-editor performed these tasks in British newsrooms.) Reporters were constantly phoning in stories, or sending dispatches by wire, to editors or rewrite men who converted them into readable copy and prepared them for the compositors. The work was mostly very intense, especially on evening papers. Irvin Cobb, who wrote for the *World*, has left behind a description of "the chopping-box method of a newspaper shop," where reporters were continuously working against time, their unforgiving enemy. "Good stuff must be slashed to the quick and the adorably little brain children of the rewrite staff lie in windows on the city room floor," Cobb observed.[9] Even when newspapers lifted stories from their competitors without attribution or baldly exaggerated the content of news items, their objective was to simulate a feeling of "real news" that would have instant appeal to the consumer. A separate department did the editorial writing, but on the majority of American newspapers this facet of newspaper work had lost much of its importance.

Speed had become fully integrated into journalism on both sides of the Atlantic. "Get there first with the most news" was an American press slogan widely adopted by now in Britain. When Nelly Bly completed her record-breaking "Around the World" stunt Pulitzer's *World* blared the headline, "FATHER TIME OUTDONE." This capsule statement seemed to speak for a generation of newspapermen and women who were working at the cusp of modernity, while striving to overcome temporal obstacles. "Money, time, the rest of the paper, sometimes even men's lives, do not seek to count against that insane desire to get something of importance in the sheet which all the rest want and can't get," complained a photographer-journalist in 1905.[10] In the years just before 1914, the *Evening News* in London customarily printed five or six editions a day and pushed its staff as hard as any American newspaper to produce fast-breaking stories about crime, sports, politics – literally anything of interest that came to hand. Reporters were usually confined to a single room where telephones were constantly ringing. The clamor never ceased. "The general chat goes on ... telephone bells jangle loudly, and a man bursts into the room, looks at the clock, and begins writing for his life."[11]

Newspapers relied increasingly upon press agencies and wire reporting for the bulk of their contents. Reuters provided most of the foreign news for the American market because of its longstanding arrangement with the Associated Press. But new agencies were coming into existence, partly in response to the restrictive control of its franchises by the Associated Press. The New York *Sun* formed the Laffan News Agency when it was excluded from AP membership by the *World,* and in 1909, under similar circumstances, Hearst established his International News Service, which combined various syndicated services. Similar examples of press rivalry and the integration of "human interest" news into agency reports occurred in Britain. Central News battled energetically against the Press Association for dominance of the domestic news market and made incursions against Reuters in the foreign field, where it was described as "more lively, colourful and, as it sometimes seemed, much faster."[12] Until 1905 Extel (Exchange Telegraph Company) dominated the reporting of sports news. Then the Press Association began to use the telephone for the purpose of speeding the delivery of football and cricket results. The Press Association also established a special News Service in 1909, covering items of ordinary interest such as fires and "startling crimes and outrages." Likewise, the London *Times* and the *New York Times* strengthened a reciprocal news-sharing arrangement that they had commenced in 1902. The upshot of these numerous changes was that by 1914 a structure of transatlantic journalism had come into existence largely built around speed and an American-inspired focus on "human interest."

Sports coverage, which was especially dependent upon the speed of the telegraph and telephone, became extremely popular during these years, though its modern efflorescence did not occur either in Britain or the United States until the 1920s, helped along by the advent of radio. In Manchester the Edward Hultons (father and son) placed a working-class passion for sports reporting at the center of their successful commercial publishing empire, which consisted of "sensationalized" Sunday and evening papers, and, beginning in 1909, of the halfpenny *Daily Sketch*, an "All-Picture Morning Paper." Saturday afternoon specials offering the latest football results began to appear with increasing regularity, and it became the common practice for newspapers to publish Football League tables and match summaries every Monday morning. Increased attention was also given to cricket, especially in the evening press, and in the *Daily News* and the *Daily Telegraph* among the morning papers. It has been estimated that by 1900 sports news constituted about 7.5 per cent of the content of the *Daily Telegraph*, a significant shift in emphasis.[13]

In America Pulitzer and Hearst greatly expanded the coverage of baseball news and often reported it on the front page. More than any other sport the reporting of baseball became tied to speed. Hearst's *Boston American,* for example, often printed its final edition at the end of the seventh inning of a Red Sox game on the assumption that the team ahead at that time would be the winner. If its conjecture as to the end result proved erroneous, it was often prepared to destroy thousands of copies and resume the process of printing all over again.[14] During the winter months American sports reporting fell off in the absence of a spectator sport sufficiently popular to act as a substitute for baseball. But horse racing secured a solid following in both the United States and Britain, despite accusations that it fostered immorality and sensationalism. Many newspapers published a torrent of information about racing, including tips, though a small number of proprietors refused to sanction the practice. George Cadbury, the Quaker owner of the London *Daily News*, excluded all racing information from his paper. When he purchased the evening *Star* in 1909, however, he wisely reversed course for commercial reasons, telling his son that, "I sought to be guided by commonsense."[15]

Crime was also widely reported in the press before 1914, with the Hearst papers providing the most sensational and entertaining coverage. As with sports, evening newspapers found it profitable to highlight crime stories because (if accompanied by bold headlines and pictures) these were frequently best poised to attract large numbers of spontaneous readers. Morning papers did not lag far behind in the coverage of crime, including such "respectable" entries as the *Times* and the *Daily Telegraph*. The *Times* occasionally criticized its competitors for exploiting the crime-oriented proclivities of its semiliterate readers. Yet it too unshackled itself from time to time, as in its coverage of the Jack the Ripper murders in 1888, when it did not hesitate to publish details of the violent nature of the homicides (while modulating some of their explicit sexuality). In the intense competition for an edge in circulation coverage of crime was often a better option for reporters and editors than sports or sex. "Even the palmy days of the late Boer War never saw so many editions on the street as that ghastly time when the terrible Whitechapel maniac was at his grisly work," commented a journalist.[16] Mass circulation newspapers were eviscerated for allegedly facilitating the commission of crimes as well as giving publicity to them. It is a charge that continues to be made against the tabloid press today, often without justification, and in the years prior to 1914 it was employed generically as a stick with which to beat proponents of New or Yellow Journalism. When a Methodist minister addressed a large crowd in Manhattan in 1897, he reiterated the point (obvious to him) that "child criminals are increasing in number, and the cause must be laid at the door of those papers which seek to picture youthful criminals and describe their doings in long accounts."[17]

News accounts of violent crimes were generally more sensationalized in the American press. As well as being placed on the front page, they sometimes fastened speculative guilt or innocence on the accused, a difficult thing to accomplish in Britain because of tighter legal restraints. However, barriers were occasionally breached in Britain, as when witnesses were identified by journalists or interviewed before the commencement of a trial, a common practice in America. In the 1890s, the *Pall Mall Gazette* staged several Hearst-style "citizens' arrests" in its offices to generate publicity and increase sales. It turned out, ironically, that the assistant editor who first conceived of this stunt, a newsman named Tommy Fielders, was an American journalist temporarily working for the paper.[18] Some crime stories attracted large-scale interest on both sides of the Atlantic. A sensational poisoning case in Manhattan in 1898–9, involving a wealthy man-about-town named Roland Molineux, generated fierce newspaper competition between Pulitzer and Hearst that produced striking headlines and a series of spectacular news stories. It also fascinated British readers, who were able to follow its salacious details in the pages of both the *Daily Telegraph* and the *Times*. In 1906, the spectacular murder of the architect Stanford White by Harry Thaw in the Madison Square Roof Garden in Manhattan, which led to two trials, created a banquet of sensationalism for the Hearst press. This "Trial of the Century" (with its numerous commercial offshoots) likewise generated enormous interest among readers of the British press.

On both sides of the Atlantic reporting techniques became ever more "Americanized" in the years leading up to 1914. American reporters were thoroughly steeped in the competitive practice of chasing after news, rather than waiting for it to come to them. It was widely affirmed that newspapers "don't want brains; they want tireless legs to make the rounds." The work of the burrowing, aggressive American newspaperman was characterized by one journalist as "the subtlest, swiftest element in the chemistry of modern civilization."[19] When Fred Wile of the *Chicago Record* was assigned to cover President McKinley, his editor warned him: "Stick to him like a leech. Sleep with him if you can, and eat with him, too. And the Lord have mercy on you if the Record is scooped."[20] American cities were divided into reporting beats and scoured systematically for news of fires, homicides or anything else out of the commonplace, an organizational technique first commenced by Charles Chapin, Pulitzer's great City Editor on the *World*. Speed was at all times the desideratum in the compilation of news stories. Aubrey White, a British reporter who worked the morgue beat for the New York *Evening Telegraph* (the sister paper of the *Herald*) in the late 1890s, has described the fierceness of the competition among "legmen," who rushed breathlessly about looking for stories. When White turned a story in to his editor a few minutes late, he was reprimanded in the following words: "Your way of writing might do very well for the London *Times*, but here you must make it more lively." A popular handbook for journalists observed: "It is a wild race between journalists as to who will get the first word. The prevailing style bears the traces of this breathless haste; it is smartly pictorial, restless, impatient, emphatic."[21]

Some British reporters (unfairly for the most part) continued to be thought of as deficient in initiative and slow of foot by comparison with their American colleagues. In the view of one pressman, their work remained "ponderous, stately, dignified." Lincoln Springfield, who covered the 1895 general election for the *Pall Mall Gazette*, filed dispatches from Oldham and neighboring constituencies, without, he subsequently admitted, spending a single minute in any of them. A rapidly diminishing number of British reporters still adhered to a "gentlemanly" approach to journalism that eschewed speed and informality. H. M. Stanley, for example, reported that while employed by the *Herald*, he was taunted and made to feel that "an American journalist was not of such fine clay, as a Briton of the same profession."[22] However, most reporters on British newspapers were prepared to engage in "rough and tumble" tactics to dig into the interstices of urban life in search of news stories, in the way American journalists did. By 1900, the majority of evening papers in London had adopted the American practice of assigning "turns" to reporters each day, depending upon where their editors believed the timeliest news stories were likely to develop. These reporters were made to submit their copy under conditions of speed, occasionally being supplemented by teams of boys who were sent out in shifts and instructed to bring to the copy room running accounts of the news.[23] In 1908 a milestone of sorts was attained. A *Herald* reporter from New York was dismissed by the paper for losing out on a scoop of the pioneering Wright Brothers flight to a journalist working for the *Daily Mail*.[24]

Throughout the transatlantic world an absorptive process involving American-inspired techniques of modern reporting and innovative content was at work. In New York the *Tribune*, a newspaper with a conservative readership edited by Whitelaw Reid and (from 1913) his son Ogden, introduced "Sunday supplements" (including comics), political cartoons, a feature-oriented Sunday magazine and a daily "Woman's Page," which it inaccurately promoted as the only existing one in the world. It also gave increased attention to crime and sports (subjects that Greeley had resisted), and to "the latent possibilities of the city as a field for news."[25] The *New York Times*, purchased in 1896 by the Southern publisher Adolph Ochs, adhered for the most part to a comparatively staid format. But it also took into account the need for change. While denigrating "the sensational, the sordid, and the over-smart," and condemning the Hearst press in particular for its "freak journalism," it lightened its typography to increase its visual appeal, reduced its price to a penny in October 1898 and introduced a halftone Sunday magazine supplement, though without a comic strip. It also increased the range of its news coverage, in an attempt to validate its celebrated motto, "All the News That's Fit to Print," which has continued to appear on the newspaper's masthead since February 1897. The sensational scoop by the *New York Times* of the sinking of the Titanic in April 1912, for which it relied heavily on wireless technology and the telephone, enormously boosted its transatlantic reputation. An editor of the *Daily Mail* in London kept a copy of the newspaper's Titanic story in his desk and described it as "an example of the greatest accomplishment in news reporting."[26] Britain's traditional press was likewise reconfigured in "Americanizing" ways, a development depicted harshly by one critic as "a sneaking fondness for fashionable fiddle-faddle." Newspapers steadily contracted the number and size of their leading articles, printed interviews with newly minted celebrities and replaced the detailed reporting of parliamentary debates with feature-oriented material. Most British newspapers also reduced their price to a penny or a halfpenny in the years before 1914 and published an increasing number of pictures as a supplement to the text.

Changes in content were seminal but so were better opportunities and working conditions for journalists, a trend given impetus by the creation of a mass circulation press. After 1900 many more journalists were hired, including large numbers of women for the first time. The bohemian vestiges of newspaper life, palpable during the middle decades of the century, gave way to an increased professional feeling among journalists. Key questions began to be debated in public venues: What did it mean to be a journalist and how did journalism differ from other forms of literature? Was it possible to create professional requirements for journalists that were sensible and, at the same time, widely agreed upon? Could salaries be raised sufficient to guarantee the establishment of a predictable career structure, thereby obviating the need for journalists to seek complementary sources of income? During the final decades of the century the position of journalists notably improved in a number of ways. Was it possible to sustain this improvement? If so, might this lead to the recognition of journalism as on a par with accepted professions such as medicine or law? To what extent did any or all of these more recent transformations derive from the American experience, as was broadly true of so many other aspects of press history during the preceding 80 years?

Journalism has never lacked for romantic associations. When Julius Chambers arrived in New York near the turn of the century, at the commencement of what was to be a fruitful career, he felt an initial frisson of excitement: "(The call of journalism) to American youth is irresistible. It is the call at once of romance and of strenuous business." David Christie Murray came to London at about the same time as Chambers, likewise searching for newspaper work and aspiring to become a successful writer, an ambition he too fulfilled. Murray recollected being suffused with "the glory, the passion, the very rage of achievement." And in 1902, when Aaron Watson, a provincial journalist, returned to London after being away for seven years, he discovered (not to his liking) that the city's newspapers were in the hands of "new men." On the plus side though, as he conceded, the prospects for amply remunerated work were much better than they had been even a decade earlier, and he felt that "anybody who could write at all might find an opening."[27]

The expansion of newspaper staffs created thousands of openings in Britain and America for prospective journalists, especially those prepared to cover speedy urban beats. Formal requirements were minimal. A young man or woman had only to demonstrate an ability to write quickly and clearly, and to work extended hours. Admittedly, the nature of the work was unpredictable and might well be brief. But the emotional and material rewards involved in becoming a journalist were often sufficient in themselves, not only in terms of fulfilling the goal of being a published writer but because of the opportunity to become a foreign reporter or even an editor. Newly empowered press lords such as Hearst and Harmsworth were much more likely to measure productivity in tangible ways than their predecessors, which worked to the advantage of press novices. An ample portion of the available work (particularly in American newsrooms) was compensated in accordance with the number of words that found their way into print, an arrangement that might be attractive to a young journalist with sufficient know-how to manipulate the system.

Throughout most of the nineteenth century journalism was regarded as an occupation of low social standing, though this was truer in Britain than America. From the earliest days of press history social background had acted as an occupational signifier for many newspapermen in Britain. Men with university degrees ("university tips") had monopolized editorial and writing positions on the majority of newspapers and magazines. A degree from Oxford or Cambridge, or residence at one of the Inns of Court in London while preparing to become a barrister, posited a means of advancement. Only at the level of basic reporting, often meaning a rote collection of facts, did a socially disadvantaged candidate stand a reasonable chance of becoming a journalist. In the United States a degree from a university embodied less social cachet, but it too opened doors to respected positions in the press. Journalists of relatively modest educational and social background did the bulk of the "mechanical" legwork on American newspapers, though they often held some of the editing jobs as well.

As opportunities increased in the late nineteenth century and competition for work from those of lower social origins intensified, the popular press in both countries tended to do the bulk of the new hiring. Opportunities were greater in the United States because such a press had emerged earlier and had spawned numerous offspring. From the outset Bennett hired untrained young journalists for his staff, or gave them an opportunity to work as freelancers. He and many other American proprietors emphasized practical training, with college graduates sometimes being dissuaded even from applying for work. Julius Chambers relates that Greeley dismissed him from the *Tribune* staff (temporarily as it turned out) when he discovered that he had a degree from Cornell University, telling him: "I'd a damn sight rather you had graduated at a printer's case." When another reporter informed his editor that he was a graduate from the University of Michigan he noticed "the look in his eye and the slight disdainful wave of his hand. I was to understand later how inconsequential in those days was a college diploma in a newspaper office."[28]

In both Britain and America most of those who started at the level of reporter could expect to end there, though this was marginally less true in America. "The training of a reporter is not the best training for the highest places," affirmed George Smalley, who nonetheless negotiated the difficult transition from reporter to editor on the *Tribune*.[29] Within newspaper offices a hierarchy existed, with editors and reporters sometimes maintaining a state of physical separation. When Louis Heren went to work for the *Times* in the 1940s he discovered that the staff of this venerable newspaper was still divided into two segments: gentlemen and players. "The gentlemen were the editors and leader writers. The players were the reporters."[30] Social distinctions of this kind did not exist to the same degree in American newsrooms. For the most part greater informality prevailed, with fewer barriers in existence. When Greeley edited the *Tribune* he worked in a large noisy room with his employees, a situation that Julian Ralph described in similar terms for the *Sun*: "No taint of caste poisons its atmosphere or forces its workers into cliques, and when its men have no work to do they play together at cards or chess or gymnastics, or whatever." Interestingly, shortly after Beaverbrook (of Canadian extraction) became proprietor of the *Daily Express* in 1915 he sought to facilitate interaction among its journalists by removing physical barriers, though within a short period of time it was reported that the editor of the paper "vanished into a room of his own."[31]

More revealing, perhaps, were the ways in which outsiders treated journalists from different kinds of newspapers. Those working for penny and halfpenny papers were sometimes denied opportunities for interviews or reporting access. As early as the 1840s, Bennett was barred from New York's inner social circles because of his dubious background (Scottish and rural) and, more relevantly, because he owned the *Herald*, an object of contempt in many literate quarters. Blumenfeld recounted a similar experience shortly after he became editor of the *Daily Express*. He was initially barred from membership in an exclusive London club because his paper sold for a halfpenny. When the price was doubled to a penny hitherto inaccessible walls began to disintegrate and he was successfully invited to apply for membership. Snobbery of this type existed on both sides of the Atlantic but almost certainly had greater resonance in Britain. Harmsworth recalled in the early 1880s, that at the outset of his career in journalism reporters from the *Times* "spoke to nobody," treating representatives of penny papers (like himself) with disparagement. According to Hannan Swaffer, the great picture editor of the *Daily Mirror*, photographers from the paper were shunned by representatives of the *Times*: "They worked for penny papers. We were a halfpenny and a picture paper. It was a dreadful crime." Most wounding to the psyche perhaps were the experiences of Edgar Wallace as a reporter for the *Daily Mail* during the Boer War. He was subjected to "gratuitous snubs" from correspondents of the "old school," including Burleigh of the *Daily Telegraph,* and believed that this was because he was regarded as a "slum child – ignorant of the very elements of English grammar."[32]

Class deference was frequently minimal on American newspapers, and proprietors like Pulitzer and Hearst (who lacked social credentials of their own) were more likely to hire journalists with little formal education and without "respectable" credentials, and to elevate them to positions of influence. The question of what constituted proper dress for a journalist is germane to this point. As late as the turn of the century, most British reporters were required to wear frock coats, top hats and pegged trousers to work, even when the bulk of their day was spent prowling around police stations or at the city morgue. Not until after 1914 was this dress requirement mostly abandoned, and according to one account, it continued to be the rule on the *Daily Telegraph* as late as 1937.[33] Harmsworth insisted that his staff always dress with a degree of formality, even while on a "hurry call" in pursuit of news. He was prepared to concede "important news for the lack of this livery," according to Phillip Gibbs, a decision that Hearst or Pulitzer would have found incomprehensible. It was generally believed that a London journalist, "must be dressed as well as a stockbroker if he wishes to make a name in Fleet Street," though newspapermen occasionally devised entertaining ways to subvert this dress code. Reporters on the *Star,* for example, were compelled to wear silk hats in the newsroom. When unobserved they invented a game of chance that involved tossing playing cards into these hats. Hard-earned wages undoubtedly shifted hands in this way.[34]

American reporters were not for the most part obligated to observe a dress standard. There was little likelihood that persons being pursued for interviews or news stories would reject the importunities of reporters based on their social position alone. On the contrary, a growing number of American newspapermen prided themselves on their informal attire: a white shirt with sleeves rolled up unaccompanied by a hat or a tie, which was intended to consecrate their addiction to speed. However, as journalists shed the conventional vestiges of earlier days they began to establish new signposts that were shaped by their evolving professional status. An indicator of this is that they were instructed to dress well, in emulation of other groups of professional workers. Lecturers in newly founded schools of journalism told them to attire themselves respectfully (a hat, cut trousers, decorative waistcoats); otherwise, their occupational status would be cast into doubt. Most American journalists accepted this advice in good spirit, if with some reluctance, and readjusted to a "proper" dress code.

The hiring of women reporters in significant numbers during the years leading up to 1914 was a striking phenomenon. Previously, British and American newspapers had employed few women, and when women did manage to be hired as journalists their work tended to fall outside the regular staff structure. As a mass circulation press created better opportunities for work, women began to compete for jobs, and by the turn of the century a growing number were beginning to be hired, especially in America. Some British editors and newspaper owners were responsive to employing women. Stead for one gave energetic support to female journalists while editor of the *Northern Echo* and the *Pall Mall Gazette*. He hired women to fill editorial positions and successfully promoted the careers of two women who became celebrated journalists: Hulda Friedrichs and Flora Shaw. Friedrichs was given a key staff position as an interviewer on the *Pall Mall Gazette* by Stead and has been described as "the first woman in journalism paid and treated (more or less) as a man." Stead also befriended and assisted Shaw, who gained fame as the colonial editor of the *Times*, even if, ironically, she was denied a request by that newspaper to travel to Africa in the 1890s because her male editors felt it was too dangerous for a woman to go there.[35]

Harmsworth was likewise receptive to employing women journalists, primarily to work on the "Woman's Page" of the *Daily Mail*, and on the *Daily Mirror*, especially in its initial incarnation as a newspaper dedicated exclusively to feminine interests. Women did scattered work in many areas of the British press: writing about fashion for London papers like the *Daily Telegraph*; preparing syndicated "Letters" on miscellaneous subjects; occasionally being given overseas assignments as special correspondents.[36] On the whole, however, by comparison with America British newspapers practised little more than token gender integration before 1914. The journalist Frances Low wrote in 1904 that she knew of only two women who were "regular reporters" on the staffs of well-established British newspapers. When the "stunt reporter," Elizabeth Banks, arrived in London from America in the early 1890s looking for work, she was peremptorily told: "You will never be able to do big things in journalism ... you're all woman and no journalist." Neither the *Daily Express* nor the *Daily Mail* – two newspapers that spearheaded the modernization of transatlantic journalism – hired women as full-time staff employees until 1904. When Emillie Marshall joined the *Daily Express* as its first full-time female staff member in that year, she was instructed to write stories about "women, food and weather."[37]

Women did considerably better as journalists in America. Pulitzer and Hearst employed a number of women to work on the *World* and the *Evening Journal*. Some specialized in interviewing because it was widely believed that feminine wiles could be put to effective use in persuading people of both sexes to talk freely. Other women journalists engaged in stunts or wrote "soft news" for the women's pages of American city newspapers. Participants in this niche journalism (referred to deprecatingly as the "Hen Coop") enjoyed lower professional status than men and were less adequately remunerated.[38] Yet, a small number of American women became highly paid journalists, notably among those employed by Hearst. They were given prestigious by-lines (as were increasing numbers of male journalists during these years) and were fully integrated into reporting and editorial staffs. Several of them were unfairly denigrated as "sob sisters," because their primary task was to explicate the emotional components of a news story from a woman's perspective. But a few of the so-called "sob sisters" were exceptionally fine journalists and garnered national recognition, including "Dorothy Dix" (Elizabeth Gilmer) and "Annie Laurie" (Winifred Black). Both women made effective use of speed and sensationalism. Gilmer won fame by commencing her "advice to the lovelorn" column for the Hearst press. She was a gifted crime reporter whose spectacular coverage of the White/Thaw/ Nesbit murder case brought her an annual income of $13,000 dollars, reportedly the highest sum earned by any woman in the United States. Black's career was spent entirely in the service of Hearst. She covered high profile murder trials, and in her emphasis on speed, scoops and sensationalism embodied the best (and worst) aspects of American tabloid journalism. Her press credo remains of considerable interest: "The ideal newspaper woman has the keen zest of a child, the cool courage of a man and the subtlety of a woman."[39]

It would be seriously misleading to overstate the advances of women in journalism before 1914. In both America and Britain familiar arguments were conveniently trotted out in opposition to their presence: that reporting was dangerous; that it was physically and emotionally too strenuous for women; that it involved night work, which compromised their social standing; and that the sexual vulnerability of women made it impossible for them to work as reporters without forfeiting claims to respectability. American press informality also sometimes clashed with the interests of women journalists, as when male reporters in several newsrooms hung up curtains around their space, so as to be able to smoke freely or work in shirtsleeves; or when women were told to write their stories at home and not intrude on the "masculine" environment of the work place.[40] Women journalists were also barred from membership in several professional organizations on the stated grounds that they were unqualified for the job, were unable to write with objectivity and, most important, took positions away from better-qualified male journalists. Still, in a comparative way and particularly with regard to the much-maligned Hearst, who was in many ways the most "Americanized" press magnate of the century, when cultural determinants such as speed and informality clashed with traditional press modes, it is safe to say that the former sometimes won the battle.

Beginning in the third quarter of the century, attempts to establish a professional status for journalists began to take definable shape. In previous decades many journalists on both sides of the Atlantic had disported themselves in a bohemian fashion, among the best known from the British side being Yates and Sala ("King of Bohemia"). These journalists cultivated an image of unstructured literary freedom: "no method, no system, no management, no earnest purpose." They spent time in taverns and theaters in London and New York, consorting with unconventional writers, actors and a medley of journalists. Several members of the New York literary coterie that introduced British newspapermen to innovative ideas about journalism congregated in the bohemian neighborhoods around Madison Square and Gramercy Park, in what then constituted northern Manhattan, while in London, companionate watering holes were to be found in refreshment bars in the vicinity of Fleet Street and Ludgate Hill Station. Justin McCarthy, a fringe member of the bohemian world in both cities, has left behind a compelling account of this life: "Late hours of conviviality, much beer, much brandy and soda, many cigars, unlimited tobacco, a good deal of temporary poverty, a common faculty for running into debt."[41]

By the turn of the century traditional bohemianism had mostly disappeared, especially in America, in the face of better work opportunities and improved income. "I cannot see that dandruff on the collar is an evidence of brains," commented one young reporter.[42] Nonetheless, in the newly emerging age of mass circulation journalism an inverted form of bohemianism developed. The image of the hard drinking, carefree, irresponsible newspaperman became synonymous with the city reporter, initially in America, where the style became closely linked to Chicago, and then in Britain, where it came to be particularly observed among pressmen in Manchester. The modern pressman (and woman) began to be conceived as a mental freelancer, though subject to the external sanction of job insecurity. It should be noted that reporters were always in a vulnerable position. They could be instantly dismissed at the whim of a proprietor (and then rehired almost as quickly).

The notion of journalism as a profession is central to the evolution of the transatlantic press because it involved a concerted effort to resolve at least two key issues. The first was the attempt to demarcate journalism from literature. Throughout most of the century critics derided newspaper work (especially that done on the cheap press) as an unproblematic task requiring little in the way of creative talent. In its swifter, modern version it was viewed as the product of a "mile-a-minute" age that did not allow sufficient time for reflection or to generate a "universal principle or emotion of human life."[43] E. L. Godkin affirmed that "American style" journalism was an example of "bad literature," while Matthew Arnold described it scornfully as "literature in a hurry."[44] In the view of Henry James, a writer required a "fine" intelligence, whereas a journalist needed little other than an inclination to undertake hard work. James believed that steady employment on a newspaper excluded even the possibility of developing cultured literary judgments because such work was earthbound, at its best little more than the "criticism of the moment at the moment."[45] Several prominent writers disagreed, including H. G. Wells and Walter Besant. They maintained that journalism was a legitimate way of communicating ideas, and that in the proper circumstances it was potentially much more than that.

In a narrow sense at least Wells and Besant were right. Many journalists were demonstrably fine writers who proved capable of making a tasteful choice of words and paragraphs and, more important, of fusing quality with speed. Richard Harding Davis, Stephen Crane, Edgar Wallace and Jack London (the latter complained that a "reporter's work is all hack from morning till night") were among a batch of established and ambitious writers on both sides of the Atlantic who coveted and achieved fame and money through newspaper work.[46] They traveled to distant locales and, making use of their reputations as celebrities, helped to increase the circulation of their newspapers. Their news reports, written with immediacy and dash, were infused with an eye for the literary brushstroke. Harmsworth, Hearst and other proprietors paid such authors top salaries and, in so doing, attracted scores of other good young writers to their stables. In her book *Narrating the News,* Karen Roggenkamp maintains insightfully that reporters often employed a "fictive" discourse that tapped into traditional narrative structures.[47] This was especially evident on the Hearst press, where the "journalism that acts" made little distinction between fact and fiction. Newspapers blurred the "truth status" of their articles (sometimes deliberately) by means of an indiscriminate intermixture of news, fiction and feature articles. In press language they applied the word "story" both to hard news and syndicated fiction, which was by 1914 becoming a central feature of mass circulation journalism, especially in the American press where a group of successful fiction syndicates had recently come into existence.

The suggested dichotomy between literature and journalism drew implicitly on two distinct press models: writing as entertainment and as a source of information. The sensationalism of Pulitzer, Hearst and Harmsworth appeared to many observers to tip the balance too far in the former direction. On the other hand, the "information" (or photographic) model of mass circulation journalism provided an important counterbalance. "Objective reporting" had received a stimulus from the widespread use of the telegraph with its emphasis on "bare and unadorned statements." It was easily denigrated for its unimaginative "facticity." But at its best, it presented something considerably better than this: an aspiration towards fairness and an attempt to extrapolate truth from a confused mass of events and opinions. It implied that news and views needed to be separated, what Jean Chalaby has characterized as the "discursive practice" whereby reporters "step back from mediating between readers and reality." More passionately, it is what C. P. Scott, the celebrated editor of the *Manchester Guardian,* had in mind when he affirmed: "At the peril of its soul (journalists) must see that the supply (of news) is not tainted." In the twentieth century, objectivity gradually became an infusing ideal of journalism, though often falling short in practice. It is, however, a segment of the rich tapestry of the modern press, as likely to be found in some of the tabloid papers as in the so-called quality press.[48]

A second key issue, more concrete in substance, involved the type of training required for a successful career in journalism. Should it derive from experience, formal education, or a combination of the two? Many newspapermen in both countries believed intuitively that the best results were likely to evolve from practical experience. This involved a stint in newsrooms, where one began either as a "sub" or (in American terminology) a "cub." By 1900, individuals with university degrees in Britain could no longer take for granted automatic success in journalism. Many of them were now required to undergo a period of provincial work, though this continued to be somewhat random in nature. George W. Steevens, who entered journalism after a brilliant undergraduate career as a classics scholar at Oxford, had to work on several local newspapers before becoming a war reporter for the *Daily Mail*. Harmsworth was skeptical about the value of a university education for journalists, as were many other proprietors. "Highly educated men as a rule have no sense of news," he commented. In effect this signified an endorsement of the view held by many New Journalists, such as O'Connor, who were attempting to transform the earlier system of social privilege into a modern version of classlessness, in the belief that newsrooms represented "the real university for the journalist." For the first time university graduates in Britain began to be actively discouraged from applying for positions in the press. The editor of the *Eastern Morning News*, a Hull newspaper, told Harold Spender: "You have had an Oxford education … and it will take you some time to get over that." Keble Howard, an ambitious novice, was afraid to reveal to the editor of the *Sketch* for two years that he had a degree from Oxford because the editor believed that "any young fellow who had been put into a newspaper office at sixteen was worth his place in London, but I was not."[49] In light of this shift in attitude, the percentage of university men on the staffs of British newspapers declined noticeably in the years before 1914.

A similar assumption was coming to be widely accepted in the United States: that, in the words of the American reporter, Julian Ralph, journalists were "born and not made." However, unlike in Britain this tended to validate the American cultural belief that ability was widely diffused and had only to manifest itself to ensure recognition. As Horace Greeley phrased it in his inimitable homespun style: "The real newspaperman was the boy who had slept on newspapers and ink." Horace White, who worked on the "old style" *New York Evening Post*, agreed with Greeley, though in a more nuanced way. White favored a prescribed training course for journalists as a means of complementing their intuitive "nose for news." But he believed that intuition could be honed more effectively on a city beat than in a classroom.[50] This "practical" conception of journalism (in respect at least to its reporting side) was a way of demonstrating that a non-elitist democratic press with acceptable cultural standards was fully in existence, and if buttressed by a proper training system, could provide the foundation for a strong professional edifice. To an extent, therefore, the hiring pattern in America was the reverse of what it was in Britain. A greater number of journalists with a formal educational background were hired, and in the years before 1914, the percentage of strictly "born not made" journalists declined. It is estimated that in 1911 about one half of the reporters in the United States and nearly 75 per cent of the editors of city newspapers were college graduates.[51]

As a byproduct of the movement towards professionalism, journalists in both countries sought to create objective criteria with which to measure the quality of reporters and editors. Efforts to do this, at a time of invigorating change, were better able to flourish amidst the social fluidity of America. As early as the 1860s, locally based press clubs began to spring up in American cities, including New York, where an organization of self-styled "reputable" journalists commenced a series of monthly meetings for purposes of companionship and conviviality. News copy was shared and exchanged by this and other associations, and a measure of professional fraternity was encouraged. A small number of press clubs published newsletters and magazines. After a series of false starts a National Press Club was commenced in Washington in 1908, which, it should be noted, barred women from membership, though the latter shrewdly formed their own organization as early as 1882 and were active in a number of local groups.[52]

Efforts to provide university-based training for journalists occurred spasmodically in the United States. As early as 1873 courses were offered at the University of Missouri, and within two decades at Cornell and the University of Pennsylvania. In 1908, the first degree-granting School of Journalism in the world was established by the University of Missouri, "a watershed year for a modern, professionalized mass media," in the opinion of one historian.[53] Walter Williams, a journalist, was a participant in these path-breaking events at Missouri, and while he espoused a high-minded approach to reporting, he was not attracted to the ideal of journalism as public service in the same way as Pulitzer. Beginning in 1902, the latter set in motion a series of events that culminated in the landmark creation of the School of Journalism at Columbia University, which opened for classes in 1912. Pulitzer championed in uncompromising terms the notion of journalism as a modern profession, one that was the equal of any other. He recognized the usefulness of practical experience as a segment of professional training, but believed that this had to be reinforced by formal training and the inculcation of a "professional pride that would enable (journalists) to work in concert for the public good." Pulitzer was determined at all costs to do what he could to "keep the counting-room in its proper place," and to harness the modern press to an emerging sense of democratic accountability. This public service conception of the press, inspiring in its formulation, aimed to "make better journalists, who will make better newspapers, which will better serve the public."[54]

In Britain the evolution of journalism as a profession took a somewhat different path.[55] A few tentative steps were begun towards the formation of press clubs and associations, including the establishment of an organization in London in 1882 and one in Manchester a few years later. In 1890, the Institute of Journalists, epitomizing the ambition of the modern professional worker to maintain controls on outsiders (though it encouraged proprietors to join), was formally chartered. Two events of special interest are connected with its early history. The first is that it allowed women to become members, an enlightened departure from the American precedent. The second is that it attempted unsuccessfully to create an examination system for journalists, a proposal condemned by Sala and other pressmen on the grounds that "a journalist is not made by test examination; he is made by industry, intelligence, and experience."[56] This view, representing a reversal of traditional thinking about the nature of journalism in Britain, continued to prevail until well into the twentieth century.

In 1907, the National Union of Journalists, an organization that viewed journalism from a trade union perspective, was founded. It took on the task of improving working conditions, including raising salaries, which remained inordinately low. The NUJ tried to prevent non-journalists (however defined) from "doing reporting work to the financial detriment of regular Press-men." However, no formal educational track was offered to journalists in Britain before 1914, other than a handful of courses provided by the City of London School and small-scale programs at the University of Birmingham and Kings College London. Proponents of training requirements began to make the case boldly for an American-style school of journalism that would create "fixed rules" and a "body of doctrine" for a newly evolving profession.[57] But an attempt by David Anderson of the *Daily Telegraph* to establish such a school in 1887, intended to teach shorthand and writing skills (in return for a substantial payment of 100 pounds), met with widespread disparagement, including a public denunciation by George Gissing, who characterized it as "vulgarity unutterable." Under pressure from a group of journalists Anderson's school was wound up within a few years.[58] Gissing's perspective was that of an accomplished writer/editor, while the self-taught Anderson sought "to elevate 'half-informed' men to a level of competence so they would no longer be the 'waste-paper basket' for all and sundry who cannot succeed in other professions."[59]

In a sense, this unresolved disagreement was at the core of the history of transatlantic journalism in the nineteenth century and of the Americanizing process that so powerfully informed it. In whatever fashion the arguments are framed – vulgarity versus elegance, new versus old, quantity versus quality, uneasiness arrayed against comfort – they were deeply enmeshed in the complexities of Anglo-American journalism as it took shape in the decades after 1830. By 1914 the press had undergone a vast number of changes in both countries. It had become "Americanized" and, to a degree, modernized. Events of enormous importance had transpired: commercial, technological, structural, cultural and, not to be overlooked, heroic. New classes of readers had been born and a mass circulation press was now in existence to service their needs. With all of its failings, this press reflected something exciting – a revolution of sorts. As we pause to look back at events from the perspective of another revolution (one driven by technology and at a speed that seems as incalculable as it is unpredictable) we should, rightfully, be critical of where the nineteenth-century revolution in mass circulation journalism went wrong – too great a deterioration of standards, too little "serious" content, sensationalism for its own sake, commercial manipulation fitfully enabled to run rampant. But we should also acknowledge the positive side of this great revolution in transatlantic journalism: the creation of a print media based on speed that, for better or worse, expressed the democratic aspirations of millions of ordinary readers and, for a time at least, brought them an enormous amount of pleasure. It would be churlish to deny that it does not still do so.

Notes

1 *Review of Reviews*, XXI (1900), 430.
2 Baxter to Blumenfeld, 3 January 1935, Blumenfeld Papers. Sydney Dark, who worked for Blumenfeld, was more critical: "He has approached every problem and every policy primarily with the idea of 'circulation value' in his mind." *Not Such a Bad Life*, 58. Hamilton Fyfe described Blumenfeld as "a genial, kindly believer in nothing (who) applied only one test to whatever might be proposed, 'Will it sell the paper?'" *Sixty Years of Fleet Street*, 97.

3   *Daily Express*, 25 and 24 April 1900.
4   *Review of Reviews*, XXI (1900), 427.
5   The comment by Jones is in Dennis Griffiths, *Fleet Street: Five Hundred Years of the Press* (London: The British Library: 2006), 129.
6   David Butler and Gareth Butler, *British Political Facts, 1900–1985* (Houndmills: Macmillan, 1986), 494–5.
7   Russell's observation is in *Sell's* (1912), 84.
8   Sidney Dark, *Mainly About Other People* (London: Hodder and Stoughton, 1925), 12.
9   Cobb, *Exit Laughing*, 120. Walter Lippmann wrote: "The news of the day as it reaches the newspaper office is an incredible medley of fact, propaganda, rumor, suspicion, clues, hopes, and fears, and the task of selecting and ordering that news is one of the truly sacred and priestly offices in a democracy." *Liberty and the News* (New York: Harcourt, Brace and Howe, 1920), 47.
10 Michael L. Carlebach, *American Photojournalism Comes of Age* (Washington, D.C.: Smithsonian Institute Press, 1997), 43.
11 Arthur Machen, in T. Michael Pope (ed.), *The Book of Fleet Street* (London: Cassell, 1930), 147.
12 Scott, *Reporter Anonymous*, 118.
13 Tony Mason, "Sporting News, 1860–1914," in Michael Harris and Alan Lee (eds), *The Press in English Society from the Seventeenth to Nineteenth Centuries* (Rutherford: Fairleigh Dickinson University Press, 1986), 174.
14 M. Koenigsberg, *King News: An Autobiography* (Philadelphia: F. A. Stokes, 1941), 333.
15 A. G. Gardiner, *Life of George Cadbury* (London: Cassell, 1923), 231.
16 Chris Healy, *Confessions of a Journalist* (London: Chatto & Windus, 1904), 342.
17 *New York Tribune*, 8 March 1897, as quoted in *Sell's* (1899), 166.
18 Springfield, *Some Piquant People*, 96.
19 The "legs" reference is to be found in "The Rewards of Writing: The Financial Ups and Downs of Authorship and Newspaper Reporting," by a Near Writer, in *Collier's*, XLVII, 25 March 1911. The quote about "modern civilization" is by Creelman, *On the Great Highway*, 61–2.
20 Wile, *News*, 43.
21 F. J. Mansfield, *The Complete Journalist: A Study of the Principles and Practice of Newspaper-Making* (London: Sir Isaac Pitman & Sons, 1936, second edition), 224.
22 Franc B. Wilkie, *Sketches Beyond the Sea* (Chicago: Belford, Clark, 1880), 77; Springfield, *Some Piquant People*, 129.
23 Healy, *Confessions of a Journalist*, 285–6.
24 Cecil Carnes, *Jimmy Hare, News Photographer: Half a Century with a Camera*, (New York: Macmillan, 1940), 193.
25 Harry W. Baehr, Jr., *The New York Tribune Since the Civil War* (New York: Dodd, Mead, 1936), 79, 235–6.
26 Leonard Ray Teel, *The Public Press, 1900–1945* (Westport: Praeger, 2006), 49; George H. Douglas, *The Golden Age of the Newspaper* (Westport: Greenwood Press, 1999), chapter 9.
27 David Christie Murray, *Recollections* (London: John Long, 1908), 103; Watson, *Newspaper Man's Memories*, 204.

28 Chambers, *News Hunting*, 3. Ray Baker was the reporter and his quote is in Fred Fedler, *Lessons from the Past: Journalists' Lives and Work, 1850–1950* (Prospect Heights: Waveland Press, 2000), 18.

29 Smalley, "Notes on Journalism," *Harper's New Monthly Magazine*, XXVII (1898), 216.

30 *The Times*, 2 January 1985.

31 Julian Ralph, *The Making of a Journalist* (London: Harper & Brothers, 1907), 179; Mansfield, *Complete Journalist*, 129.

32 Blumenfeld, *Press in My Times*, 196; Wallace, *People*, 116. Swaffer's statement is in Horrie, *Tabloid Nation*, 31.

33 Wintour, *Rise and Fall of Fleet Street*, 37.

34 Cosmo Hamilton, *People Worth Talking About* (Freeport: Books for Libraries Press, 1970), 110; Healy, *Confessions of a Journalist*, 271; Springfield, *Some Piquant People*, 55–6.

35 Scott, *'We' and Me*, 123; E. Moberly Bell, *Flora Shaw (Lady Lugard D. B. E.)* (London: Constable, 1947), 171.

36 See two interesting articles by Laura Alex Smith in *Mitchell's* (1897, 1900), which survey women's work in journalism. Also, Ishbel Ross, *Ladies of the Press: The Story of Women in Journalism by an Insider* (New York: Harper & Brothers, 1936), especially chapters 1–4.

37 Francis H. Low, *Press Work for Women: A Text Book for the Young Woman Journalist* (London: L. Upcott-Gill, 1904), 13; Barbara Onslow, *Women of the Press in Nineteenth-Century Britain* (New York: St. Martin's Press, 2000), 21. The quote about Marshall is in Anna Sebba, *Battling for the News: The Rise of the Woman Reporter* (London: Hodder, Stoughton, 1994), 52.

38 See Jean Marie Lutes, *Front Page Girls: Women Journalists in American Culture and Fiction, 1880–1930* (Ithaca: Cornell University Press, 2006) and Patricia Bradley, *Women and the Press: The Struggle for Equality* (Evanston: Northwestern University Press, 2005), especially 115–39.

39 See Harnett T. Kane and Ella Bentley Arthur, *Dear Dorothy Dix: The Story of a Compassionate Woman* (Garden City: Doubleday, 1952). Her credo is in Ross, *Ladies of the Press*, 67.

40 Some of these conditions are described in Elizabeth L. Banks, *The Autobiography of a "Newspaper Girl"* (London: Methuen, 1902).

41 McCarthy, *Reminiscences*, I, 311. On the bohemian climate in New York, see Congdon, *Reminiscences* and Stedman, *Life and Letters*, I. For London, see Cross, *Common Writer*.

42 Quoted in Ritchie, *Press Gallery*, 199.

43 H. W. Boynton, *Journalism and Literature and Other Essays* (Boston: Houghton, Mifflin, 1904), 12.

44 E. L. Godkin, "Newspapers Here and Abroad," *North American Review*, CL (1890), 202.

45 For a cogent expression of the views of James on this subject, see his essay, "The Art of Fiction," in William Veeder and Susan M. Griffith (eds), *The Art of Criticism: Henry James on the Theory and the Practice of Fiction* (Chicago: The University of Chicago Press, 1986).

46 The quote by London is taken from Ronald Weber, *Professional Writers in America's Golden Age of Print* (Athens: Ohio University Press, 1997), 126.

47   See also Shelley Fisher Fishkin, *From Fact to Fiction: Journalism and Imaginative Writing in America* (New York: Oxford University Press, 1985); Rubery, *Novelty of News*, chapter 9.

48   Chalaby, *Invention of Journalism*, 129. Scott's statement is in Smith, *Newspaper*, 130. For an interesting discussion of objectivity and differing models of journalism, see Stephen J. A. Ward, *The Invention of Journalism Ethics: The Path to Objectivity and Beyond* (Montreal: McGill-Queen's University Press, 2004), chapter 5.

49   Lemahieu, *Culture for Democracy*, 20; T. P. O'Connor, "How to Become a Journalist," *Royal Magazine*, VII (1901), 244; J. A. Spender, *New Lamps and Ancient Lights* (London: Cassell, 1940), 231; Keble Howard, *My Motley Life: A Tale of Struggle* (London: T. Fisher Unwin, 1927), 113.

50   Ralph, *Making of a Journalist*, 175. Greeley is quoted in Charles A. Dana, *The Art of Newspaper Making* (New York: D. Appleton, 1900), 28. Nicholas Tomalin has commented that the only prerequisites needed for a good journalist are "a plausible manner, rat-like cunning and a little literary ability." (Ann Leslie, "Female 'Firemen'," in Stephen A. Glover, *Secrets of the Press: Journalists on Journalism* (London: Allen Lane, 1999), 233.)

51   Irwin, *Collier's*, 6 May 1911.

52   Maurine Beasley, "The Women's National Press Club: Case Study of Professional Aspirations," *Journalism History*, XV (winter 1988).

53   Betty Houchin Winfield, "Emerging Professionalism and Modernity," in Winfield (ed.), *Journalism 1908: Birth of a Profession* (Columbia: University of Missouri Press, 2008), 1.

54   Pulitzer, "College of Journalism," 650, 655; James Boylan, *Pulitzer's School: Columbia University's School of Journalism, 1903–2003* (New York: Columbia University Press, 2003), 19.

55   An interesting article is Phillip Elliott, "Professional Ideology and Organisational Change: The Journalist Since 1800," in Boyce, *Newspaper History*, 172–91.

56   Interestingly, the Institute of Journalists tried to get a parliamentary bill passed in the 1930s that would have made it an offence for an unregistered person to describe himself as a journalist. (Cyril Bainbridge (ed.), *One Hundred Years of Journalism: Social Aspects of the Press* (London: Macmillan, 1984), 88–9.)

57   Henri Stephen de Blowitz, "Journalism as a Profession," *Contemporary Review*, LXIII (1893), 37–46.

58   Philip Waller, *Writers, Readers and Reputations: Literary Life in Britain, 1870–1918* (Oxford: Oxford University Press, 2006), 400.

59   *Journalist*, 8 April 1887.

Selected Bibliography

Note: Complete information about all of the works listed in this section can be found in the relevant chapter footnotes.

Contemporary Newspapers

Answers to Correspondents (London)
Chicago Daily News
Chicago Times
Daily Express (London)
Daily Graphic (London)
Daily Graphic (New York)
Daily Mail (London)
Daily Mirror (London)
Daily News (London)
Daily Paper (London)
Daily Telegraph (London)
Echo (London)
Evening News (London)
Frank Leslie's Illustrated Newspaper (New York)
Gleason's Pictorial Drawing-Room Companion (Boston)
Harper's Weekly (New York)
Illustrated London News
Illustrated Times (London)
Morning Courier and New-York Enquirer
Morning (London)
Morning Leader (London)
Morning Star (London)
New Orleans Picayune
New York Evening Journal
New York Herald
New York Times
New York Transcript
New York Tribune
Northern Echo (Darlington)
Pall Mall Gazette (London)
Pearson's Weekly (London)
Penny Magazine (London)
Pictorial Times (London)
Review of Reviews (London)
Reynolds's Newspaper (London)
Sketch (London)

St. Louis Post-Dispatch
Star (London)
Sun (London)
Sun (New York)
The Times (London)
Tit-Bits (London)
Truth (London)
Weekly Sun (London)
Westminster Gazette (London)
World (London)
World (New York)

Books and Journal Articles

Abbot, W., *Watching the World Go By* (1933)
Andrews, J., *The North Reports the Civil War* (1955)
Armstrong, W., *E. L. Godkin: A Biography* (1978)
Arnold, M., *Civilization in the United States: First and Last Impressions of America* (1880)
Arnold, M., "Up to Easter," *Nineteenth Century*, XXI (1887), 629–43
Ashley, M., *The Age of the Storytellers: British Popular Fiction, 1880–1950* (2006)
Aucoin, J., *The Evolution of American Investigative Journalism* (2005)
Bailey, P., *Popular Culture and Performance in the Victorian City* (1998)
Bainbridge, C. (ed.), *One Hundred Years of Journalism* (1984)
Baldasty, G., *E. W. Scripps and the Business of Newspapers* (1999)
Baldasty, G., *The Commercialization of News in the Nineteenth Century* (1992)
Banks, E., *The Autobiography of a "Newspaper Girl"* (1902)
Baxter, B., *Strange Street* (1935)
Bell, E., *Flora Shaw (Lady Lugard D. B. E.)* (1947)
Bell, E., *The Life & Letters of C. F. Moberly Bell* (1927)
Bennett, A., *Those United States* (1912)
Berger, M., *The Story of the New York Times, 1851–1951* (1951)
Besant, W., *Autobiography* (1902)
Blatchford, R., *My Eighty Years* (1931)
Blathwayt, R., *Through Life and Round the World* (1917)
Blouët, P., *A Frenchman in America: Recollections of Men and Things* (1891)
Blumenfeld, R., *The Press in My Time* (1933)
Bonsal, S., *Heyday in a Vanished World* (1937)
Boston, R., *The Essential Fleet Street: Its History and Influence* (1990)
Bourne, H., *English Newspapers*, 2 volumes (1887)
Boyce, G., J. Curran and P. Wingate (eds), *Newspaper History: From the 17th Century to the Present Day* (1978)
Boylan, J., *Pulitzer's School: Columbia University's School of Journalism, 1903–2003* (2003)
Bradley, P., *Women and the Press: The Struggle for Equality* (2005)
Brake, L. and M. Demoor (eds), *Dictionary of Nineteenth-Century Journalism* (2009)
Brake, L., *Print in Transition, 1850–1910: Studies in Media and Book History* (2001)
Brake, L., "Who is 'We'?: The Daily Paper Projects and the Journalism Manifestos of W. T. Stead" in Demoor, M. (ed.), *Marketing the Author* (2004)

Brendon, P., *The Life and Death of the Press Barons* (1982)

Brian, D., *Pulitzer: A Life* (2001)

Brittain, H., *Happy Pilgrimage* (1946)

Brown, C., *The Correspondents' War: Journalists in the Spanish-American War* (1967)

Brown, F., *Raymond of the Times* (1951)

Brown, J., *Beyond the Lines: Pictorial Reporting, Everyday Life and the Crisis of Gilded Age America* (2002)

Brown, L., *Victorian News and Newspapers* (1985)

Brown, R., *Knowledge is Power: The Diffusion of Information in Early America, 1700–1865* (1989)

Bryce, J., *The American Commonwealth*, 3 volumes (1888)

Campbell, W., *Yellow Journalism: Puncturing the Myths, Defining the Legacies* (2001)

Carey, J., *The Intellectuals and the Masses: Pride and Prejudice Among the Literary Intelligentsia, 1880–1939* (1992)

Carlebach, M., *American Photojournalism Comes of Age* (1997)

Carlson, O., *Brisbane: A Candid Biography* (1937)

Carlson, O., *The Man Who Made News: James Gordon Bennett* (1942)

Carlson, O. and E. Bates, *Hearst: Lord of San Simeon* (1936)

Carnes, C., *Jimmy Hare, News Photographer: Half a Century with a Camera* (1940)

Chalaby, J., *The Invention of Journalism* (1998)

Chambers, J., *News Hunting on Three Continents* (1921)

Christiansen, A., *Headlines All My Life* (1961)

Churchill A., *Park Row* (1931)

Clayton, C., *Little Mack: Joseph B. McCullagh of the St. Louis "Globe-Democrat"* (1969)

Cobb, I., *Exit Laughing* (1941)

Cohen, P., *The Murder of Helen Jewett: The Life and Death of a Prostitute in Nineteenth-Century New York* (1998)

Conboy, M., *Journalism, a Critical History* (2004)

Conboy, M., *Tabloid Britain: Constructing a Community Through Language* (2006)

Congdon, C., *Reminiscences of a Journalist* (1880)

Cooper, C., *An Editor's Retrospect* (1896)

Copeland, F., *Kendall of the Picayune* (1943)

Cortissoz, R., *The Life of Whitelaw Reid*, 2 volumes (1921)

Creelman, J., *On the Great Highway* (1901)

Cross, N., *The Common Writer: Life in Nineteenth-Century Grub Street* (1985)

Crouthamel, J., *Bennett's New York Herald and the Rise of the Popular Press* (1989)

Crouthamel, J., *James Watson Webb: A Biography* (1969)

Cudlipp, H., *The Prerogative of the Harlot: Press Barons & Power* (1980)

Curl, D., *Murat Halstead and the "Cincinnati Commercial"* (1980)

Curtis, L., *Jack the Ripper and the London Press* (2001)

Dana, C., *The Art of Newspaper Making* (1900)

Dark, S., *Mainly About Other People* (1925)

Dark, S., *Not Such a Bad Life* (1941)

Desmond, R., *The Information Process: World News Reporting to the Twentieth Century* (1978)

Dicey, E., *Six Months in the Federal States*, 2 volumes (1863)

Dickens, C., *American Notes for General Circulation* (1842)

Douglas, G., *The Golden Age of the Newspaper* (1999)

Dreiser, T., *A Book About Myself* (1929)

Driberg, T., *'Swaff': The Life and Times of Hannen Swaffer* (1974)

Edwards, P., *Dickens's 'Young Men': George Augustus Sala, Edmund Yates and the World of Victorian Journalism* (1997)

Escott, T., *Masters of English Journalism* (1911)

Escott, T., *Platform, Press, Politics and Play* (1894)

Emery, E., *The Press and America*, 7th edition (1992)

Fedler, F., *Lessons from the Past: Journalists' Lives and Work, 1850–1950* (2000)

Fishkin, S., *From Fact to Fiction: Journalism and Imaginative Writing in America* (1985)

Forbes, A., *Memories and Studies of War and Peace* (1895)

Forster, J., "The Newspaper Literature of America," *Foreign Quarterly Review*, 30 (1842), 197–222

Fortenberry, S., S. Garner and R. Woodward, *The Correspondence of Harold Frederic* (1977)

Friedrichs, H., *The Life of Sir George Newnes, Bart.* (1911)

Furneaux, R., *The First War Correspondent: William Howard Russell of "The Times"* (1944)

Fyfe, H., *Press Parade* (1936)

Fyfe, H., *Sixty Years of Fleet Street* (1949)

Fyfe, H., *T. P. O'Connor* (1934)

Gardiner, A., *Life of George Cadbury* (1923)

Gibbs, P., *Adventures in Journalism* (1923)

Glover, S., *Secrets of the Press: Journalists on Journalism* (1999)

Goddard, M., *What Interests People and Why* (1935)

Goodman, M., *The Sun and the Moon: The Remarkable True Account of Hoaxers, Showmen, Dueling Journalists, and Lunar Man-Bats in Nineteenth-Century New York* (2008)

Gramling, O., *AP: The Story of News* (1940)

Grant, B., *To the Four Corners: The Memoirs of a News Photographer* (1933)

Grant, J., *The Newspaper* Press, 2 volumes (1871)

Gray, V., *Charles Knight: Educator, Publisher, Writer* (2006)

Greeley, H., *Recollections of a Busy Life* (1869)

Greenwood, J., *A Night in a Workhouse* (1866)

Greenwood, J., *Unsentimental Journalist* (1867)

Griffiths, D., *Fleet Street: Five Hundred Years of the Press* (2006)

Griffiths, D., *Plant Here "The Standard"* (1996)

Griffiths, D. (ed.), *The Encyclopedia of the British Press, 1422–1992* (1992)

Gross, J., *The Rise and Fall of the Man of Letters: Aspects of English Literary Life Since 1800* (1969)

Hampton, M., *Visions of the Press in Britain, 1850–1950* (2004)

Harmsworth, A., "The Newspapers of the Twentieth Century," *North American Review*, 152 (1901), 72–90

Harris, F., *My Life and Loves* (1925)

Harris, M. and A. Lee (eds), *The Press in English Society from the Seventeenth to Nineteenth Centuries* (1986)

Hart-Davis, D., *The House the Berrys Built* (1990)

Hatton, J., *Cigarette Papers* (1902)

Hatton, J., *To-Day in America: Studies for the Old World and the New* (1881)

Haywood, I., *The Revolution in Popular Literature: Print, Politics and the People* (2004)

Healy, C., *Confessions of a Journalist* (1904)

Henkin, D., *The Postal Age: The Emergence of Modern Communications in Nineteenth-Century America* (2006)

Herd, H., *The Making of Modern Journalism* (1927)

Herd, H., *The March of Journalism: The Story of the Present Press from 1622 to the Present Day* (1952)

Hibbert, H., *Fifty Years of a Londoner's Life* (1916)

Hindle, W., *The Morning Post, 1772–1937* (1937)

Hodgson, P., *The War Illustrators* (1977)

Hogarth, P., *The Artist and Reporter* (1986)

Hollis, P., *The Pauper Press: A Study in Working-Class Radicalism of the 1830s* (1970)

Hoole, W., *Vizetelly Covers the Confederacy* (1957)

Horrie, C., *Tabloid Nation: The Birth of the Daily Mirror to the Death of the Tabloid* (2003)

Hudson, F., *Journalism in the United States, from 1690 to 1872* (1873)

Hughes, H., *News and the Human Interest Story* (1940)

Humpherys, A. and L. James (eds), *G.W.M. Reynolds: Nineteenth Century Fiction, Politics and the Press* (2008)

Hutt, A., *The Changing Newspaper: Trends in Britain and America, 1622–1972* (1973)

Irwin, W., "The American Newspaper: A Study of Journalism in Its Relation to the Public," *Collier's*, 15 articles (1911)

Jackson, K., *George Newnes and the New Journalism in Britain, 1880–1910* (2001)

Jackson, M., *The Pictorial Press: Its Origin and Progress* (1885)

James, L., *Fiction for the Working Man* (1963)

Jeal, T., *Stanley: The Impossible Life of Africa's Greatest Explorer* (2007)

Johanningsmeier, C., *The Role of Newspaper Syndicates in America, 1860–1900* (1997)

Johnson, P., *Front Line Artists* (1978)

Jones, A., *Press, Politics and Society: A History of Journalism in Wales* (1993)

Jones, K., *Fleet Street & Downing Street* (1919)

Juergens, G., *Joseph Pulitzer and "The New York World"* (1966)

Kaul, C., *Reporting the Raj: The British Press and India, c. 1880–1922* (2003)

Kenin, R., *Return to Albion: Americans in England, 1760–1940* (1979)

Kielbowicz, R., *News in the Mail: The Press, Post Office, and Public Information, 1700–1860s* (1989)

King, H., *Pulitzer's Prize Editor: A Biography of John A. Cockerill* (1965)

Kluger, R., *The Paper: The Life and Death of the "New York Herald Tribune"* (1986)

Knightley, P., *The First Casualty: From the Crimea to Vietnam: The War Correspondent as Hero, Propagandist and Myth Maker* (1975)

Koenigsberg, M., *King News: An Autobiography* (1941)

Koss, S., *The Rise and Fall of the Political Press in Britain: The Nineteenth Century* (1981)

Kroeger, B., *Nelly Bly: Daredevil, Reporter, Feminist* (1994)

Kunzle, D., *The History of the Comic Strip: The Nineteenth Century* (1990)

Lee, A., *The Daily Newspaper in America: The Evolution of a Social Instrument* (1937)

Lee, A., *The Origins of the Popular Press in England, 1855–1914* (1976)

Lehuu, I., *Carnival on the Page: Popular Print Media in Antebellum America* (2000)

LeMahieu, D., *A Culture for Democracy: Mass Communication and the Cultivated Mind in Britain Between the Wars* (1989)

Lent, J., *Comic Books and Comic Strips in the United States: An International Biography* (1994)

Leonard, T., *News for All: America's Coming-Of-Age With the Press* (1995)

Leonard, T., *The Power of the Press: The Birth of American Political Reporting* (1986)

Levine, L., *Highbrow/Lowbrow: The Emergence of Cultural Hierarchy in America* (1988)

Linton, D. and R. Boston (eds), *The Newspaper Press in Britain: An Annotated Bibliography* (1987)

Lucy, H., *Lord and Commons* (1921)

Lucy, H., *Sixty Years in the Wilderness* (1911)

Lutes, J., *Front Page Girls: Women Journalists in American Culture and Fiction, 1880–1930* (2006)

Mackay, C., *Through the Long Day, Or, Memorials of a Literary Life During Half a Century* (1887)

Marbut, F., *News from the Capital: The Story of Washington Reporting* (1971)

Markham, J., *Bovard of the Post-Dispatch* (1954)

Martineau, H., *Society in America*, 3 volumes (1837)

Massingham, H., *The London Daily Press* (1892)

Mathews, J., *George W. Smalley: Forty Years a Foreign Correspondent* (1973)

Mayer, M., *Making News* (1987)

McCarthy, J., *Reminiscences*, 2 volumes (1889)

Memoirs of Henry Villard, Journalist and Financier, 2 volumes (1904)

Milton, J., *The Yellow Kids: Foreign Correspondents in the Heyday of Yellow Journalism* (1989)

Moncrieff, C., *Living on a Deadline: A History of the Press Association* (2001)

Morison, S., *The English Newspaper: Some Account of the Physical Development of Journals Printed in London between 1622 and the Present Day* (1932)

Morphet, D., *Louis Jennings MP: Editor of the New York Times and Tory Democrat* (2001)

Morris, J., *The Rose Man of Sing Sing: True Tale of Life, Murder, and Redemption in the Age of Yellow Journalism* (2003)

Morris, J. M., *Pulitzer: A Life in Politics, Print, and Power* (2010)

Mott, F., *American Journalism: A History of Newspapers in the United States Through 250 Years; 1690–1940* (1947)

Mulvey, C., *Anglo-American Landscapes: A Study of Nineteenth-Century Anglo-American Travel Literature* (1983)

Mulvey, C., *Transatlantic Manners: Social Patterns in Nineteenth-Century Anglo-American Travel Literature* (1990)

Murray, D., *Recollections* (1908)

Nasaw, D., *The Chief: The Life of William Randolph Hearst* (2000)

Norris, J., *Advertising and the Transformation of American Society, 1865–1920* (1990)

Northrop, W., *With Pen and Camera* (1904)

O'Brien, Frank, *The Story of "The Sun": New York: 1833–1928* (1928)

O'Connor, T., *Memoirs of an Old Parliamentarian*, 2 volumes (1929)

O'Connor, T., "The New Journalism," *The New Review*, I (1889), 423–34

Ogden, R. (ed.), *Life and Letters of Edwin Lawrence Godkin*, 2 volumes (1907)

Onslow, B., *Women of the Press in Nineteenth-Century Britain* (2000)

O'Shea, J., *Leaves from the Life of a Special Correspondent*, 2 volumes (1885)

Palmegiano, E., "'BABY-BEER-BULLETS!!!': British Perceptions of American Journalism in the Nineteenth Century," *American Journalism*, XXIV (2007), 37–66

Pearson, H., *Labby: The Life and Character of Henry Labouchere* (1936)

Pebody, C., *English Journalism and the Men Who Have Made It* (1882)

Pemberton, M., *Lord Northcliffe: A Memoir* (1922)

Pope, T. (ed.), *The Book of Fleet Street* (1930)

Poore, B., *Perley's Reminiscences of Sixty Years in the National Metropolis* (1886)

Pope, W., *The Story of the "Star", 1888–1938* (1938)

Potter, S., *News and the British World: The Emergence of an Imperial Press System* (2003)

Pound, R. and G. Harmsworth, *Northcliffe* (1959)

Pulitzer, J., "The College of Journalism," *North American Review*, CLXXVIII (1904), 641–80

Ralph, J., *The Making of a Journalist* (1907)

Rammelkamp, J., *Pulitzer's Post-Dispatch, 1878–1883* (1967)

Raymond, E., *Portraits of the Nineties* (1921)

Read, D., *The Power of News: The History of Reuters, 1849–1989* (1992)

Reid, A., "The English and the American Press," *Nineteenth Century*, XXII (1887), 219–33

Reid, S. (ed.), *Memoirs of Sir Wemyss Reid, 1842–1885* (1905)

Richardson, J., *From the City to Fleet Street: Some Journalistic Experiences* (1927)

Ritchie, D., *Press Gallery: Congress and the Washington Correspondents* (1991)

Rogers, J., *The American Newspaper* (1909)

Roggenkamp, K., *Narrating the News: New Journalism and Literary Genre in Late Nineteenth-Century American Newspapers and Fiction* (2005)

Ross, I., *Ladies of the Press* (1936)

Roth, M., *Historical Dictionary of War Journalism* (1997)

Rubery, M., *The Novelty of Newspapers: Victorian Fiction and the Invention of the News* (2009)

Russell, W., *The War: From the Landing at Gallipoli to the Death of Lord Raglan* (1855)

Sala, G., *The Life and Adventures of George Augustus Sala Written by Himself*, 2 volumes (1896)

Salmon, L., *The Newspaper and the Historian* (1923)

Schudson, M., *Discovering the News: A Social History of American Newspapers* (1978)

Schudson, M., *The Power of News* (1995)

Schults, R., *Crusader in Babylon: W. T. Stead and the Pall Mall Gazette* (1972)

Schwarzlose, R., *The Nation's Newsbrokers*, 2 volumes (1989)

Scott, G., *Reporter Anonymous: The Story of the Press Association* (1968)

Scott, J., *The Life and Death of a Newspaper* (1952)

Scott, J., *The Story of the Pall Mall Gazette* (1950)

Sebba, A., *Battling for the News: The Rise of the Woman Reporter* (1994)

Seitz, D., *Joseph Pulitzer: His Life and Letters* (1924)

Seitz, D., *The James Gordon Bennetts, Father and Son: Proprietors of the New York Herald* (1928)

Sell's Dictionary of the World's Press (1883–1914)

Seymour-Ure, *Press, Politics and the Public* (1968)

Simon, M., *Jazz Journalism: The Story of the Tabloid Newspapers* (1938)

Sims, G., *My Life: Sixty Years' Recollections of Bohemian London* (1917)

Sloan, D. and L. Purcell (eds), *American Journalism: History, Principles, Practices* (2002)

Smalley, G., *Anglo-American Memories* (1911)

Smith, A., *The Newspaper: An International History* (1979)

Sparrow, A., *Obscure Scribblers: A History of Parliamentary Journalism* (2003)

Spender, H., *A Briton in America* (1921)

Spender, H., *The Fire of Life: A Book of Memories* (1926)

Springfield, L., *Some Piquant People* (1924)

Stanley, D. (ed.), *The Autobiography of Sir Henry Morton Stanley* (1909)

Starr, L., *Bohemian Brigade: Civil War Newsmen in Action* (1954)

Starr, P., *The Creation of the Media: Political Origins of Modern Communications* (2004)

Startt, J., *Journalists for Empire: The Imperial Debate in the Edwardian Stately Press, 1903–1913* (1991)

Stead, W., *If Christ Came to Chicago!: A Plea for the Union of All Who Love in the Service of All Who Suffer* (1894)

Stead, W., *The Americanization of the World, or the Trend of the Twentieth Century* (1901)

Stead, W., "Government by Journalism," *Contemporary Review*, 49 (1886), 653–74

Stealey, O., *Twenty Years in the Press Gallery* (1906)

Stedman, L. and G. Gould, *Life and Letters of Edmund Clarence Stedman*, 2 volumes (1910)

Steed, W., *The Press* (1938)

Steed, W., *Through Thirty Years, 1892–1922* (1923)

Steele, J., *The Sun Shines for All: Journalism and Ideology in the Life of Charles A. Dana* (1993)

Steevens, G., *The Land of the Dollar* (1897)

Stephens, M., *A History of News: From the Drum to the Satellite* (1988)

Stevens, J., *Sensationalism and the New York Press* (1991)

Stoddard, H., *Horace Greeley: Printer, Editor, Crusader* (1946)

Stone, C., *Dana and the Sun* (1938)

Stone, M., *Fifty Years a Journalist* (1921)

Storey, G., *Reuters' Century, 1851–1951* (1951)

Swanberg, W., *Citizen Hearst: A Biography of William Randolph Hearst* (1961)

Swanberg, W., *Pulitzer* (1967)

The History of The Times: "The Thunderer" in the Making, 1785–1841 (1935)

The History of The Times: The Tradition Established, 1841–1884 (1939)

Thomas, F. (ed.), *Fifty Years of Fleet Street: Being the Life and Recollections of Sir John R. Robinson* (1904)

Thomas, W., *A Traveller in News* (1925)

Thompson, C., *I Lost My English Accent* (1939)

Thompson, J., *Northcliffe: Press Baron in Politics, 1865–1922* (2000)

Thompson, R., *Wiring a Continent: The History of the Telegraph Industry in the United States 1833–1886* (1947)

Thorold, A., *The Life of Henry Labouchere* (1913)

Trollope, A., *North America*, 2 volumes (1862)

Trollope, F., *Domestic Manners of the Americans* (1832)

Tucher, A., *Froth and Scum: Truth, Beauty, Goodness, and the Ax Murder in America's First Mass Medium* (1994)

Tunstall, J., *The Media are American: Anglo-American Media in the World* (1977)

Tunstall, J. and D. Machin, *The Anglo-American Media Connection* (1999)

Villard, O., *Some Newspapers and Newspaper-Men* (1923)

Villiers, F., *Villiers: His Five Decades of Adventure*, 2 volumes (1920)

Vizetelly H., *Glances Back Through Seventy Years: Autobiographical and Other Reminiscences*, 2 volumes (1893)

Waller, P., *Writers, Readers and Reputations: Literary Life in Britain, 1870–1918* (2006)

Walker, D., *Januarius MacGahan: The Life and Campaigns of an American War Correspondent* (1988)

Wall, J., *Henry Watterson: Reconstructed Rebel* (1956)

Wallace, E., *People: A Short Autobiography* (1926)

Walsh, J., *To Print the News and Raise Hell* (1968)

Ward, S., *The Invention of Journalism Ethics: The Path to Objectivity and Beyond* (2004)

Watson, A., *A Newspaper Man's Memories* (1925)

Weber, R., *Professional Writers in America's Golden Age of Print* (1997)

Weisberger, B., *The American Newspaperman* (1961)

Whitehouse, R., *The Other Fleet Street* (2004)

Whiteing, R., *My Harvest* (1915)

Whitt, J., *Women in American Journalism* (2008)

Whyte, F., *The Life of W.T. Stead*, 2 volumes (1925)

Whyte, K., *The Uncrowned King: The Sensational Rise of William Randolph Hearst* (2009)

Wiener, J. (ed.), *Innovators and Preachers: The Role of the Editor in Victorian England* (1985)

Wiener, J. (ed.), *Papers for the Millions: The New Journalism in Britain, 1850s to 1914* (1988)

Wiener, J., *The War of the Unstamped: The Movement to Repeal the British Newspaper Tax, 1830–1836* (1969)

Wiener, J. and M. Hampton (eds), *Anglo-American Media Interactions, 1850–2000* (2007)

Wile, F., *News is Where You Find It: Forty Years' Reporting at Home and Abroad* (1939)

Wilentz, S., *Chants Democratic: New York City & the Rise of the American Working Class, 1788–1850* (1984)

Wilkes, R., *Scandal: A Scurrilous History of Gossip* (2002)

Wilkie, F., *Pen and Powder* (1888)

Wilkinson, H., *Thirty-Five Years, 1874–1909* (1933)

Williams, R., *Horace Greeley: Champion of American Freedom* (2006)

Wilkinson-Latham, R., *From Our Special Correspondent: Victorian War Correspondents and Their Campaigns* (1979)

Williams, K., *Get Me a Murder a Day: A History of Mass Communication in Britain* (1998)

Williams, R., *The Long Revolution* (1961)

Winfield, B. (ed.), *Journalism 1908: Birth of a Profession* (2008)

Wingate, C. (ed.), *Views and Interviews on Journalism* (1875)

Wintour, C., *Pressures on the Press: An Editor Looks at Fleet Street* (1972)
Wintour, C., *The Rise and Fall of Fleet Street* (1989)
Yates, E., *Celebrities at Home* (1877–79)
Yates, E., *His Recollections and Experiences*, 2 volumes (1884)
Young, J., *Men and Memories*, ed. May D. Russell (1901)

Index